Ralph Metzner

EXPLORER OF CONSCIOUSNESS

"A remarkable and lovingly warm tribute to a true 20th-century pioneer in psychedelic, transpersonal, and consciousness studies whose cultural influence and scholarly contributions to our understanding of psychedelics and altered states have led to the reemergence of psychedelic research today. Ralph's incredible life is beautifully told in these pages."

ANTHONY P. BOSSIS, PH.D., CLINICAL
ASSISTANT PROFESSOR, DEPARTMENT OF PSYCHIATRY
AT NYU GROSSMAN SCHOOL OF MEDICINE

"Over the sixty years I knew Ralph, he remained the best educated, most curious, and most open man I've ever known. Where others saw walls, he not only saw doors but propped them open and urged us to follow him to experience new facets of our interconnections and underlying unity."

JAMES FADIMAN, PH.D., MICRODOSE RESEARCHER AND
AUTHOR OF *THE PSYCHEDELIC EXPLORER'S GUIDE*

"A vibrant palette of inspiration and lived experience that documents Ralph Metzner's multifaceted legacy. This book will remain alive and vibrant as an influence on the field of psychedelics."

JANIS PHELPS, PH.D., DIRECTOR OF THE CENTER FOR
PSYCHEDELIC THERAPIES AND RESEARCH,
CALIFORNIA INSTITUTE OF INTEGRAL STUDIES

"Ralph Metzner helped give birth to the psychedelic Sixties—witnessing, shaping, and intelligently commenting on this movement's tumultuous life for more than half a century. This collection of loving remembrances humanizes and deepens our understanding of him as a consciousness-raising pioneer."

DON LATTIN, AUTHOR OF *THE HARVARD PSYCHEDELIC CLUB*
AND *GOD ON PSYCHEDELICS*

"Ralph Metzner has been a mentor to countless psychedelic explorers, and this is an inspiring celebration of Ralph's influence on the many people whose lives were touched deeply by his mentorship. Ralph's legacy offers an important reminder of the visionary aspects of psychedelic use that cannot be contained within a medical model."

MARY GOMES, PH.D., COEDITOR OF *ECOPSYCHOLOGY*

"Ralph Metzner was a pioneer 'explorer of consciousness' who stood steadfastly for the integrity of psychedelic work, service, community, and right livelihood. This book, with contributions from other psychedelic pioneers, provides a wonderful opportunity for us all to keep learning from Ralph."

MICHAEL MITHOEFER, M.D., MDMA RESEARCHER

"The lifelong imprints left on those one touches with their presence, words, and actions make a person unforgettable. This book is a tribute to an unforgettable Ralph, whose unique and vast range of imprints is beautifully portrayed in this collection of writings by those who met him along their paths. May Ralph's legacy keep inspiring new generations committed to the ever-expanding dance of consciousness. In gratitude, Maestro!"

SUSANA BUSTOS, PH.D., DIRECTOR OF ESCUELA DE PSICOVEGETALISMO AND COAUTHOR OF *THE SHAMANIC ODYSSEY*

"It is with great pride and honor that I hold my position at the University of California San Francisco in Ralph's name. I so appreciate the depth and breadth of Ralph's knowledge and expertise as a scientist, artist, healer, and more."

ROBIN CARHART-HARRIS, PH.D., RALPH METZNER DISTINGUISHED PROFESSOR OF NEUROLOGY, PSYCHIATRY AND BEHAVIORAL SCIENCES AT THE UNIVERSITY OF CALIFORNIA SAN FRANCISCO

"As a treasured professor, author, lecturer, mentor, therapist, and administrator, Ralph Metzner made significant contributions to transpersonal and psychedelic research and therapy. This volume is a complement to his vision and makes the case for his most important ideas on expansion and deepening of consciousness, alchemy, shamanism, human development, mythology, death and afterlife, family, and friendship."

ROBERT MCDERMOTT, PH.D., PRESIDENT EMERITUS AND PROFESSOR EMERITUS, CALIFORNIA INSTITUTE OF INTEGRAL STUDIES

"In the lineage he leaves behind, the fire of Ralph's commitment to ending suffering lives on. The potency of his alchemical divinatory practices as pathways for radical transformation reflect his unending passion for the liberation of awakened consciousness and the proactive co-creation of a more peaceful and just world."

VALERIA MCCARROLL, PH.D., LMFT, FOUNDER OF SOMADELICS

"Reading this book, I am reminded again and again what a fabulous human being Ralph was. He was a holistic thinker, a courageous explorer, a comic who made us laugh, and a human being with an utterly dependable grasp on all levels of reality. This book captures so much of him and is a gift for all spiritual seekers."

BRIAN THOMAS SWIMME, PH.D., PROFESSOR EMERITUS, CALIFORNIA INSTITUTE OF INTEGRAL STUDIES AND AUTHOR OF COSMOGENESIS

"This book highlights Ralph's academic and experiential contributions to healing and visionary states using various entheogens, meditations, and shamanic techniques. It describes his dedication to the field of green psychology for the preservation of the natural world. It is an indispensable read for all practitioners who are exploring altered states of consciousness."

ALEXANDER SHESTER, M.D., AUTHOR OF VISIONARY HEALING

"Ralph Metzner made a significant contribution to the exploration of psychedelic worlds. This book honors a great master, teacher, and humanitarian friend."

ROGER LIGGENSTORFER, PUBLISHER, AND CHRISTINE HEIDRICH, TRANSLATOR

"Like the shaman whose traditions he both studied and extended, Ralph was a traveler between worlds. And not only a traveler, but a guide, interpreter, and defender. A truly integral individual, his expertise and passions spanned the common divisions between science and spirituality, the personal and the political, the esoteric and the ecological. This volume of tributes will give the reader a tangible sense of the exceptional range of fields to which Ralph made significant and lasting contributions."

SEAN KELLY, PH.D., AUTHOR OF *BECOMING GAIA*

"Ralph Metzner dedicated his life to the exploration of consciousness and the one energy that we all are. This book honors his great spirit and provides inspiration for our own explorations of the source from which we all spring."

MARKUS BERGER, ETHNOBOTANIST, DRUG RESEARCHER, AND EDITOR-IN-CHIEF OF *LUCY'S RAUSCH*

"This tribute to Ralph Metzner's life conveys so eloquently how skillfully Ralph used his profound understanding of the world's wisdom traditions to touch so many so deeply. This book is an invitation to share in Ralph's journey to consciousness."

ALLEN KANNER, PH.D., COEDITOR OF *ECOPSYCHOLOGY*

"Ralph Metzner guided many people through profound experiences and altered states of consciousness. Here is a well-deserved tribute to this impressive intrepid pioneer, psychonaut, guide, and author."

ROGER WALSH M.D., PH.D., PROFESSOR, UNIVERSITY OF CALIFORNIA, AND EDITOR OF *HIGHER WISDOM*

"A fitting tribute to a man who touched so many around the world with his wisdom, love, intellect, heart, and creative flow. So many wonderful voices reveal different aspects of Brother Raoul's self. Take the time to read them all and gain good medicine about a good medicine man that showed up and went for the gold of transformation."

TOM "TOMÁS" PINKSON, PH.D., PSYCHOTHERAPIST AND AUTHOR OF *THE PSYCHEDELIC SHAMAN*

Ralph Metzner

EXPLORER OF CONSCIOUSNESS

THE LIFE AND LEGACY OF
A PSYCHEDELIC PIONEER

Edited by
Cathy Coleman, Ph.D.

Park Street Press
Rochester, Vermont

Park Street Press
One Park Street
Rochester, Vermont 05767
www.ParkStPress.com

Text stock is SFI certified

Park Street Press is a division of Inner Traditions International

Note to the Reader: *The information in this book is for historical, cultural, and educational interest only and should not be construed as a guide to or advocacy of the use or ingestion of psychoactive medicines. In no way should the material in this book be taken to advocate, explicitly or implicitly, the use of illegal substances. Neither authors nor publisher assume any responsibility for physical, psychological, or social consequences resulting from ingesting any of the substances described in this book.*

Cataloging-in-Publication Data for this title is available from the Library of Congress

ISBN 979-8-88850-050-7 (print)
ISBN 979-8-88850-051-4 (ebook)

Printed and bound in the United States by Lake Book Manufacturing, LLC
The text stock is SFI certified. The Sustainable Forestry Initiative® program promotes sustainable forest management.

10   9   8   7   6   5   4   3   2   1

Text design and layout by Virginia Scott Bowman
This book was typeset in Garamond Premier Pro, Gill Sans, and Legacy Sans with Orpheus Pro and Glodok used as display typefaces

To send correspondence to the author of this book, mail a first-class letter to the author c/o Inner Traditions • Bear & Company, One Park Street, Rochester, VT 05767, and we will forward the communication, or contact the author directly at **info@greenearthfound.org**.

Scan the QR code and save 25% at InnerTraditions.com. Browse over 2,000 titles on spirituality, the occult, ancient mysteries, new science, holistic health, and natural medicine.

⑥

*This book is dedicated to Ralph's life purpose of
expanded consciousness, and to fellow explorers,
including those who have come before
and those who will follow.*

Shaman's Song

During the first half of my life
I wove the threads and textures
Of my experience
Into a multi-colored tapestry that
In the ending half of this journey
Has become a magic carpet
On which I shall sail away
Over the mountains
Into the worlds
Of the mystery.

RALPH METZNER

Contents

Psychedelic Medicines for Healing and Visions

Foreword

David Presti

Endlessly curious, eternal student, intrepid adventurer—courageous and creative explorer of the wild frontiers of consciousness.

Healer, shaman, magician—one who welcomed ancestors and spirits as allies.

Pioneer in the therapeutic utility of psychedelic substances—innovator in the importance of set and setting, master of ritual and ceremony. One who courageously developed, transmitted, and mentored others in the therapeutic use of psychedelics.

Cartographer of consciousness expansion—exploring, shaping, and transmitting ancient and modern methods to deeply connect with mind and expand awareness in service of attunement to community, society, and planet.

A visionary and precise scholar—who, as he appreciated the boundaries of the academic establishment, helped guide the creation of an academic institution (California Institute of Integral Studies) that transcended those bounds, a place where psyche—mind, soul, spirit—is respected as irreducible in the study of psychology.

Master teacher and gifted storyteller—who guided, influenced, and mentored, directly and indirectly, generations of shamanic practitioners and psychedelic therapists.

A life rich in varied experience—from childhood in war-ravaged Germany to a famously innovative school in Scotland attended by members of the British royal family to Oxford, the oldest English-language university in the world, to graduate studies and life-long collaborations and friendships that began when he was the junior member of an infamous Harvard trio.

A key player in transpersonal psychology—in crafting the contemporary academic discipline of taking seriously the transcendent; he authored two dozen books and influenced multitudes through direct encounters with his uniquely quiet and powerful style.

A pioneer of ecopsychology—of what has also become known as green psychology, terrapsychology, nature religion, dark green religion. Taking lessons from the personal to the global, from the individual psyche to the collective, from work with the personal shadow to work with societal shadows that contribute to driving our current great planetary derangement. One who knew that Gaia is alive and sentient, and commands our respect and collaboration, if we are to survive and flourish.

Alchemist extraordinaire—re-enlivening a concept often dismissed as primitive and prescientific. Alchemy as a quest for knowledge, wisdom, and healing. Alchemy as transformation of consciousness, of the body, and of its subtle energy field. Alchemy as ritual and profoundly respectful relationship with the natural world.

Traveler in service of experiential learning—and sharing knowledge with others. Catalyst for an extended community, appreciating that lasting benefits of transformative experiences are best attained through ongoing practice within a supportive community, a tribe, a circle. The circle can be more important than the medicine.

Devoted to family and community—caring husband, father, family and community citizen. Friend to many.

Truly a life well-lived, living as if the kind of world many of us would like to have is indeed possible. One who has left the world a far better place for his having lived.

This book is filled with stories speaking to all these qualities of this truly remarkable being. Reading it will take you on a journey through an extraordinary life.

It will also give perspective on the role psychedelic medicines had in Ralph's life and work. As psychedelics are currently undergoing a rapid and somewhat rampant movement into contemporary society—a society perhaps not well prepared to receive these complex and powerful substances—it is particularly instructive to appreciate how for him psychedelics were aids, not ends, to expanding consciousness.

For Ralph, it was all about opening one's awareness in service of personal transformation and global transformation—addressing the personal and interpersonal, and also the most important societal and planetary crises of our era. This perhaps is the most important message of Ralph Metzner's life and work, and of this wonderful collection of essays.

Enjoy!

DAVID PRESTI, PH.D., teaches biology, psychology, and cognitive science at the University of California, Berkeley, where he has been on the faculty in molecular and cell biology for thirty years. For the past two decades David has been teaching neuroscience and conversing about science with Tibetan Buddhist monastics in India, Bhutan, and Nepal. His areas of expertise include human neurobiology and neurochemistry, the effects of drugs on the brain and the mind, the clinical treatment of addiction, and the scientific study of mind and consciousness. He is the author of several books, including *Foundational Concepts in Neuroscience: A Brain-Mind Odyssey* and *Mind Beyond Brain: Buddhism, Science, and the Paranormal*.

Preface

Cathy Coleman and Simon Warwick-Smith

Ralph Metzner was a visionary scholar who led a long and illustrious life. The inspiration for this book was seeded by the tributes given at Ralph's memorial in San Francisco on May 24, 2019; by an unsolicited written tribute by Alan Levin; and by the suggestion of Friedrich Rehrnbeck of Germany. This memorial collection of essays comprises personal homages as to how Ralph impacted the contributors' lives. Known as a *Gedenkschrift* in German, the more common term is *Festschrift*, which is a celebration of writings to honor a respected person while they are alive. While some collections are strictly academic works focusing on themes of the person's life work, this compilation includes both academic and more personal essays.

The pieces fell into place to proceed with the project when we—Cathy Coleman, Ralph's wife of thirty-one years, and Simon Warwick-Smith, Ralph's friend and editor/agent of twenty-five years—joined forces. We put out the call for contributions and were touched by the enthusiastic response and support. It is truly an acknowledgment of a life well lived. We are deeply grateful for each of the eighty-seven essays that we received. Due to space constraints, not all of them could be included in this volume. We encourage readers to visit the Green Earth Foundation website at www.greenearthfound.org, where you can find the additional tributes to Ralph that are not contained in these pages. With appreciation, the authors of those contributions can be found listed in the acknowledgments at the back of this book.

The essays herein offer insights, anecdotes, and observations from people worldwide, each connected to the various aspects and stages of Ralph's life—those he touched and those who touched him. He had German and Scottish roots, and he made teaching trips for several decades to Germany, Italy, Sweden, Switzerland, and Brazil, as well as to locations within the United States.

We have loosely grouped the contributions to correspond with Ralph's broad influences and impact: Overview and Early Life; A Scholar, Educator, and Mentor; Psychedelic Medicines for Healing and Visions; Esoteric Modalities and Sacred Storytelling; Green Psychology; Artistic Expression; Death, Conscious Dying, and the Afterlife; and Family.

OVERVIEW AND EARLY LIFE

We begin with a few contributions that highlight the key points of Ralph's biography and the connections to the rest of his life's work. One especially important aspect is the roots of war and reconciliation.

Ralph's life-long, almost obsessive, focus on the causes of war and reconciliation was rooted in his early family life. His parents endured their respective countries being at war, his mother being Scottish and his father German. Ralph's childhood was enmeshed with the suffering and deprivation of World War II as he was born in 1936 in Berlin and remained there until the end of the war in 1945, taking shelter in their home basement during bombing raids. The piece from Ralph's brother, Robin Metzner, describes Ralph's roots, childhood, and teenage years.

Aware of the widespread repression people of German descent had about Germany's WWII history, Ralph conducted workshops and storytelling rituals on the Nazi Holocaust and war, which resulted in profound healings and shifts in relationships, especially between older and younger generations. Ralph noted that "Only once the hurt received and inflicted is openly and truthfully acknowledged can authentic healing take place."[1]

---

1. Ralph Metzner, *Ecology of Consciousness* (Oakland, CA: New Harbinger, 2017), 236.

Ralph guided groups in reconciliation processes with their ancestors. He studied family constellation therapy with its founder, Bert Hellinger, who became a mentor for him. In this work individuals are guided to the complex family soul of living and deceased family members and ancestors through "representatives."

Ralph wrote: "I have come to believe that the kind of civilized transition that is required of us all will involve far-reaching transformations of consciousness in individuals, their families and their communities, and ultimately the global social order."[2]

A SCHOLAR, EDUCATOR, AND MENTOR

An academic, Ralph Metzner harnessed education as a platform for promoting personal, social, and cultural transformation. He had an expansive view of education, perhaps first formed from his early years at Gordonstoun School in Scotland, an avant-garde experiment in its field.[3] He was a gifted teacher who experimented with ideas, courses, and methodologies. His academic rigor was further honed at Oxford.

Ralph's lifework included his pioneering role in building an accredited institution of integral education. In his role as the academic dean at the California Institute of Integral Studies (CIIS), he integrated an Eastern-oriented curriculum with Western psychology. Ralph was among the founding practitioners and teachers of the transpersonal psychology field. CIIS was among the few leading institutions where transpersonal psychology was taught in the late twentieth century.

Ralph introduced courses in the divine feminine, laying the groundwork for the later emergence of a Women's Spirituality program. He incorporated esoteric healing arts such as astrology, alchemy, and the I Ching into mainstream academic studies. He championed phenomenological as well as empirical research. One of Ralph's students, Roger Marsden, noted: "He didn't teach about a system; he

---

2. Ralph Metzner, *Ecology of Consciousness* (Oakland, CA: New Harbinger, 2017), 83.
3. See Alastair McIntosh's essay in this volume.

taught an integration of multiple systems across time, cultures, and disciplines."[4]

Ralph expanded the school's courses and programs, incorporating new psychology and cultural anthropology programs. Michael Flanagin's contribution "Ralph's Animation of the Academy" describes Ralph's initiating role in building an accredited institution of integral education.

Chiron, the centaur, is a key archetype for Ralph about which Monika Wikman and I (Cathy) wrote. In Greek mythology, Chiron became a teacher and mentor to various mythological heroes, imparting to them the values and knowledge that they would later need to pursue their quests. Chiron strove to make each one a whole person, skilled in music, astrology, herbal medicine, hunting, and riding. His students came to him to gather the skills to fulfill their own destinies. Chiron was a maverick thinker.[5] My discovery of the archetypal symbolism of Chiron coincided with Ralph's and my first date. As this volume illustrates, Ralph played out the archetype of Chiron with the many students and colleagues whom he mentored.

PSYCHEDELIC MEDICINES FOR HEALING AND VISIONS

Ralph gained renown for his pioneering role in the study of psychedelics at Harvard with Timothy Leary and Richard Alpert (Ram Dass). They coauthored the infamous book *The Psychedelic Experience: A Manual Based on the Tibetan Book of the Dead*, first published in 1964. His prolific psychedelic exploration—and teaching, writing, and healing work—continued until his death in 2019.

Charles Grob notes that "Ralph maintained a strong focus on scholarly and intellectual rigor, comprehending the powerful implica-

---

4. Quote from Roger Marsden's essay in this volume.
5. Richard Nolle, *Chiron: The New Planet in Your Horoscope* (Tempe, Arizona: American Federation of Astrologers, 1983), 11.

tions these compounds might have for both individual and collective healing."[6]

Ralph preferred the term *entheogen* to *psychedelic*, due to the cultural baggage that accumulated with the use of the word *psychedelic*. "*Entheogenic*," he wrote, "refers explicitly to the capacity of these experiences to put one in touch with the sacred or divine dimensions of our existence."

Ralph continued, "Scientific studies have shown that given favorable conditions of set and setting, these substances can aid and support healing or psychotherapy; they can function as allies in overcoming addictions and compulsions; they can assist those who are dying in their preparations for the final passage; they can further understanding of states and dimensions of consciousness and the nature of reality; they can enhance creativity—and they can increase the openness to and likelihood of spiritual or mystical experience."[7] This is noteworthy validation.

In addition to *The Psychedelic Experience*, Ralph wrote on psychedelic (or entheogenic) medicines, including books on MDMA, ayahuasca, mushrooms, and *Bufo alvarius* and 5-methoxy-dimethyltryptamine (5-MeO-DMT). He also spelled out guidelines for the productive and safe use of these substances. The titles of his works are listed in the back of this book.

Today we are seeing rapid growth in the legitimacy and acceptance of psychedelic-assisted therapies, and their employment for certain intractable health issues such as PTSD, treatment-resistant depression, and anxiety. Ralph's extensive research and documentation of the effects of different substances and their usefulness for expanded consciousness and healing have been foundational to the field.

Stan Grof observed, "Ralph was an early harbinger in the current

---

6. Quote from Charles S. Grob's essay in this volume.
7. Ralph Metzner, *Allies for Awakening: Guidelines for Productive and Safe Experiences with Entheogens* (Berkeley, CA: Regent Press, 2015; Sonoma, CA: Four Trees Press, 2022), 8.

psychedelic renewal. During the period when psychedelics were illegal he studied new and not yet illegal or semilegal medicines . . . Many of these new substances came from the laboratory of Sasha Shulgin and Jungian therapist Leo Zeff. Ralph introduced useful knowledge about MDMA to therapists and interested members of the public in his coauthored book *Through the Gateway of the Heart*."[8]

Visionary circles in North America and Europe were conducted by Ralph for the last forty years of his life, in which many people engaged in deep work with him for a long period of time. His impact was profound in terms of their personal transformations and their consequent flowering growth and creativity. There are a number of contributors on this topic, including Mark Seelig's extraordinary piece, "Life-Changing Work with Sacred Medicine Circles."

We offer a glossary of psychoactive medicines in this book as a starting point for those who are less familiar with this topic and to show the range of medicines with which Ralph worked.

ESOTERIC MODALITIES AND SACRED STORYTELLING

Ralph's timeless book *Maps of Consciousness*, first published in 1971, described six esoteric systems—I Ching, tantra, tarot, alchemy, astrology, and Actualism—and how they can be applied for personal growth. (This classic for exploring the mind and expanded awareness was republished by Inner Traditions in 2023.)

Ralph sought substance-free methods and techniques for gaining insights and revelations. He developed and taught Metzner Alchemical Divination Training (MAD), a three-year training program (using no substances), for approximately a decade from about 2002–2012. His writings, teachings, and trainings opened brand-new horizons to his students. Jamy Faust, Paul Müller, and Friedrich Rehrnbeck wrote on their experiences in this training.

---

8. Quote from Stan Grof's essay in this volume.

Several of the essays describe Ralph's deep involvement in the School of Actualism in the 1970s. Actualism, or Agni Yoga, was developed by Russell Schofield, one of Ralph's mentors. "In Agni Yoga, the living fire is used to bring light into darkened areas of consciousness, and the consuming fire aspect is used to burn out obstructions to the free flow of energy from other sources."[9] The term *Light-Fire yoga* used herein refers to this process.

In addition to Agni Yoga, as a psychotherapist Ralph used many different healing approaches, such as meditation, guided imagery, divination, sand tray therapy, past life regression, family constellation work, and entheogens, to complement his repertoire of more traditional methods. Some of the more impactful ways in which he influenced his clients' lives is described here.

There are contributions from American and European colleagues and friends, including academic colleagues from the CIIS; from various aspects of psychedelic research; from work with the International Transpersonal Association (ITA) on conferences; and from friendships forged.

GREEN PSYCHOLOGY

Ralph was a pioneer in the field of ecopsychology. He had an early understanding of the environmental crisis and re-envisioned psychology as inclusive of an ecological context and an integral part of human life. Craig Chalquist pointed out that Ralph preferred the term *green psychology* to *ecopsychology* because he did not want the sprouting field to devolve into just another academic department or subdiscipline within psychology (which is what happened). "What he offered was new visions of who we are and how to be here with each other," noted Chalquist.

Ralph was a fearless advocate of the radical shift in consciousness that is needed to turn around the human relationship to the environment.

---

9. Ralph Metzner, *Maps of Consciousness* (New York: Collier-Macmillan, 1971), 142–3. Republished in 2023 by Inner Traditions.

In the words of Sam Mickey, "Ralph's writings and teaching lay out guidelines for transitioning to an ecological worldview, including ecological reorientations of science, philosophy, politics, economics, and religion, drawing on diverse sources of knowing, such as alchemy, yoga, mysticism, shamanism, and psychoactive plant medicines."[10]

During his lifetime of nearly eighty-three years, the limitations and self-concepts held by society have evolved, transformed, and expanded. We live in a more aware, nuanced culture with a heightened sense of responsibility and connectedness. Ralph Metzner made his contribution to these new foundations of our unfolding world.

ARTISTIC EXPRESSION

In addition to being a researcher, professor, therapist, and author, it would come as no surprise that Ralph was also a poet and musician who inspired creativity in colleagues, associates, and friends. A section on artistic expression is included. We are happy to include some pieces of art that were created by the contributors for Ralph.

DEATH, CONSCIOUS DYING, AND THE AFTERLIFE

Conscious dying was important to Ralph. This hearkens back to the beginning of his career with the publication of his coauthored book *The Psychedelic Experience: A Manual Based on the Tibetan Book of the Dead*, which describes experiences to be expected at the time of death and the following forty-nine days. In addition, it is a manual for the living. Ralph held that the most important use of psychedelics and consequent experience of expanded states of awareness was to prepare for conscious dying.

Ralph's dying process was indeed conscious. He was courageous, pragmatic, and without fear in the face of his impending death. He had a firm conviction about life after death and reincarnation. He had his

---

10. Quote from Sam Mickey's essay in this volume.

personal, financial, and work affairs in order. He was complete. He died peacefully in his sleep.

Ralph proposed that a positive, less fearful attitude toward death is a necessary preparation for a transformed state of heightened aliveness. He encouraged us to confront our fear of death and to embrace the process of dying as liberating and bringing wisdom.[11]

Simcha Paull Raphael's "Afterlife Journey of the Soul in Jewish Mysticism and Tradition" is a penetrating exploration of the stages of life after death in Judaism, with insights for the dying and bereaved. Ralph was Simcha's dissertation chair on this topic, of deep interest to him.

FAMILY

Finally, there is a section with contributions from his family: his daughter Sophia Metzner, his stepson Elias Jacobson, and myself (Cathy), his wife.

◆ ◆ ◆

A few other notes about this book as a whole: Many of the contributions could be classified in several sections. For example, Susan Wright's "Conversations with Ralph" is placed in the "Artistic Expression" section, but it could fit just as well in "Death, Conscious Dying, and the Afterlife." We have tried to build a full and rich experience for readers within each section.

You will find some repetitious phrases throughout the book such as "So it is," the title of Charles Grob's essay. Such phrases were key to Ralph's worldview. *So it is* refers to Ralph's acknowledgment of the reality of a situation, allowing it simply to be what it is.

The variety of styles and tones throughout the book represent an intentional decision to enable each author's authentic voice to shine through.

Simon notes, "Reading these thoughtful and heartwarming stories, I gained unexpected personal epiphanies."

We hope that you, too, get as much pleasure as we did reading the tales of this remarkable man.

---

11. Ralph Metzner, *The Unfolding Self* (Santa Fe, NM: Synergetic Press, 2022), 159–86.

.

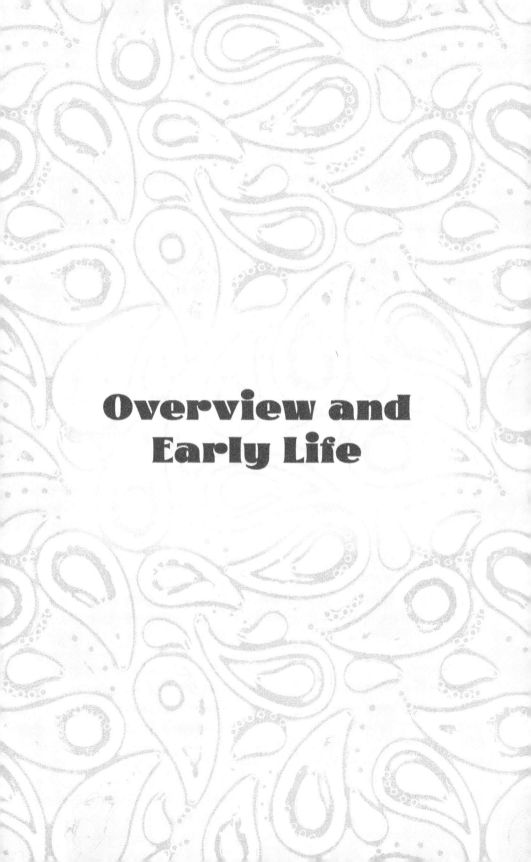

Overview and Early Life

Ralph Metzner
May 18, 1936–March 14, 2019

Ralph Metzner was a recognized pioneer of psychological, philosophical, and cross-cultural studies of consciousness. He was born on May 18, 1936, the second son of Wolfgang Metzner, owner of a successful publishing house in Berlin, Germany, and Jessie (known as "Jill") Laurie, a Scotswoman from Stewarton, Ayrshire, in Scotland. His parents met in 1932 in Geneva, Switzerland, when Wolfgang was a student at the University there and Jill was employed by the League of Nations. After their marriage, they lived in Berlin and had three sons.

In 1944 they fled Berlin to Husum in Schleswig-Holstein, northern Germany, to escape wartime bombing and destruction and the advance of the Russian armies. There they saw the war out in considerable penury. At the end of the war in 1945, in view of the breakdown of education in Germany, they decided that Jill should return to Scotland temporarily with the boys while Wolfgang rebuilt his business in Frankfurt. The separation of Ralph's parents eventually caused their marriage to break down.

In 1948, Wolfgang's business and the education system in Germany were recovering, and they agreed that the younger boys, Ralph and Robin, should return to live and be educated in Germany, and the eldest, Ken, continue his education at Fettes College in Edinburgh, Scotland. Jill had meanwhile moved to Paris, France, where she was on the staff of UNESCO. So Ralph and his younger brother, Robin, went to school at Germany's top boarding school, Salem. But in 1950 Ralph made clear his wish to return to Scotland. His parents agreed and his father was able to arrange with Salem for him to move to Gordonstoun School in Scotland as an exchange student (the two schools were associated).

Ralph was not happy at Gordonstoun, but he knew it was an excellent place to get an education, and he wanted to be there. He bore the burden of being despised as an enemy German, yet he won respect as a top scholar. In due course Ralph was admitted to Oxford University's Queen's College. There he obtained a first class honours degree[1] in politics, philosophy, and economics. He subsequently attended Harvard University from 1958 to 1962 where he obtained his Ph.D. in clinical psychology and personality and a postdoctoral NIMH fellowship in pharmacology at the Medical School. Ralph's adversity in his childhood and teens had a profound and lasting influence on his personality and thinking. His life-long interest both in the causes of war and how to end it gave rise to his book *The Roots of War and Domination*.[2]

While at Harvard in the late 1950s and early 1960s he collaborated with Timothy Leary and Richard Alpert in classic studies of psychedelics. He coauthored *The Psychedelic Experience* with Leary and Alpert in 1964 and became editor of *The Psychedelic Review*. His conversational memoir of the Harvard projects in the early 1960s, with Ram Dass and Gary Bravo, *Birth of a Psychedelic Culture*, was published in 2010 by Synergetic Press. In the 1970s he became a student, and then a teacher, of Actualism. *Actualism* refers to "the actual design of Man as a Cosmic Being." The method it employs is called Agni Yoga. *Agni* means "fire" and *yoga* means "union," so "union by fire." The practitioner envisions a point of white light six inches above his or her head and directs it down to fill the body. The idea is that this purifies the individual with observable positive effects on well-being and general perceptivity, and the benefits continue to accrue with ongoing practice.[3] These Light-Fire energy purification techniques are used to increase joy, solve problems, heal oneself and others, and enhance creative expression.

In 1962 he married Susan Homer, and they lived together in the Millbrook Community in upstate New York. They divorced in 1964.

---

1. A first class honours degree is the equivalent to a U.S. bachelor's degree with highest honors.
2. Ralph Metzner, *The Roots of War and Domination* (Sonoma, CA: Four Trees Press, 2022).
3. Ralph Metzner, *Maps of Consciousness* (New York: Collier-Macmillan, 1971), 141–60.

In 1966 he had a son, Ari Krishna Metzner, from a brief relation-ship. Ralph was a single parent for much of Ari's childhood. Ari died at age eight in a bicycle accident in 1974—a tragedy that shook Ralph to his core.

Ralph was a psychotherapist in private practice in the San Francisco Bay Area and professor emeritus at the California Institute of Integral Studies (CIIS) in San Francisco, where he taught psychology and con-sciousness studies for thirty-one years, and where he served as academic dean and academic vice-president. Throughout his long working life Ralph was an indefatigable traveler in many parts of the world and a fascinating scholar, teacher, researcher, and author.

In 1988 Ralph married Cathy Coleman, a colleague at CIIS. Ralph and Cathy had a daughter, Sophia Marija Metzner, in 1989, and together with Cathy's son, Elias (Eli) Jacobson, they lived as a family in Sonoma, California.

■ Fig. I. Green Earth Foundation board's last meeting with Ralph, November 2018; from left: Joseph Friedman, Jack Silver, Ralph, Michael Ziegler, Kathleen Silver, Leigh Marz, Cathy Coleman (Photo by Sophia Metzner)

In 1989 Ralph and Cathy cofounded the Green Earth Foundation, an educational, research, and publishing organization.

In his sixties Ralph ignited his musical and poetic talents. He began taking jazz piano lessons as an adjunct to his earlier classical piano training. He composed words and music for numerous songs and recorded them on an album titled *Bardo Blues and Other Songs of Liberation*. He published some of his poetry in *Diving for Treasures* (2015), and recorded some of the poems with musical accompaniment with collaborators in an album titled *Spirit Soundings*. In 2018 he produced a narrative recording with musical accompaniment, *Völuspa*, with Byron Metcalf.

His life was rich in friendships and collegial relationships.

He died peacefully on March 14, 2019, at his home in Sonoma, California, at age eighty-two from the lung disease idiopathic pulmonary fibrosis (IPF). His older brother, Ken Metzner, died in California in 2020. He is survived by his younger brother, Robin Metzner, and by his half-brothers, Guenther Metzner and Otto Metzner, and his half-sister, Anna Metzner, all in Germany; and by their respective families, including eleven nieces and nephews.

Remembering Ralph Metzner:
Scholar, Teacher, Shaman
David Presti

This essay is adapted from and reprinted with permission of *The Journal of Transpersonal Psychology*.[4]

Ralph Metzner was a visionary alchemical explorer, rigorous academic scholar, and uniquely gifted shamanic teacher. His contributions to

---

4. David E. Presti, "A Memorial Tribute to Ralph Metzner: Scholar, Teacher, Shaman (18 May 1936 to 14 March 2019)," *The Journal of Transpersonal Psychology* 51, no. 1 (2019), 1–5.

■ Fig. 2. David Presti, his wife Kristi Panik, and Ralph in March 2018
(Photo courtesy of David Presti)

transpersonal psychology, consciousness research, and contemporary psychedelic studies are myriad. Throughout his life he engaged in a deep study of mind, and he distilled his findings into words and practices he communicated to others through his many writings, teachings, and counsel. The study of consciousness, now an acceptable topic of investigation in mainstream science, will surely benefit as ideas he explored continue to penetrate into academic discourse. And the growing contemporary field of psychedelic science—currently undergoing a blossoming of clinical and neurobiological investigation—has been and will continue to be profoundly influenced by Ralph's contributions over the last more than half-century.

Following graduation from Oxford in 1958, Ralph came to the United States to attend graduate school in psychology at Harvard University. After a couple years studying behaviorist learning theory and psychoanalysis, dominant forces in academic psychology at that time, he encountered the research project of Harvard faculty members Timothy Leary and Richard Alpert, who were conducting an innovative investigation into the psychological effects of psilocybin.

Psilocybin had recently been identified—by Albert Hofmann[5] of the Swiss pharmaceutical company Sandoz—as the primary psychoactive chemical in psychedelic (genus *Psilocybe*) mushrooms. Ralph had his first psychedelic-drug experience in March 1961, about which he would later write, with deep sincerity, in the preface to his *Maps of Consciousness* (1971, 2023): "I shall always be grateful to Harvard for providing me with that extremely educational experience."

Ralph joined the psilocybin research project, although he and other graduate students were informed the following year by senior faculty in the psychology department that they could not use psilocybin-related research in their doctoral dissertations. In part this related to deep opposition to a paradigm that drew upon the study of subjective experience rather than measurement of behavioral action. American psychology at the time was only beginning its emergence from decades of domination by behaviorism. And perhaps even more egregious was the fact that the researchers in the psilocybin project were generating ideas and protocols via taking the drug themselves. This was considered by some to be an unacceptable manner of conducting scientific investigation.

While continuing to participate in psychedelic research, Ralph also engaged in another project in reward-delay learning and used that work to complete a doctorate in clinical psychology. He followed with an NIMH postdoctoral fellowship in pharmacology at Harvard's medical school. Shortly thereafter, his mentors were famously dismissed from Harvard—a testament to the power of psychedelics to shake up the psyche and potentially lead to problematic consequences when this power is not effectively contained and channeled.

Ralph, together with Leary and Alpert, moved to a communal living setting in Millbrook, New York, where they continued their

---

5. Although Albert Hofmann is known best for being the first person to synthesize LSD, he was also the first person to isolate, synthesize, and name the principal psychedelic mushroom compounds psilocybin and psilocin. "Psilocybin und Psilocin, zwei psychotrope Wirkstoffe aus mexikanischen Rauschpilzen," *Helvetica Chemica Acta* 42 (1959): 1557–72.

exploration of the impact of psychedelics on consciousness. By this time psilocybin had become difficult to obtain from Sandoz and their primary focus of exploration had switched to LSD. From these investigations came Ralph's first book, a collaborative project together with Leary and Alpert (and inspired by Aldous Huxley), based on a translation of Tibetan texts known in English as the Tibetan Book of the Dead. In Tibetan spiritual traditions, these texts have been interpreted as a guide to negotiating the intermediate state (*bardo*) between one life and the next. In *The Psychedelic Experience: A Manual Based on The Tibetan Book of the Dead* (1964), the bardo prayers were reformulated by Ralph, Leary, and Alpert as guides to harnessing states of consciousness experienced during a psychedelic trip for psychospiritual growth. It was and is a beautiful notion, poetically executed.

Their communal research program at Millbrook eventually dissolved. Leary went on to become a provocative activist for social change, proponent of personal exploration with psychedelics, and highly visible lightning rod for targeting by establishment powers. Alpert journeyed to India, connected strongly with Hindu spirituality, and returned to America as Ram Dass. He authored a widely read book—*Be Here Now*—and through his lectures and writings contributed to introducing ideas from Asian spiritual traditions into American culture.

Ralph moved to California where he assumed a position as a staff clinical psychologist at Mendocino State Hospital in Ukiah, California—an institution for the "criminally insane" and other chronically mentally ill, housing nearly two thousand patients at the time. Subsequently, he worked as a staff clinical psychologist at Kaiser Permanente, Stanford University, and Fairview State Hospital in Southern California.

All along, Ralph continued his scholarly activities, editing a periodic publication called *The Psychedelic Review* (1963–71) and a book, *The Ecstatic Adventure* (1968), addressing the psychological and societal impact of psychedelics. While Ralph's initial connection with transpersonal psychology was catalyzed by years of intense exploration with psychedelics, he quickly expanded into other territory. His quest throughout was to draw upon the rich bodies of knowledge and wisdom emergent from European and Asian spiritual and mystical traditions and bring this to bear to both expand a modern science of human perception and develop and disseminate practices conducive to psychospiritual growth and healing.

In 1971 he published *Maps of Consciousness*, a magnum opus of scholarly and personal-practice investigation into a variety of esoteric divinatory and psychospiritual traditions—including the I Ching, alchemy, tarot, and astrology—speaking to the deepening of one's capacity to explore the boundaries of the mind. For Ralph, it was always about how to apply the knowledge and practices learned from these traditions to reduce suffering at the individual, societal, and planetary levels. His interest in extending the results of personal transformation to planetary health is articulated in his 1999 book, *Green Psychology: Transforming Our Relationship to the Earth* and is the stated mission of the Green Earth Foundation, a nonprofit organization created by him and his wife Cathy.

In the early 1970s Ralph studied Actualism, an esoteric yogic teaching of working with inner light, from Russell Schofield at the School of Actualism in Southern California. Ralph was among the pioneering teaching staff of Actualism. He was an active member of the Actualism community for nearly a decade, and this served as a foundational aspect of his work and his own practice throughout his life.

In 1975 Ralph took a job as professor at a small graduate school in San Francisco known at the time as the California Institute of Asian Studies. In 1980 the school's name changed to the California Institute of Integral Studies (CIIS) and the institution grew in size and stature. Today CIIS is at the forefront of psychology graduate training programs encouraging and supporting investigation of frontier areas of humanistic and transpersonal psychology and consciousness research.

Ralph served as professor on the CIIS faculty for three decades. He took on positions as academic dean and academic vice-president, during which time he contributed to the expansion of the school and its programs. I had the good fortune to meet Ralph in the early 1990s, and thereafter paid a number of visits to his classes at CIIS, offering instruction and facilitating discussion related to neuroscience and psychopharmacology.

Ralph researched, taught, and wrote continuously—in academic settings and in widely delivered lectures, seminars, and workshops. His teachings were profoundly influential to a large number of psychotherapeutic practitioners, and the web of his students was vast. And to his last days, he maintained a small psychotherapy practice.

Ralph's work with psychedelics that began when he was a graduate student at Harvard continued throughout his life. He worked with and wrote about the powerful psychotherapeutic utility of MDMA (3,4-methylenedioxy-N-methylamphetamine) in the 1980s, well before it became an illegal Schedule I controlled substance in 1985. In the early 1980s, he proposed the term *empathogenic* to describe the distinctive "heart-opening" quality so often associated with MDMA and distinguishing its effects from those of other psychedelics. Only now, after decades of perseverance, is the psychotherapeutic use of MDMA again becoming accepted in academic clinical science.

For three decades, prior to it becoming an illegal Schedule I substance in 2011, Ralph researched the psychotherapeutic utility of 5-MeO-DMT, a psychedelic substance present in a number of Amazonian plants and also in secretions from the Sonoran Desert toad (*Bufo alvarius*). He summarized a number of his methods and observations related to working with this substance in his book *The Toad and the Jaguar* (2013).

Ralph was a gifted and prolific writer. During his lifetime, he wrote twenty-four books and more than a hundred published essays, journal articles, and book chapters. His last published book—*Searching for the Philosophers' Stone: Encounters with Mystics, Scientists, and Healers* (2018)—describes his relationships with and gratitude for important teachers in his life, and appeared in print only weeks before he died.

In the days immediately prior to his death, Ralph posted small notes near his bed in which he had written: "intention ➞ attention ➞ awareness"—reminders to remain alert and aware along his dying trajectory—and a testament to the shamanic advice he frequently offered in working with visionary states: stay connected with your intention, your ancestors (those who have gone before, those who have mapped the terrain), your ground, and your light. Good medicine, indeed.

Ralph leaves an extensive legacy of written scholarship and teaching, and a widely distributed circle of students and friends, deeply grateful for what he gave to the global community of transpersonal psychology. Thank you, Ralph!

> Gate gate pāragate pārasaṃgate bodhi svāhā
> Gone, gone, gone all the way over,
> everyone gone to the other shore,
> enlightenment, svāhā![6]

---

6. This mantra is spoken by the bodhisattva Avalokiteshvara at the end of the delivery of the Prajnaparamita Sutra or Heart Sutra. This is the great Buddhist teaching on the emptiness, dependent origination, the deep interconnection of all things, what Thich Nhat Hanh beautifully calls "interbeing." Thich Nhat Hahn's description: "Gate means gone: gone from suffering to the liberation from suffering. Gone from forgetfulness to mindfulness. Gone from duality to nonduality. Gate, gate means gone, gone. Pāragate means gone all the way to the other shore. In pārasaṃgate, saṃ means everyone, the sangha, the entire community of beings. Bodhi is the light inside, enlightenment, or awakening. Svāhā is a cry of joy and triumph, like Eureka! or Hallelujah!"

The Unusual Second Son
Robin Metzner

Robin Metzner is Ralph's younger brother, born not quite two years after Ralph, in January 1938. Robin studied jurisprudence at Geneva University and at Jesus College, Oxford. He and Ralph were both at Oxford during the 1957–58 academic year. Robin then practiced law as a barrister and judge.

Ralph's wife, Cathy, asked me to write about Ralph's early family life before his move to the United States and about the influence of his father, Wolfgang, on his later development there.

Ralph's paternal ancestors were working-class Prussians living in Berlin. In 1936 Ralph's father was working in Berlin in a junior capacity in the family publishing business. Ralph was the second of three sons from Wolfgang's marriage to Jill Laurie, a Scotswoman.

The Nazis were in power. The German government had become a dictatorship. Wolfgang had been a social democrat and therefore anti-Nazi from the outset. He and Jill were both committed pacifists, tolerant and decent, energetic and hardworking.

From his days in Geneva, Wolfgang had come to believe in the principles of the League of Nations: notably international cooperation and disarmament. He became a lifelong Francophile and Anglophile and learned the languages. Since the election of Hitler in 1933 he had realized that he and Jill had to abandon politics and to keep their views to themselves if they did not want to prejudice the family's livelihood, liberty, or lives. He was severely conflicted. He had come under suspicion of disloyalty to the Nazi ideals. The Nazis were popular then. I should add that Wolfgang was a highly intelligent, cultured, and scholarly type. In middle age it became apparent that he was also an astute and energetic businessman.

By luck or design during the war years he was not at any time involved in any military or violent action or secret service work or with criminals, detainees, deportations, or interrogations. By the end of the war, the business premises had been bombed out of existence. The family was impoverished. Ralph was nine years old at that time and experienced wartime bombing. Luckily the family home was not hit. With Russian armies approaching, Jill and we boys fled Berlin to a village near Denmark.

Soon after the war in May 1945 Jill obtained employment and was granted the use of a house from the British Military Occupation Forces. Wolfgang was not often there. He was striving to rebuild the business amid the ruins of Germany. In 1948, aged 39, he obtained the necessary license to reestablish the business in Frankfurt. It soon prospered again. In time, it became his life and soul until he died at age eighty-two in 1992, one of the grand old men of postwar German publishing.

Because of the breakdown of the economy and lack of schooling in Germany after the war, it was agreed that Jill should return with us boys to Britain temporarily. We left in December 1946 and did not see Wolfgang again for two years. He was not then allowed to leave Germany. We first stayed with Jill's sister in a roughhouse village in Scotland. Later, Ralph moved to a boarding school near London. Jill was the only breadwinner. In 1948 she obtained work with UNESCO in Paris and, as a result, Ralph returned to Germany to attend a boarding school there.

The family got together most holidays. At about that time I first realized that Ralph was different—he had interests way beyond his contemporaries, like reading serious stuff. In 1950, age fourteen, at his wish, he returned to Britain and attended a well-known boarding school in Northern Scotland called Gordonstoun. He would meet his parents and brothers only during holidays. In those halcyon days (1950s) that meant skiing or mountaineering in the Alps, or trips in Germany or France (where our mother, Jill, lived). One thing caused Ralph's parents concern. He was reported by his teachers not to be much interested in science or useful subjects for any future career. During one holiday in Paris, I was in awe to find Ralph reading the Bible from end to end, taking me to cheap afternoon sessions in the Comedie Francaise, playing the *flaneur* (idler) on the Boul'Mich, and enjoying live early soul and country music sessions in a bar in St. Germain.

Ralph excelled in his school exams and won a scholarship in 1954 to the Queen's College, Oxford. He studied psychology, physiology, and philosophy for the next three years. The focus was on psychology, at

■ Fig. 3. From left: Young brothers Ralph, Robin, and Ken, with their mother, Jill, in 1947 (From the collection of Ralph Metzner)

■ Fig. 4. Brothers Ken, Ralph, and Robin in 1969 (From the collection of Ralph Metzner)

■ Fig. 5. Brothers Ralph, Robin, and Ken at Robin's home in London on Ralph's seventy-fifth birthday, May 18, 2011 (From the collection of Ralph Metzner)

the time probably largely theoretical, as opposed to experimental psychology. The faculty, under Professor George Humphrey, was probably quite small. The philosophy in question was principally J. L. Austin and Gilbert Ryle's philosophy of language (meaning, in reality, the English language). It was an ideal venue and those were ideal subjects for him. I visited him there in 1957 and learned from his tutor that he was producing outstanding essays. He was also reading widely outside his course work, for instance (as he told me), Gurdjieff. In 1958 he obtained a first class degree. After a few months in Germany, and after doing more examinations, he departed with a scholarship to Harvard. There he ploughed his own furrow, remote as he then was from his parent's influence. The rest is history . . .

Wolfgang's business life as a publisher seemed to have little relevance to Ralph's later professional development, except that it was a similar broad profession, in part connected to academia, and it paid for his education and holidays. Wolfgang's publishing business was a highly specialized business and profitable. By far the main part was publishing books, journals, and forms for the information, education, reference, and use of civil registries.

Wolfgang did not discuss business decisions at home, nor bring any of his publications home. He liked to keep his business and family lives separate. Occasionally an author came for dinner. Jill and we boys only had a general idea. We rarely visited the office during holidays.

To my mind, the legacy that Ralph took away from his father was more his scholarly bent of mind and reading habit, his disciplined phenomenal memory and thorough work ethic; and from both his parents their internationalist democratic pacifist opinions. The crucial relevant influence on his future surely came from his time at Oxford and Harvard. His parents were sometimes puzzled about their unusual second son in the United States, but they tried to understand. Wolfgang and Jill divorced in 1954, but remained good friends for life. The relationship between Ralph and his parents was excellent throughout their lives, for Ralph had much in common with each of them.

There Are No Winners in War
Richard Strozzi-Heckler

Richard Strozzi-Heckler, Ph.D., is a psychologist, author, and a seventh-degree Shihan in Aikido. He is the founder of the Strozzi Institute, the Center for Leadership and Mastery, and Two Rock Aikido Dojo.

Ralph came to the Two Rock Dojo[7] in Northern California on two occasions, which gave me the good fortune and pleasure of engaging with him in a number of far-ranging conversations. He led a ceremony at the dojo for a small group of like-minded men that was spiritually impactful and highly illuminating for all. In the debrief the following morning, Ralph made known that he underestimated the mixture he put together for us, and as he surrendered to the strength of the medicine himself he didn't think he fully performed his role as guide. I (and I think I can speak for the other participants) had no experience of what he said as he was energetically and verbally present, grounded in his role, while skillfully guiding us through multidimensions of consciousness. What moved me by his transparent self-reflection was the genuineness and honesty in which he shared himself. In that moment he was a model of an authenticity that eclipsed role, identity, and ego.

Shortly after that I invited Ralph to speak at the Strozzi Institute's annual alumni gathering. When he asked what he should present I told him to speak about the influences, good and bad, that shaped him in who he is now; in other words, I asked him to tell us about his journey. I could see that a number of attendees were surprised by his demeanor: a somewhat frail, slow moving, older gentleman, yet in no apparent distress. As he spoke everyone was instantly engaged as he presented his extraordinary life and work. The light of his wisdom,

---

7. Two Rock Dojo, founded in 1987 by Richard Strozzi-Heckler Shihan, is affiliated with the California Aikido Association and trains in Aiki principles with a sensibility of a martial context emphasizing taking Aiki training and principles into everyday life.

compassion, and love transformed the space, holding us in a single undivided attention.

At some point I asked him what formed his strong antiwar position. He told me that he had lived in Germany during World War II and he had seen firsthand the horrors of war. He explained that there was no food, clean water, or sanitation, and all the streets and houses were rubble from the bombing. His mother had fled Germany with her three sons in December of 1946 and moved to her homeland, Scotland. "My first thought was that I was going to the winner's country," he said. "I was so elated to be in the country that had won the war and I assumed this meant plenty of good food to eat, water safe to drink, and to have a clean bed to sleep in." He then described the shock of arriving in London to see that it looked just like Germany. "It was then," he said, "that I realized there are no winners in war."

As he spoke, Ralph embodied this powerful insight his nine-year-old self had experienced decades ago; and its truth emanated from him like a thunderbolt reverberating throughout the room. Yes, the attendees in the room would say they were against war and violence, but to hear this truth transmitted in this simple but powerful way touched us deeply.

Ralph's teachings came not only from knowledge, which he had plenty of, but the metabolizing of his rich life into an embodied wisdom. This was the gift he left for me. Thank you, Ralph.

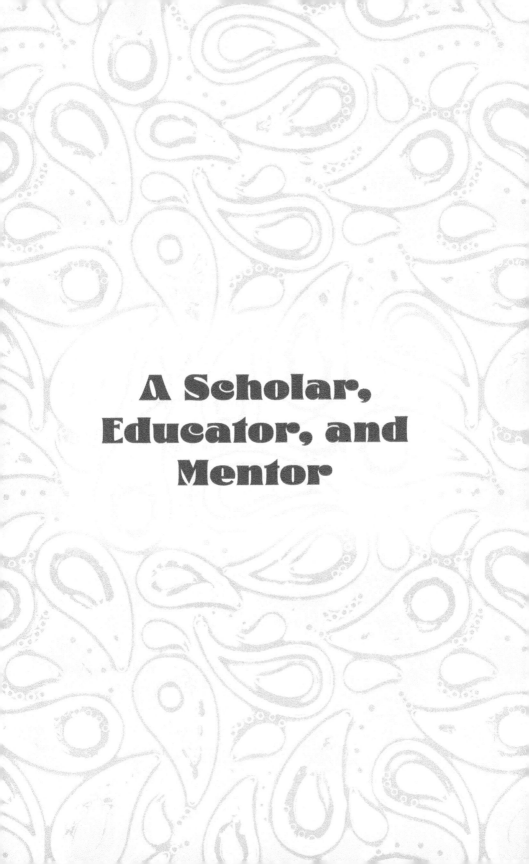

A Scholar, Educator, and Mentor

Entertaining Gods and Goddesses
Stanley Krippner

Stanley Krippner, Ph.D., has held numerous faculty appointments and authored several books and over one thousand peer-reviewed articles on psychology, dreams, hypnosis, psychedelics, mythology, and parapsychology. He received the 2002 Award for Distinguished Contributions to the International Development of Psychology from the American Psychological Association.

In 1962, I was invited to Harvard and participated in one of Timothy Leary's last "authorized" psilocybin sessions. It was a memorable event, and I recently wrote about it for an anthology on the topic.[1]

Once Leary left Harvard and established his Castalia organization at Millbrook, New York, I was again invited to participate in an event, but this time without psilocybin or any other psychedelic substance. This event lasted for three days; Ralph, who had recently returned from India, led a sunrise yoga session on the second day. This workshop was quite memorable. I found most of the exercises unique, and adapted some of them into my own workshops, especially those on the theme of "personal mythology," which was the title of a book I later coauthored with David Feinstein, another psychologist.[2]

My first contact with Ralph was during my tenure at Kent State University as director of the Child Study Center. I was pleasantly surprised when Ralph invited me to write a chapter for his book *The Ecstatic Adventure*, a collection of first-person accounts. For Ralph's book I described an adventure that was far from ecstatic, one that resulted from consuming a large number of psychotropic morning glory

---

1. Zalman Schacter-Shalomi and Stanley Krippner, "Personal Experiences with Psychoactive Agents: Our First Time," in *Seeking the Sacred with Psychoactive Substances: Chemical Pathways to Spirituality and to God*, vol. 2, ed. J. H. Ellens (Westport, CT: Praeger, 2014), 147–67.
2. David Feinstein and Stanley Krippner, *Personal Mythology: The Psychology of Your Evolving Self* (Los Angeles: Jeremy P. Tarcher, 1988).

seeds. I titled it "Of Hell and Heavenly Blue," the latter term a reference to one of the three varieties that had mind-altering effects. (Indeed, the company that produced these species sprayed them with a chemical that eliminated their ability to evoke psychedelic tripping.)

When my family and I moved to New York City, my contact with Ralph continued. At that time, I was conducting dream research at Maimonides Medical Center in Brooklyn, New York. I invited Ralph to participate in a content analysis of dreams that was part of an experiment involving putative telepathy, an attempt by participants to dream about art prints that had been randomly selected once they had retired to a soundproof room. The results, though controversial, provided data strongly supporting the telepathy hypothesis.

Leary had established an educational center in Manhattan, one that I occasionally visited. During those years, Leary was castigated by politicians, ridiculed by much of the media, and deserted by some of his former friends and colleagues. I admired Ralph for continuing his contact loyally with Leary and for emphasizing the positive contributions that the infamous Harvard Psilocybin Project had made to an understanding of set and setting in evoking responses to these substances.

■ Fig. 6. Stanley Krippner and Ralph
(From the collection of Ralph Metzner)

Ralph and I both relocated to the San Francisco Bay Area and continued our contact. His academic appointment at CIIS was of great benefit to that institution, for which I taught a few courses while employed by neighboring Saybrook University.

My friend Ron Boyer and I attended a gathering in Ralph's honor not long before his passing. We managed to have a brief visit, during which he noted that I was his "oldest living friend." For me that was an honor and a privilege.

In retrospect, I found it remarkable that Ralph survived the Harvard tempest with his academic credentials and standing intact. Leary had become a countercultural icon, a fugitive from justice, and—upon his release from jail—an author and lecturer. The other member of that Harvard trio, Richard Alpert, had become Baba Ram Dass, a spiritual leader whose books inspired thousands of seekers. I maintained contact with both of them, and I was present at a Stanford University conference when Leary and Ram Dass had an incredible reunion after an absence of contact of several years.

Ralph had chosen a different path, working not only in academia but founding the Green Earth Foundation. Ralph's activism regarding the environment was only one way in which he expressed his concern for what can be called "the world *problématique*." Much more proactive than either Leary or Ram Dass, Ralph was a signatory of the 9/11 Truth Commission and wrote about the roots of war.[3]

Both of us were interested in unidentified aerial objects and several topics outside the psychological mainstream such as reports of past lives.

Ralph's knowledge of Eastern thought was impressive, first expressed in the adaptation of the Tibetan Book of the Dead, coauthored with Leary and Ram Dass, and later developed more thoroughly when he wrote about the I Ching and Buddhism. His book *The Well of Remembrance* used his Northern European roots as a stimulus for

---

3. Ralph Metzner, *The Roots of War and Domination* (Sonoma, CA: Four Trees Press, 2022).

his readers to examine their own ethnic heritage. The books *Maps of Consciousness* and *Know Your Type* display a mastery of several fields of knowledge that seemingly would take decades to assimilate; however, he was only age thirty-four and forty-two respectively when they were published. Ralph was a poet, a songwriter, and a raconteur with an engaging sense of humor. His final book, *Searching for the Philosophers' Stone*, was autobiographical in nature. He presented penetrating portraits of Albert Hofmann and others in a way that not only illuminated their contributions but revealed aspects of their personalities unknown to me (and others) who had also known them.

When Ralph was admitted to Harvard, he had little idea as to how his time there would affect his life. It not only provided a solid grounding in mainstream psychology, it provided him with unique opportunities that would have derailed a lesser graduate student. Ralph took it all in stride, constructing a personal myth that I have always found incomparable. Whatever gods and goddesses there are will be entertained by this life well-lived.

Climbing the Ladder of Spiritual Awakening
DeLee Lantz

Dorothy "DeLee" Lantz, Ph.D., is a licensed psychologist. She was in the same clinical psychology graduate class as Ralph Metzner. She taught at the University of California, Santa Cruz; California Institute of Integral Studies; and several other universities. DeLee is in private practice in psychotherapy and biofeedback in San Francisco and Marin County, California.

1958. The first year of Harvard graduate school. A young man in his early twenties, straight from Oxford, Oxford haircut, English accent, wise to the world of fast-paced seminar discussions. A young woman in her early twenties, straight from a small town of ten thousand in Oklahoma, state university graduate, Oklahoma accent, style, and . . . horror! painted fingernails. Uncertain what she was doing there. Certainly not used to fast-paced seminars with expectations of insightful contributions. Ralph Metzner and DeLee Lantz.

We were the opposite ends of the spectrum of our ten-person class. Seemingly little in common. Yet Ralph and I became friends quickly. I received a somewhat condescending reception from some other classmates, with whom I later became friends, but to whom I had to "prove" myself. (And I learned from the other women to stop painting my nails, which was a sign of . . . what, I never figured out, but certainly not acceptable in this setting.) I never felt any of this from Ralph. And throughout the rest of his life, I saw how accepting Ralph was of both surface differences and deeper ones in people.

In hindsight, I have guessed that this was an outcome of having been "different" himself and having to "prove" himself. Born in Germany, relocated to Scotland at the end of the war (December 1946) and attending an elite boarding school, with little English, Ralph was an outsider who often experienced suspicion or downright hostility for his nationality. He had to endure, prevail, and excel. He could have identified with the aggressor. Or he could have become dedicated to accepting the outsider and being interested in their differences. He became the latter, of course. I don't believe that this was a consciously made choice. That would have the flavor of condescension, of sympathy. I believe it stemmed from some deeper part of himself.

Academically speaking, Ralph was a shining star of our class. I marveled at how he would respond so quickly and fluently to something as though he'd had plenty of time to ponder it, fashioning a witty, insightful response. This, of course, remained an ability of his throughout his life. But Ralph never, ever, acted arrogant, smart-ass, or better than. He never tried to one-up his classmates—as some others did, seeming to believe that's what you did in seminars.

That his superior intelligence was fully recognized in graduate school was clear when I overheard two professors talking to one another. One said, "Ralph is one of the brightest students ever to go through the program." The other responded, "No, he's one of the brightest students ever to go through the Graduate School."

Then, of course, there was the life-changing meeting and collaboration with Timothy Leary, that force who arrived during our second year and profoundly affected the trajectory of Ralph's life work. The threesome of Ralph, Tim, and Dick Alpert were to create a revolutionary change. I was not a part of that work. However, Tim affected all of us and most of us were introduced to the mind-expanding experience of psychedelics. I was a participant/subject in the first research study and here again, Ralph played a major role for me.

Ralph and George Litwin were the guides for three of us, fellow graduate students, as we took psilocybin for the first time. Set and setting were carefully and skillfully attended to. That, plus the safety that I felt with them, allowed for that mind-expanding experience from which one never fully returns. It set the stage for most of us who experienced this to seek an understanding of this profound departure from ordinary consciousness. We voraciously sought to know more of that expanded world.

We read Huxley's *The Perennial Philosophy*. We studied Eastern spiritual traditions, naively at first, to be sure. We took more psychedelics. The experience and the search led some of us to India. I spent four years there, over three trips, studying both Hinduism and Tibetan Buddhism.

After graduate school and leaving Cambridge, we continued to be friends, as our lives intertwined through the next sixty-one years. And counting. We connected through his New York time, my occasional visits to Millbrook, and eventually we both wound up in California. During a visit to Santa Cruz, where I was teaching, he introduced me to Actualism and Agni Yoga and I spent many a weekend at Russell Schofield's home and school in Southern California. I continue to use some of those practices in my own meditation and with my clients.

I eventually landed in San Francisco. Ralph, by then, was the academic dean of CIIS. He recruited me as adjunct faculty there. Thus,

I had occasion to witness how his leadership and teaching helped the graduate school flourish as a seat of spiritual searching and learning. Through his many books he shared with readers both his geographical and inner quests to uncover the many ways that mind and reality can be understood. It is impossible upon reading them and hearing him talk ever to think that "mind," "consciousness," and "the real world" are more or less the same for all. They are not.

In Plato's *Symposium* the topic of Love was chosen for the conversation for an evening of drinking (*symposium* literally meant "drinking party" in ancient Greek). Socrates shared insights about the Ladder of Love, with each step of the ladder leading to a higher expression. I believe Ralph's experience with the use of entheogens in this same way. We may first use drugs for recreation, to "get high," have fun, or "blow our minds." Having learned that there is another level of consciousness, we then yearn to go to a higher rung on that ladder, ever seeking greater spiritual development. Thus, rung by rung, we climb a Ladder of Spirituality, seeking further spiritual awakening. Ralph's life was a determined journey up that ladder, teaching others as he climbed.

Ralph's Animation of the Academy
Michael Flanagin

Michael Flanagin, Ph.D., earned his doctorate at CIIS in East-West Psychology where he served as the assistant to the dean (Ralph Metzner) and director of public programs for many years. Ralph was the committee chairman of his dissertation on serpent symbolism, a subject Ralph himself suggested. Upon graduation, he joined the staff of the Jung Institute in San Francisco and was one of the main writers of *The Book of Symbols*, a project of the New York Jung Institute's *Archive for Research in Archetypal Symbolism*.

The first time I saw Ralph Metzner was through the front window of the California Institute of Asian Studies (as it was known in 1980). I was about to enter my new graduate school and encountered him as the instructor of my first class. I had arrived in San Francisco the day before, fresh from a seminary in Minnesota. I found his style of teaching was as abrupt a contrast as the snowy fields I had left behind were with the butterflies in January in the Bay Area.

I went on to study with Ralph in an unbroken sequence for many years, and to discover what an original personality he was. I believe he welcomed someone coming into his sphere from what he perceived as a more conservative academic background: it revealed his widening influence. Others may recall Ralph in shorter and more concentrated presentations as his enchanted cosmology matured in later years. I draw my reflections from prolonged observation of his day-to-day self in those earlier years, observing less spectacular details like his neatly stylized handwriting, his orderly filing system, his reasonableness—all vestiges of a Germanic youth. As William James insisted, one learns personality theory from remarkable personalities, not from ordinary cases. One could learn an extraordinary amount from Ralph.

As his assistant, I noticed people would often approach Ralph with a sly, conspiratorial smile, as if they were privy to his esoteric arcana and a radical new world opened up by psychedelics and expect an immediate acknowledgment. But Ralph was a sensitive person best approached with a measure of reserve, allowing his deeper capacity for emotional engagement to emerge and a trust to be gradually established.

Although I had sampled LSD before I met him, I never sampled a single psychoactive molecule during our decade of active propinquity. Ralph's willingness to teach someone who still attended weekly Mass or who could decipher ancient Greek made me wonder if this broadmindedness was not a key to a significant, but easily overlooked, attribute of his long career. How much of that was owed to his fortuitous encounter at Harvard with Leary and Ram Dass is anyone's guess, but that it began at a time when that revolution meant academic expulsion for Leary and Ram Dass is pivotal. By 1980, Ralph had positioned himself as an academic dean in a graduate school pioneering degree programs that brought psychedelic consciousness into the limelight, drawing content from the rich maps and metaphors that he found in traditional symbolic cultures. Ralph had turned the tables on Harvard, albeit in a new, fresh, and exciting milieu.

Working on a daily basis side by side, I pondered Ralph's educated speech, his occasional Oxford-era Britishisms or his fluency in German. I quietly pieced together a profile that helped explain him to me: the son of a well-educated German father and a Scottish mother, both from whom he was separated as he attended boarding school in Scotland after the war ended. Not only was he inwardly highly sensitive, but he kept various poignant memories in his private core. The visionary inspiration of a dramatically expanded horizon in his mastery of pharmacopeia made sense in this profile.

In 1980, not all of Ralph's ideas were fully developed; his emphasis on the divine feminine and the ecology of a living planet had yet to surface. As the archetypal scholar, he was drawn to systems of typology. I recall sitting nervously as he walked around a table of his students during a class on William Sheldon's body types. As this slender ectomorph looked suspiciously at the few innocent pounds that I had added to my thirty-year-old waist, I, by contrast, saw him as a skein of thinly enfleshed nerves.

In Ralph's presentation, modern psychology flowed naturally from continuities with ancient knowledge. It made the alchemical marriage of opposite elements a powerful metaphor for him: his ideas presupposed polarity to make them vital. I found the easiest rapport with him came by adopting a neutral midpoint, but never opposing. And the thing to remember is that Ralph was very, very intelligent: it paid to just listen.

During the years of our working together, he brought some of the most colorful celebrities of his wider world into the institute's public programs that he had me coordinate. I observed how he positioned himself with his many students—a rather soft-spoken authority that was not easily brooked—but also his stance with the faculty as their dean. In the early years at such a "cutting-edge" school (as CIIS described itself), incoming faculty might expect great liberality and laissez-faire approaches, but Ralph held to standards from his Oxford education that resulted in accreditation, while ironically remaining the standard bearer of a Leary-era revolt.

His early years with a literate German father, a leader in the German publishing industry, left him with an interesting alchemy all his own. He was one of the most interesting personalities I've ever encountered. Yet if I would consider him as my main teacher, I only rarely adopted his ideas. What I adopted was the reasoning behind his ideas, the willingness to apply historical scholarship to new fields, as well as a bent for the comparative studies of symbols. For example, I did not share his enthusiasm for the wilderness outings of a vision quest. His past was the key to his futuristic mind.

For many of us, the decade of the 1980s when Ralph was academic dean and one of the main professors in the East-West Psychology program was a golden age. Outside our school walls, of course, it was the Reagan years and the high-water mark of the AIDS crisis in San Francisco. But inside, a luminary of sorts was crafting an array of lapidary teachings, a person I could easily imagine in that seventeenth-century woodcut, depicting an alchemist following the footprints of Sophia lit by his lantern of arcane wisdom. Ralph was also thoroughly modern, an early adopter of technology, delighted by new ideas and engaged by claims that a more conservative person, like myself, would require proofs that made acceptance come more slowly.

Ralph introduced shamanism to what was then a mainly Eastern-oriented curriculum, yet he guarded the conventions of Western psychological research, including the widely loathed courses in statistics, being sensitive to a graduate's professional credentials. He also introduced what might be broadly called the "sacred feminine," best represented by his championing the work of Marija Gimbutas, Susan Seddon Boulet, and Hildegard of Bingen with her famous *viriditas*, the greening power of the spirit. For Ralph, these ideas complemented, substantiated, and integrated the inspiration received from entheogens.

As I prepared to move on in my career, I saw him become transformed. His life's work included not only his pioneering role in building an accredited institution of integral education, but in his role in preserving the planet, whose green mantle of life was perhaps more alive to him than those lost in the mental structures of an exhausted civilization.

The last time I saw Ralph was in 1996 when I invited him and the Swedish curator of the New York Jung Institute ARAS collection to speak on Norse mythology. (I was her counterpart at the San Francisco Jung Institute, where the program took place.) Ralph's mixed feelings around his German identity had benefitted from his recent investigation of Germanic myths. He suggested that similar benefits awaited any modern German who might have erected a protective barrier between their conscious mind and their deeper ancestral roots due to painful associations with the Wotanism of wartime ideology. He developed these ideas in a most persuasive application of the therapeutic potential of archetypal symbolism, his book *The Well of Remembrance*.

Over dinner following this program I had no premonition that this would be our final encounter in person, although we corresponded until

■ Fig. 7. Ram Dass, Michael Kahn, and Ralph at CIIS graduation 1989; Michael was a CIIS professor and was in graduate school at Harvard with Ralph with Ram Dass as faculty (From the collection of Ralph Metzner)

his death. But I felt a sense of completion in witnessing how Ralph had healed something profound in his inner world through his assimilation in these old Germanic myths. By drawing on such a feminine and ter-restrial image as the "well of remembrance," taken from Norse mythol-ogy, he drew up the waters that were for him personally healing and laid the inner groundwork for an expanded global attitude that would ultimately defend and protect a green Earth.

A true teacher enlists the lesson of his own life, not his syllabus, to guide followers onto their own paths, and Ralph's embodiment of his discoveries guided all of us beyond our intellect into the long-forgotten depths of human nature.

Master Teacher
Peter Faust

Peter Faust, M.A., is an acupuncturist, healer, teacher, and author. Peter coau-thored *The Constellation Approach: Finding Peace Through Your Family Lineage* with his wife Jamy, and he has written two books of poetry.

As a young man I desired three things: to be happy, to have an interest-ing life, and, as I got older, to become a teacher. Intuitively, upon meet-ing Ralph I was aware he knew how to connect with students.

He imparted sacred and ancient knowledge passed along in an oral tradition. His teaching went way beyond any linear comprehension of alternate states of consciousness or understanding ways of mapping the human journey. Ralph shared with us what it meant to be a multidi-mensional being and how to live consciously. He showed us how to free ourselves from limiting belief systems and how to connect with an eter-nal source of knowledge that is hidden yet accessible to all who seek. *His classes freed my psyche from the Western medical psychological para-digm and propelled me into the realms of ancestors, spirits, energy fields, and divine experience.*

A quote of Ralph's I always enjoyed was from Odin, one of his favorite teachers: "Knowledge is not free: at the very least you must pay with attention." Studying with Ralph was not easy, and I saw many people come and go because they were uncomfortable with some aspect of his personality. I learned that he was not there to be your friend. However, I can honestly say he was one of the friendliest men I have ever met. Openhearted and inquisitive, he was willing to hear your opinion on almost any subject. He just did not have a lot of patience for superficiality. He took his role as teacher seriously, and expected you to take your role as student in kind.

The unspoken assumption was that he was there to teach, and you were there to learn. You could not find a better friend in a teacher if you took his work seriously. There was always plenty of room and time for laughter and lightheartedness, but when the candles were lit and the ceremony began, it was time for business. As I saw it, a big facet of his business as a master teacher was twofold. He would reinforce this teaching over and over in his classes. We were there to seek *healing* and *guidance*: healing the past and looking toward our future. His role was to teach, help, and guide us in this twofold path of inquiry.

As every serious teacher and student knows, the students must do their own personal work to grow and evolve. He was not going to do your homework for you. This was another reason that students came and went. The more you attended his gatherings, the deeper your personal process went. A slow separation and dissolving of ego occurred, until you were left with a choice: *to surrender even more or leave*. Sometimes I wondered if I was going mad. Ralph had a way of directing and focusing my consciousness on the people, events, and circumstances that were unresolved and buried deep within me: those troubling things that held me back from being truly free. In most sessions I cried, or cringed, more than I laughed. Yet to be able to release judgments of my childhood, shame for unconscious actions, insecurities, limiting beliefs, and to glimpse, for a few brief moments, the interconnectedness of life was true healing. Ralph, the master teacher, provided me a space to go to those depths of profound healing. He led us all there, and he brought us all back.

Guidance, the other half of his twofold process, was equally as challenging. In most of his classes I would receive some direct guidance from an inner teacher showing me the next right action I should take on the great red road of life. Ralph would often ask during the integration rounds what we had been shown to do after we left the class. Then at the beginning of the next course he would check in and see if we had put our guidance into practice. I noticed he never shamed or demanded any of us follow the guidance we had received. However, I did notice he was pleased when we had. Early on I realized he was trying to encourage personal liberation. Heal what needs to be healed and follow the guidance you received from the well of your deep inner wisdom.

Without integrating what you received, it was just an experience, he often said. Slowly implementing the guidance that I received, during the years I studied with him, my life improved immensely. Relationships with parents, sisters, nieces, and nephews became better. My marriage went to depths I did not know were possible. I took more responsibility for my personal health and well-being. I began a yoga and meditation practice. I committed to being a leader in my men's community. My wife and I wrote a book on ancestral healing and began a program of healing family wounds that is currently in its twentieth year. His teaching and personal example of embracing our inner artist stimulated me to write two books of poetry. These are just a few of the ways Ralph guided me along the path of becoming a different person from who I was before I sat in his presence and paid attention to his teachings.

Another extremely important aspect of his mastery and contribution to sacred knowledge was his comprehension of the soul and his ability to provide a direct personal experience of soul consciousness. Ralph was unapologetic about his conviction of the existence of the soul within each of us and the possibility of communing with one's soul and the souls of others. Through my studies with him and the Soul Processes he had us practice in his retreats I was able to translate that knowledge into my vocation with family constellations. It was as if Ralph did not just teach didactically, but he was somehow able to impart this knowledge so that I could bring it forward to my students. He taught an understanding of soul that transcended religious and psychological explanations or definitions. We could say he was a priest, a psychologist, and a shaman in that regard.

The Teachers

My life has changed in 100 ways
Since meeting the teachers
My body has changed
My mind grown and
My desires shrunken to
The precious few
The gifts of this path subtle
But true
My Soul awakened and
In control of my life
No longer stumbling
Through the darkness
No longer pushing
Boulders uphill
With the teachers as my guide
I see the pitfalls
Once so easily I fell in
Alive and aware of the road
I am traveling upon
Effortlessly gliding around
All that blocks my way
The teachers have changed
My life in 100 ways
No wonder
They must live underground

For if they lived in the
Light of day
The powers that believe
They run this madhouse
Would surely try to burn
These wonderful teachers alive

PETER FAUST

Reflections on a Life Well-Lived
Roger Marsden

Roger Marsden, Ph.D., earned his degree in clinical psychology at CIIS in 2001. His doctoral dissertation was "Structured, Group Use of Psychedelic or Entheogenic Substances: Experience of Guides and Participants." The work of Ralph Metzner was one of his primary inspirations. He recently retired from work as a mental health clinician for Social Services in Oakland, California.

Ralph Metzner was an immensely influential teacher, friend, a sort of uncle, and guide. My relationship with him is so varied I barely know where to begin, although it did begin in the classroom, so I'll begin there. My first class at CIIS with Ralph was Altered States of Consciousness. It was quickly clear to me that I would take whatever other classes he offered. He didn't teach about a system; he taught an integration of multiple systems across time, cultures, and disciplines.

Ralph was instrumental in bringing amazing people to CIIS in his years as professor and academic dean; for example, Stan Grof and Fritjof Capra. For several years he created an annual full weekend with Terrence McKenna, Rupert Sheldrake, and Jill Purce. Marija Gimbutas was another; when he introduced her lecture, it was clear that he wanted to convey that she was a special person with important teachings. I still reference Professor Gimbutas in conversations when people say that humanity has always been aggressive and war-oriented. I point out that Gimbutas's work shows us that there was a time when humans showed a different capacity.

Ralph would often participate with special teachers he brought to the Institute. He did not seem to need the spotlight, but was interested in the collaboration. I recall him co-teaching a workshop on ecology with Australian John Seed. Ralph was instrumental in bringing a deeper environmental consciousness to the CIIS community in the 1980s.

When CIIS moved from Dolores Street to Ashbury Street, as part of making the old elementary school our own, Ralph fully participated in a tiling project led by Rowena Pattee, another awe-inspiring, creative person Ralph brought to the school. In the basement there were large, round foundational pillars. We tiled one as a "tree of life" and four others as each of the four elements. This is not a pompous professor sitting behind the desk. Ralph modeled creativity and playfulness as part of an integrated life.

Ralph as shamanic guide/medicine guide/psychospiritual guide knew how to set boundaries, as well as fully bring himself to the teaching. Some nearly forty years ago our men's group invited him to lead a circle for/ with us. It is a point of pride that the invitation and circle caused Ralph to "come out" after the crazy '60s, and he began his quiet inner work with groups. That he liked and respected the group enough for that to happen was very meaningful to us. In that first circle he wanted to model radical openness. Most of us were new to this format, and when it was time to do a first round of sharing, he went first and shared the story of the loss of his son. It was a powerful share and left little room for superficiality. He did not give directions; he set them by example.

I would love to do another round of the profound visualizations in those medicine circles. Although I did not have the experience and maturity to fully take in and integrate these amazing teachings, as I express them in this writing I realize how much I learned and grew. They are part of my own internal map. I recall a guided visualization about the resilience of bacteria over hundreds of thousands of years;

regressive visualization to our incarnation; visualization through our anatomical/biological systems, tuning into and appreciating the individuality of each organ; and visualization of the elements and how fire, water, air, and earth are all within us.

I recall the Psychedelic Conference in Basel, walking around with Ralph at a lunch break, looking for a place to sit down—it was like being with a rock star. Every few feet someone would come up to him to share a bit of information, an insight, a remembrance, or ask a question. He was patient and polite and available, up to a point.

I appreciate how there were these times when with all his brilliance he would be amusingly imperfect. I love the fact that when Ralph invoked the four directions at our wedding he faced the "wrong" direction—perfectly imperfect, I muse.

Finally, back to those amazing guided visualizations. One of my favorites is the Cave of the Heart, which is that inner place where special people, like Ralph, are always welcome to return so that we can converse, ask questions, and seek wisdom. Many times Ralph stressed the importance of being conscious of our relationships with our ancestors. They are available, just waiting to be engaged and acknowledged.

Thank you, Ralph! I'll see you in the Cave of the Heart.

Toward Healing and Transformation:
A Letter to Ralph
Scott Hill

Scott Hill, Ph.D., is an independent scholar specializing in the intersection of psychedelic experience and Jungian psychology, now living in Sweden. He is the author of *Confrontation with the Unconscious: Jungian Depth Psychology and Psychedelic Experience*, which Ralph endorsed as a "brilliant book that presents a sophisticated analysis of how psychedelic experiences may be understood from the standpoint of Jung's archetypal psychology."

Dear Ralph,

Even though we were in close contact for only a relatively short time, your impact on my life has been substantial and long-lasting. As I sat down to write about you, as I started to recall you and your spirit, I felt affection rising in my heart. I felt almost as though I was recalling my own father. I suppose I shouldn't be surprised that you became a kind of father figure for me considering my need to connect with you at a critical point in my life and draw on the experience, erudition, and wisdom you embody.

In 1998, when I was fifty, I was intently focused on coming to terms with a series of traumatic LSD trips I had taken in 1967. After several peaceful ecstatic trips had opened me to the exquisite beauty of the natural world, things turned dark, very dark.

It was those experiences that eventually led me first to your work and later to you, in person. I first learned of you through the book you wrote with Timothy Leary and Richard Alpert, *The Psychedelic Experience: A Manual Based on the Tibetan Book of the Dead*. Then, in 1998, I attended your book launch event in San Francisco for *The Unfolding Self: Varieties of Transformative Experience*.

Leafing now through my well-marked copy of that latter book, which describes experiences of psychospiritual transformation in terms of universal spiritual metaphors such as death and rebirth, I'm struck again by how revelatory I found it on my first reading, and how clearly it still speaks to me today. I could cite a hundred passages that helped me understand and come to terms with those life-changing trips I'd taken so long ago. But I'll focus here on your concluding chapter, "Returning to the Source," in which you describe the sense of alienation and exile one can experience when one's consciousness is expanded.

The three LSD trips that turned my life around all took place in 1967, when I was nineteen and living in Carmel. I began the first trip by swallowing a tab of acid at the mouth of an expansive bridged canyon on the Big Sur coast, after which I slid down a steep cliff to the beach far below. When the acid came on, I realized I wouldn't be able to climb up that same cliff back to the highway overhead. After a surreal walk into an enchanted forest at the base of the canyon and a frightening hike on a long winding dirt road back to the highway, I hitchhiked a ride north up the coast. On acceleration, I felt the car lift just above the road and glide forward. As we came around a wide bend high above the sea, the view of the coast ahead opened as if we were soaring over the folds of hills and bays receding into the distance, and I became absorbed in the otherworldliness of this scene. Then the realization hit me like a death blow that I had come up out of the canyon into the wrong world. When I stepped out of the car in Carmel, I felt I should return to the canyon and retrace my steps back to the world I had left behind. But I didn't have the courage to go back.

My next acid trip accentuated the sense that I was in the wrong world, and I became convinced that the world—the so-called real world—was inherently evil.

On the third trip I recalled once again that I was in the wrong world. Despite the lack of any previous religious inclination, I became convinced that God was challenging me to sacrifice my life in this world to prove my spiritual integrity and reach Him in Heaven, a demand I attempted to honor with nearly tragic consequences.

I stopped using psychedelics soon after that. But those trips continued to haunt me for many years as deeply disturbing flashbacks during which I felt called to kill myself to free my spirit from this world.

Given this history, I think you can appreciate the kind of revelation I experienced when I discovered *The Unfolding Self*. In its concluding chapter you describe transformative experiences that cause one to see "ordinary life as a kind of exile, where we are separated from our true spiritual home." Then you quote the fourteenth-century Flemish mystic Jan van Ruysbroek, who had written "We come from God and we are in exile." In this metaphor, you say, "transformation to a new way of being is compared to the process of one who leaves exile or leaves imprisonment and slavery," an experience that is consonant with recollection and anamnesis, the overcoming of forgetfulness.

You also write of individuals who experience "profound existential alienation," finding themselves "in the wrong place" or "adrift on an ocean of illusions." And you explain how all this "can provide motivation for the spiritual homeward journey [because] estrangement leads to questioning, searching, and wondering" that may lead to an awakening. As I reread your book now, I find so many passages that lightened my heart twenty years ago as I gained a new perspective on all that I had endured during those terrifying psychedelic experiences in 1967.

My own questioning, searching, and wondering led me in the spring of 2002 to your Ecological Consciousness course at the California Institute of Integral Studies. I knew I wanted to study with you, but I could never have imagined how valuable your course would be for me. By the end of the semester I had enrolled at CIIS for what would be perhaps the most fulfilling years of my life. I've recently been rereading the final paper I wrote for your Ecological Consciousness course: "Ancient Knowledge: Loss and Remembrance." My paper's subtitle indicates the way I applied what I had learned in your course to understanding my destructive LSD vision: "A Personal Reflection on the Rise of Christian Transcendental Monotheism and the Suppression of Pre-Christian Spirituality." In that paper, I cited your *Green Psychology: Transforming Our Relationship to the Earth*, and now I recall what was for me your healing suggestion that nature religions have especially relevant insights to offer anyone crippled by transcendental monotheism's removal of the sacred from the natural world.

Reading now your insightful and confirming comments throughout my paper, I feel like I am in conversation with you again. Your comments helped me then to understand my experiences as a spiritual emergence and not *merely* madness. "They were consciousness-expanding experiences," you wrote, "which set you on the path of self-exploration you are still on." And you helped me understand that I had misinterpreted the messages that called me to sacrifice my life in this world when you commented that "the spiritual messengers were telling you to get over your attachment to and identification with the limited conception of human and other realities that you unconsciously absorbed." Your understanding and insights meant a great deal to me, Ralph.

That summer I took your course Shamanic Divination and Holotropic

Breathwork: Exploring the Dynamics of Transformative Experience. The following experience illustrates the culmination of the work we did together that year. At one point in my breathwork experience I started wondering what I should do: should I return to vigorous breathing or what? Then I remembered your advice, and I invited my spirit teachers to guide me. I quote here from the course paper I wrote:

> Within a short time of silently asking for guidance, I felt something touch the top of my head, and I realized someone was laying a hand there. Then I felt another hand touch my chest, just above my heart, and I heard Ralph's voice, "Breathe from your chest." I started to breathe deeply—but gently—feeling my heart center and feeling an energy field expanding from my heart in all directions. A deep peace settled over me, and I started to gently shake with a weeping that felt like a soft summer rain cleansing away all tension and doubt from my mind. I knew then I was on the right path. I was getting the guidance I had sought—both within the breathwork session and since I had started my studies with Ralph.

As I reread those two papers and your comments, and as I reflect on the impact my work with you had on me, I'm struck again by how healing that time was and how relevant those papers and your responses are to me to this day. My work with you confirmed for me, as you put it, that I was "definitely on a powerful journey of transformation."

My subsequent participation in one of your entheogenic-shamanic circle rituals naturally took this work to another level. I think we both were anticipating a deepening of the healing that opened for me during my holotropic breathwork experience. But as you no doubt recall, it turned out to be a painfully challenging experience, I think for both of us. But despite the challenges, or because of them, it proved to be a critical step in the work I needed to do to further integrate and heal my traumatic LSD experiences.

As the full effects of the entheogenic medicine enveloped me and I entered another realm that night, I experienced an overwhelming regression into darkness, alienation, and a call to death that separated me from the ritual structure and guidance you so carefully provided us. At one point, for instance, I was only momentarily drawn back into the group ritual when someone apparently put a talking staff in my hand. I opened my eyes and looked at the staff, oblivious to everything else around me, and saw a puppet-like jester's head atop the stick. (I assume that was a hallucination!) I could only stare speechless at this mocking figure until someone gently took the staff from my hand and I withdrew again into solitary struggle.

After the next day's integration session, as we were about to close the weekend's ceremony with a dancing circle and you were putting on the music, I walked through the circle and out the door to the deck outside. And I refused your admonitions to return to the circle. It is painful to recount parts of that weekend, and I regret some things I did. But I am grateful, nevertheless, for the way the experience pushed me deeper into integration and maturation. And I am grateful that you and I met soon afterward to talk about what had happened and to confirm our mutual respect and friendship.

I came away from that entheogenic session with the valuable insight that I needed to give more attention to facing and coming to terms with my own shadow. That realization led, as you know, to a significant theme in the book I would eventually write, *Confrontation with the Unconscious: Jungian Depth Psychology and Psychedelic Experience.*

The description in my book of my MDMA session at Burning Man in 2006 gave me the opportunity to articulate my deepening awareness of and reconciliation with, as you have put it, "the inner enemy." Indeed, during that MDMA session at Burning Man, I had to deal with the projection of my own unconscious darkness after I saw an observer of my session as Satan himself. From that MDMA experience, I came to appreciate the significance of the shadow in my difficult psychedelic experiences, and I felt I had started to understand the concept of the shadow, and its projection onto others, for the first time. As you put it in *The Unfolding Self,* "When we recognize the devil as an aspect of ourselves, this deity can function as teacher and initiator: he shows us our own unknown face, providing us with the greatest gift of all—self-understanding."

And so, as it happened, that challenging entheogenic circle experience with you initiated yet another chapter in a lifelong process of integration. Given the archetypal, numinous core of negative shadow complexes, says Jungian analyst Lionel Corbett, therapeutic engagement with one's anger, destructiveness, and terror is as much a spiritual practice as attending to the positive aspects of the numinosum.

And the work continues.

In gratitude,
Scott

Mentor and Father Figure
Daniel Sloan Brown

Daniel Sloan Brown, Ph.D., has worked in the mental health field for over fifty years and is certified in Vivation Breath Work. He is the founder of New Earth Counseling and Consulting, which offers alternatives for healing, insight, and accessing spirit.

It is hard to believe that it was almost forty years ago when I first met Ralph Metzner. During those four decades he came to embody many different roles in my life: dean of my graduate school, esoteric teacher, ecopsychologist, shamanic practitioner, family man, and, most dear to my heart, he came to be a father figure for me after I had lost my father.

My initial impression of Ralph was that he was a stern academic dean, and a bit distant and demure. Other students who had been at the school for a while also reinforced that notion; they described him as a mystery of sorts. When I found out what kind of classes he was teaching, such as Altered States of Consciousness, I couldn't resist finding out more about this man that seemed so inaccessible at times—and yet was known as a master of esoteric knowledge. He was indeed a demanding teacher with high academic standards, and as dean he promoted those standards to apply to all students and professors. As a student wanting to pursue the esoteric myself, I was excited to see that such things were taken seriously at such an alternative graduate school, and that I had discovered that the most learned of the esoteric professors was the dean himself.

Another asset to my early years at CIIS was meeting so many other students that had the interests and aspirations that I did. One of those interests was the use of psychedelic medicines for expanding consciousness and for healing emotional suffering. Most of us were too young to have participated in the psychedelic revolution of the '60s, but at the beginning of the '80s we were getting to have our own version of another kind of revolution. MDMA had arrived on the altered-state scene. In the early 1980s recreational circles it was called ADAM, and I assume that may be because the experience people had then was like one being transported to the Garden of Eden for a few hours. As graduate students in psychology we were yearning to find ways to apply it to psychotherapy and healing. We created our own peer group to explore this new discovery outside of CIIS, but as young twenty-somethings we also yearned for guidance from a more experienced mentor.

During our group meetings the suggestion arose that we approach Ralph for at least one such event. It felt risky because we assumed that he had walked away from such things in the 1970s. Also, there was the fear factor of approaching a stern academic dean, requesting his participation, and possibly suffering some heavy consequences in the process. However, having read about his involvement in the '60s I felt that I could approach him. Several of us graduate students met with him in his office at CIIS, and we delicately made the request. He was hesitant; yet he was not disturbed or resistant either. He wanted some time to think about it. Soon thereafter his answer was "yes." We didn't know it at the time, but he was coming out of psychedelic retirement, and years later he would often refer to that experience with us as a turning point in his work and career. As the 1980s progressed, many of us were blessed to be able to participate in some of Ralph's visionary circles. Some continued to work with him.

As I was about to graduate from my M.A. program at CIIS, my father died abruptly, and I submerged into the mourning and suffering of losing a parent. That is when Ralph opened up to me in a surprising way, and we began a thirty-year conversation about death and dying. He became a father figure for me.

Three years later I asked Ralph to speak at my wedding, which in part came from my yearning to fill the hole left by my deceased father. In June of 1988, on a very windy day outdoors on Mount Tamalpais, he gave one of his uniquely shamanic presentations connecting our wedding ceremony to the Earth and to our ancestors. It was somewhat of a preview of his growing explorations into ecopsychology and shamanism. A month later, Ralph and his partner Cathy Coleman married on the same spot on Mount Tamalpais.

In 1990, Ralph and I drove together to a transpersonal psychology conference in Oregon. Driving there and back would be the most extended time I would ever have with him on my own. He began sharing more details about the death of his young son who died in a bicycle accident in 1974. I think it was easier for him to actually talk about his loss and suffering from the past as he was now in the process of beginning a new family. This was also the point at which we began a recurring discussion about death and the "other side," and how through all of his experiences and experiential research he had come to a confident conclusion about consciousness beyond death. It was an uplifting ride to and from Oregon, and it was when my attitude toward death shifted from fear and sorrow to hope and curiosity.

Ralph had a way of convincing me of the possibility of mystical matters that no one else could. His powers of persuasion were always compelling. With my never-ending paternal transference, there was a part of me that always wanted him to be right.

For a couple of decades before the advent of his illness, Ralph and I would periodically meet for lunch in San Rafael at various Indian restaurants. Walking through the buffet was always an interesting process because he would employ his trusty pendulum to choose which foods were a yea or a nay. I would stand behind him in line so that he could take his time with his choices and not be bothered by anybody trying to rush him from behind. It was one of those things that only he could convince me of the sacredness of such a ritual.

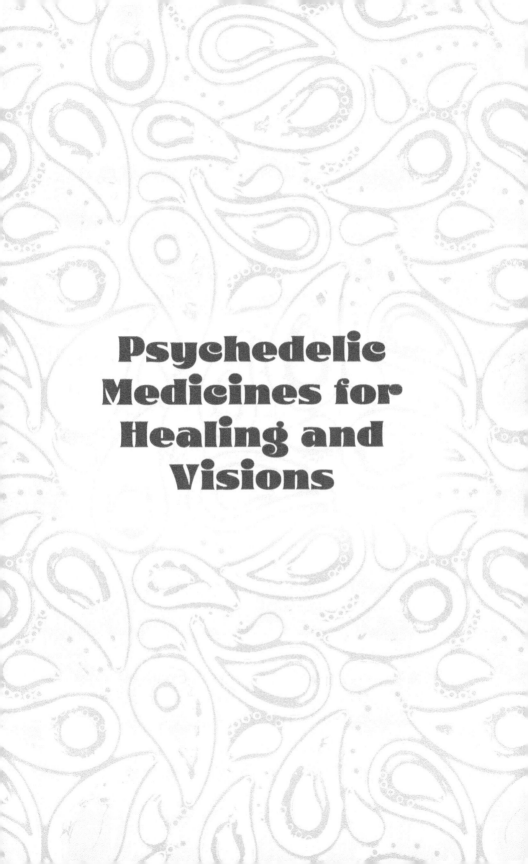

Psychedelic
Medicines for
Healing and
Visions

Meteor Showers of Synchronicities
Stanislav Grof

Stanislav Grof, M.D., Ph.D., is a psychiatrist with more than sixty years of experience in research of holotropic states of consciousness. He was principal investigator in a psychedelic research program at the Psychiatric Research Institute in Prague, Czechoslovakia, and chief of psychiatric research at the Maryland Psychiatric Research Center. He conducts professional training programs in holotropic breathwork and transpersonal psychology and gives lectures and seminars worldwide. He is one of the founders and chief theoreticians of transpersonal psychology and the founding president of the International Transpersonal Association (ITA). Stan is the author of numerous books and publications, including his life's work, *The Way of the Psychonaut: Encyclopedia for Inner Journeys* (2019).

Several months before Ralph's death, he and I realized that we had known each other more than half of a century. Looking back, meeting Ralph was one of the amazing synchronicities that accompanied me during my first visit to the United States. In May 1965, I participated and presented at a conference in Amityville, New York, organized by Harold Abramson titled "The Use of LSD in Psychotherapy and Alcoholism."

When the conference ended, I needed to get to New Haven to visit the Lidzs' and I didn't have any money. I went to the microphone and asked if anybody could give me a ride. The first participant who offered me a lift was Peter John.[1] At this point, my journey had an unexpected, extraordinary twist. It turned out that Peter John needed to make a detour. This stop was at Millbrook, the estate that was owned by Peggy Hitchcock, the Mellon family heiress. Peggy and her brothers had offered Tim Leary and his friends and colleagues a place where they could carry on their psychedelic experimentation.

---

1. Peter John was an editor of the *Psychedelic Review* 5 (1965) with Ralph Metzner, Timothy Leary, Richard Alpert, and Gunther Weil.

I could not believe my good fortune. I got the chance to see this extraordinary psychedelic community and meet Tim Leary and Ralph. Unfortunately, I missed Ram Dass who was out of town. Tim and Ralph gave me a signed copy of their book, *The Psychedelic Experience: A Manual Based on the Tibetan Book of the Dead*. It is one book that survived our February 1, 2001, house fire, and I still have it. Ralph and I spent a few hours that day talking about psychedelics behind the Iron Curtain. This was the beginning of our half-century of close friendship.

■ Fig. 8. *The Psychedelic Experience* inscribed and given to Stan by Timothy Leary and Ralph Metzner at Millbrook, New York, in 1965
(Photos courtesy of Stanislav Grof)

Since I mentioned that I experienced remarkable synchronicities during this American journey, I will describe what happened after Millbrook and New Haven. I gave a lecture at Yale University on psychedelic therapy; Dean Fritz Redlich offered me a one-year scholarship in the United States. From there continued what Arthur Koestler called "meteors of synchronicities." I had an invitation from family therapist Virginia Satir in Palo Alto. My journey continued to San Francisco and I visited Mental Research Institute (MRI) in Palo Alto and lived for about ten days as a guest in Virginia's house. I took a bus every morning to San Francisco and spent the day sightseeing, and returned late at night.

On Friday, Virginia told me: "Stan, on the weekend, you will be here alone; I have an appointment and I will have to drive a few hours south." Everything in America was new for me, interesting, and exciting. I asked Virginia to take me along; the place we were going was Esalen Institute in Big Sur. Esalen in the first years of its existence was the most exciting place I could imagine. We arrived late at night; Virginia had reserved Michael Murphy's room in the Big House and could not find a night guard to get a cabin for me. So we shared the only bed in Michael's house, which was king-size. You cannot imagine Michael's face when he opened his door and found Virginia and me in his bed!

We spent an awe-inspiring weekend and Michael took me to a rugged cape, Point 16, that was at the time for sale. I looked over the magical Big Sur Coast and dreamed how incredible it would be if I ever could live here. That weekend Michael and I formed a friendship that also has lasted now over fifty years. In 1973 Michael invited me to live at Esalen where I spent fourteen years. During this time, I had the opportunity to offer month-long workshops with stellar guest faculty. Ralph participated in some thirty of them and we had a chance to share what we were working on and writing at the time.

Ralph was one of the very important people of the psychedelic movement of the 1960s, and he continued to be a major force of this movement throughout the decades of the dark ages of psychedelics—mass hysteria, ignorant and mendacious propaganda, and discrimination against the psychedelic Renaissance. He was a true psychedelic pioneer and consciousness researcher, experienced transpersonal psychotherapist, prolific writer, shaman, healer, spiritual teacher, and unrelenting explorer of the Beyond.

Ralph was an early harbinger in the current psychedelic renewal. During the period when psychedelics were illegal he studied new and not yet illegal or semilegal medicines or those that it was possible to use because of legal loopholes. Many of these new substances came from the laboratory of Sasha Shulgin and Jungian therapist Leo Zeff. Ralph introduced useful knowledge about MDMA to therapists and

■ Fig. 9. Sasha Shulgin and Ralph (From the collection of Ralph Metzner)

interested members of the public in his coauthored book *Through the Gateway of the Heart* under the pen name of Sophia Adamson. Ralph also published a book of the underground research of tryptamines DMT and 5-MeO-DMT under the title *The Toad and the Jaguar*.

During the decades of psychedelic prohibition, we were part of an "alchemical conspiracy." We tried new substances, shared inner and outer journeys, exchanged our books, participated in many Esalen month-long seminars, and created programs and presented for numerous ITA conferences all over the world. We were also friends in a social circle and enjoyed casual time together. Ralph was an advocate for world peace and of our planet. He was a global citizen and had a passion for ecology and a profound love for the Earth.

Five years ago, when Brigitte and I got married, she joined Ralph and Cathy in our circle of friends who share our worldview, vision, and mission. Brigitte creates regular costume parties in which our transpersonal friends meet at our home. Ralph and Cathy participated in the last meeting; five of our circle of friends had died and were represented by their photographs on a little table (Christina Grof, Angeles Arrien, Frances Vaughan, Bokara Legendre, and Michael Harner). At our next party there will be one more photograph: Ralph. We miss them very much. It crossed our minds that our deceased friends from our costume parties might now be joining parties in alternate realities.

■ Fig. 10. Ralph Metzner and Stan Grof, 2018 (Photo by Brigitte Grof)

Personal Inspiration and
True Psychedelic Pioneer
Rick Doblin

Rick Doblin, Ph.D., is the founder and executive director of the astonishingly successful Multidisciplinary Association for Psychedelic Studies (MAPS).

I first experienced LSD in 1971 when I was a seventeen-year-old college freshman at New College in Sarasota, Florida. I had a series of difficult trips with LSD and mescaline and went to the school's guidance counselor for assistance. In a stroke of great luck, the guidance counselor took my request seriously and handed me a manuscript of Stan Grof's *Realms of the Human Unconscious: Observations from LSD Research*, which wasn't even published until 1975!

Reading that book changed my life and inspired me to devote my life to work with psychedelics. I dropped out of college, attended a workshop with Stan in the summer of 1972, tried Primal Therapy, and participated in a month-long encounter group, only to discover that wasn't where I wanted to be psychologically. I realized that I had undervalued the importance of integration.

I learned construction, built houses, and spent the next decade working on getting grounded enough to benefit from my experiences. During that period, I continued to learn about psychedelics through books, some LSD and mescaline experiences, and occasionally meeting psychedelic researchers.

Around 1973–74 I took a workshop taught by Ralph on Agni Yoga, and I read and was inspired by Ralph's book *Maps of Consciousness*. In 1982 I returned to college and during my first semester went to Esalen for a month-long workshop with Stan Grof called "The Mystical Quest." It was there that I also learned about MDMA.

During the 1980s, I participated in several events at Esalen arranged by Stan and others. Ralph was at some of these events. I began to get to know him more and more as a person and was able to develop an appreciation for the depth of his work. I had thought the psychedelic movement and the aspirations it had fostered had been crushed by the drug laws, and I began to realize that the movement was alive, though not so public.

Around the mid-1980s I conceived an organization that would gather resources to protect the therapeutic use of psychedelics, with a focus on MDMA. What would be the name of this organization? All I knew was that a "P" had to be in the name, for "psychedelic," as I was going to be explicit about what we were doing, no hidden agendas.

What things could I put together that contain the letter P? I remembered *Maps of Consciousness*, the book written by Ralph, and I remembered Stan's writing about the cartography of the unconscious. This is what we are doing with psychedelics—developing maps of the mind, and also maps of the future.

Thus I got the name: MAPS. Then I had to come up with things for the other letters to stand for, which I did: Multidisciplinary Association for Psychedelic Studies.[2] I really owe a debt of gratitude to Ralph for the title of his book and how it inspired the name of MAPS.

It was at one of those gatherings at Esalen where I got what would be the essential focus of MAPS. Those ideas came from two powerful circles where Ralph was also present, one with DMT and one with ketamine. Experiences in those circles led directly to the core strategy of MAPS: drug development and drug policy reform in the service of societal mental health. It's not just about treating illness; it is about providing spiritual growth opportunities for millions of people.

In 1985 the book *Through the Gateway of the Heart*, coauthored by Ralph, was published. That book was very important, full of actual clinical stories of therapeutic experiences using MDMA—such a range of stories and an incredible number of different people telling those stories. One of the chapters was from a woman who in 1984 I had helped overcome PTSD using MDMA and then a combination of LSD and MDMA. The book also speaks to how difficult things were in the mid-1980s. In publishing the book, Ralph and his coauthor, Padma Catell, felt it necessary to use a pen name (Sophia Adamson) to protect themselves.

The next year, 1986, I started MAPS.

There is one more very significant interaction I enjoyed with Ralph. In 1991 I published in the *Journal of Transpersonal Psychology* the

---

2. Founded in 1986, the Multidisciplinary Association for Psychedelic Studies (MAPS) is a 501(c)(3) non-profit research and educational organization that develops medical, legal, and cultural contexts for people to benefit from the careful use of psychedelics and marijuana.

results of a twenty-five-year follow-up to the Good Friday experiment, conducted by Walter Pahnke and Timothy Leary in 1962. At the time of that publication there was an associated op-ed in the *Boston Globe*. I received a call from someone in the Massachusetts Department of Corrections who had read the op-ed and wanted to know if I had interest in records related to another study done under the supervision of Timothy Leary in the early 1960s.

This person indicated there was a room full of old files that included material on the individuals who were subjects in the Concord Prison Experiment, including all the names of the people involved. That was incredible, because it had been thought that all these names were lost. I had spoken with Ralph and with Tim Leary, and no one any longer knew the names or had any idea how to contact the subjects. The Department of Corrections official asked if I was interested in using these files to do a follow-up study, and I replied that I'd love to do so.

The Concord Prison Experiment was one of the most important studies in psychedelic therapy. Leary, together with Ralph and Gunther Weil, who were graduate students at the time, gave psilocybin in therapeutic group settings to inmates who were eligible to be paroled shortly thereafter. As one measure of outcome, they monitored recidivism (return to prison). This provided an objective behavioral index, going beyond the subjective criteria generally used in measuring impact of psychedelic experiences.

I wanted to bring more light to this important study. It took a year to get permission to look into those records. When I was finally able to do that, the more research I did, the more disturbing the conclusions were. The recidivism data did not support the prevailing belief that this had been a tremendously successful study.

For example, Ralph and Gunther Weil had done an excellent study of recidivism base rates that was published in an obscure British criminology journal. In this study, recidivism was reported at thirty months (2.5 years) after release. However, in the Concord Prison study, recidivism at ten months was used and compared to the thirty-month base rate.

Obviously, the longer someone is out of prison the more likely he is to return.

Comparing recidivism at ten months with recidivism at thirty months is not a proper comparison. So that was a big problem. Moreover, the positive conclusions from the Concord Prison Experiment kept getting better as Tim Leary continued to talk and write about the project over the years.

What was I going to do? How is it that me, an advocate for psychedelics, was to criticize one of the most important experiments in the contemporary history of psychedelics? But I thought it important to publish my findings.

I spoke with Ralph. He provided excellent counsel when I was writing up my work, which was published in the *Journal of Psychoactive Drugs*.[3] And then he published a two-page essay reflecting on the results that was published immediately following my piece in the same issue of the *Journal of Psychoactive Drugs*.[4]

It was so gracious, so beautiful, the way he did that. He acknowledged the errors; he said this is part of the human tendency to see what we want to see. And he also said it doesn't prove that the idea of using psychedelic therapy to improve post-prison outcome doesn't work. Rather, what it suggests is the critical importance of continuing-care programs following release from prison to facilitate success. In fact, Ralph and his colleagues at Harvard had even started work to set up such continuing care when Leary and Alpert got kicked out of Harvard and everything came to a halt.

I thought Ralph was a true gentleman in the way he responded to my critique. He was deeply thoughtful.

Over the years Ralph wrote many scholarly articles. He also wrote many books. He really saw the importance of public education. I have

---

3. Rick Doblin, "Dr. Leary's Concord Prison Experiment: A 34-year Follow-up Study," *Journal of Psychoactive Drugs* 30 (1998): 419–26.
4. Ralph Metzner, "Reflections on the Concord Prison Project and the Follow-up Study," *Journal of Psychoactive Drugs* 30 (1998): 427–28.

always had the greatest admiration and respect for him for the way he continued the work ever since the days when he was graduate student at Harvard—and during the period when there was much social pressure to not speak positively about psychedelics. I didn't know until much later about the depth and breadth of his work.

Ralph was a major inspiration to many, me included. His work contributed in a central way to the current flowering in psychedelic research. He was a true psychedelic pioneer.

And So It Is, Raoul. And So It Is!
Charles S. Grob

Charles S. Grob, M.D., is professor of psychiatry and pediatrics at the UCLA School of Medicine and the director of the Division of Child and Adolescent Psychiatry at Harbor-UCLA Medical Center.

Ralph Metzner was a valued friend, mentor, and teacher of mine for over thirty years. He was also a gifted scholar, a highly innovative and effective psychotherapist, and a legendary explorer of altered states of consciousness. He made vital contributions to our understanding of how to optimally utilize a range of mind-expanding plant and synthetic drugs.

From LSD to MDMA, DMT to ayahuasca, and pulverized iboga to the dried secretions of the *Bufo alvarius* toad,[5] Ralph systematically explored a myriad of psychoactive compounds across cross-cultural

---

5. The *Bufo alvarius* toad, commonly known as the Sonoran Desert toad or Colorado River toad, has a toxic, milky-white venom that it secretes to poison its predators, which include the indigenous raccoons, birds, and other critters found in the Sonoran Desert region (parts of California, Arizona, and northern Mexico). The substance derived from that venom is 5-MeO-DMT, an extremely potent psychedelic. It's also a Schedule I drug, but in Mexico it isn't regulated. Smoking the substance can be a powerfully transformative experience, causing intense effects that last about thirty minutes.

■ Fig. 11. Charlie Grob giving tribute to Ralph on his eightieth birthday
(Photo by Cathy Coleman)

sources, derived from both ancient plants and fungi as well as novel laboratory-sourced chemicals. From my first encounter with Ralph in 1988 to his passing in 2019, I had the great fortune to participate in many of his groups and workshops, not to speak of adventures abroad, without which my life would have most certainly taken a very different course.

In the late 1980s, I embarked on a project with my colleagues Gary Bravo and Roger Walsh, methodically interviewing as many of the early psychedelic research pioneers from the 1950s and 1960s that we could locate. We called this the Elders Project, and after a false start or two, and after many years, it evolved into a published book of interviews and commentaries titled *Higher Wisdom: Eminent Elders Explore the Continuing Impact of Psychedelics* (SUNY Press, 2005). After we conducted a few initial interviews in Los Angeles and the Bay Area, Gary suggested we contact Ralph and arrange to meet with him. Gary had met Ralph a couple of years previously and felt comfortable reaching out to arrange such a meeting. At this point, I had yet to meet Ralph, though I was aware of his well-documented role in much of the early and renowned Harvard psychedelic research led by Timothy Leary, and enthusiastically embraced Gary's suggestion that we arrange for an interview with Ralph for inclusion in our planned book.

In the fall of 1988, we met with Ralph at his home in Fairfax, California. Introductions were made, and we sat down at a large table facing a densely wooded area. We began to talk, and talk. Or I should say Ralph began to talk, and I listened, and was simply fascinated with the depth of his knowledge, his evident passion for learning, and his intimate understanding of how to work with the various psychoactive chemicals with which he had such deep experiences.

We talked for hours, well into the afternoon, before I realized Gary and I had forgotten to turn on the tape recorder to memorialize our interview. I also suspect Ralph was more than happy not to receive our designation as an elder. We never again formally interviewed Ralph to elicit his story for inclusion into our book, though Ralph did join Gary and I on several occasions when we conducted and recorded interviews with those elders whose stories do populate it. This initial meeting with Ralph was also pivotal in laying the foundation for many more meetings, discussions, and collaborations to come over the next three decades.

Spending time with Ralph was a never-ending opportunity to learn, particularly about a topic that I had long considered to be of compelling interest, albeit at that time for me still somewhat hidden and elusive: the world of psychedelics. For me, it was a time of great discovery, opening up to this remarkable realm of inner experience to which we and our ancestors had long been in ignorance, denied access, and were hardly aware of, throughout much of history. With Ralph as a guide and teacher for these deep inner dives, the great mysteries vividly revealed themselves. It was also clear from joining Ralph for these events that strong safety parameters needed to be observed. Much of this was in the form of ritual, and I often appreciated Ralph's emphasis on maintaining structural coherence and group cohesion, gently containing tendencies of some to behave in more rambunctious and intrusive manners.

Ralph would take some good-natured ribbing, including being dubbed the Teutonic Shaman, but his patient admonitions to the group to maintain the personal discipline and decorum that the situation called for, and above all to stay in their own space, I always appreciated. Perhaps it was because I had a German mother and valued order, or perhaps it was that I could appreciate that ritual structure, wisely applied, is a strong protective factor to preserve safety and increase the likelihood of positive and salutary outcomes of the experience.

Ralph's groups always felt safe, and they provided both the necessary outer structure and the inner space needed to pursue one's own deep work. And, listening in an altered state to Ralph's long renditions of the great world myths, I found the value of staying grounded and focused.

Furthermore, hearing these myths and gaining insight into their multileveled meaning allowed me to envision these ancient stories and legends transcending time and space, coming to life and resonating with our own lives in the here and now. These were extraordinary experiences facilitated by one of the great masters of the realm of what Ralph would call "alchemical divination."

THE CONCORD PRISON EXPERIMENT

It was at Harvard, beginning in 1960, that Ralph made the acquaintance of Tim Leary. While many of Tim's graduate students and colleagues would come and go over the course of the turbulent 1960s, Ralph loyally stayed by his side as an important colleague and collaborator. Ralph's scholarly bent and exacting writing skills led him to take the lead with many of the academic publications that were generated from the Leary research group. For years, Ralph also maintained his position as editor of one of the first academic publications to focus on this new and promising field, *The Psychedelic Review.*

Working closely under Tim's supervision, Ralph had one of his first psychedelic experiences in a highly unusual setting, the Concord State

Prison, a medium-security institution in Massachusetts. The treatment model, as devised by Tim, was for prisoners to take psilocybin together with their psychotherapist/facilitator in a designated room in the prison.

Ralph would later describe how for the first few hours both he and his assigned prisoner/patient sat there, each in terror of the other. But, at a certain point in time, they both became aware that they were each harboring the identical fearful thoughts of the other—and then they were able to work together to achieve a profound and joyful therapeutic breakthrough.

It was always my impression that the insight he gained from this rather harrowing experience led him to further elaborate and articulate the importance of optimizing set and setting for psychedelic use. This was a critically important contribution that Ralph made to the field and to the safety and well-being of many seekers who were not only drawn to these altered state experiences but who also had had the foresight to read on the topic in preparation for their deep dive into this most unusual inner landscape.

Together with his two senior colleagues, Tim Leary and Richard Alpert (later renamed Ram Dass), Ralph was at the pinnacle of the psychedelic movement both in academia and the culture at large throughout the 1960s. But, to a greater degree than his better-known and more provocative older associates, Ralph maintained a strong focus on scholarly and intellectual rigor, comprehending the powerful implications these compounds might have for both individual and collective healing.

After the rollercoaster ride he had with Tim Leary, from Harvard to Zihuatanejo to Millbrook, exploring the personal and cultural implications of psychedelics, Ralph retreated to the West Coast in the late 1960s where he continued to explore altered states of consciousness, though without using psychedelics. Ralph went nearly a decade abstaining from psychedelic substances and immersed himself in Agni Yoga and meditation through the School of Actualism in Southern California.

PSILOCYBIN TREATMENT:
MAKING ROOM FOR THE SPIRIT REALM

In the early 2000s I had the opportunity to conduct a psilocybin treatment research investigation at Harbor-UCLA Medical Center of individuals with advanced-stage cancer and reactive existential anxiety and depression.

Our initial treatments, beginning in 2004, went well enough; however, I felt something was missing. I gave it some thought and consulted with Ralph and other senior leaders in the field, and I came to the conclusion that I was neglecting a vital part of the necessary structure for such an intense and existential treatment. *What became clear was that I needed to make room for the spirit realm,* given we were working with a powerful plant-based psychedelic alkaloid.

What I had learned from Ralph over many years of study was to not neglect the spirits but rather to call upon them for guidance, safety, and sustenance in achieving the intentions of the treatment. So, with properly obtained permission from the subjects (no one said no after I explained the purpose, and all appeared to benefit from the added experience), I began to incorporate a ritual that I had observed Ralph implement on many occasions: calling in the spirits of the four directions along with the spirits of the upper realms and the lower realms.

While somewhat unorthodox for a modern research study, I observed that this ritual calling in of the spirits had a profound effect of allowing the subject to become more grounded, centered, and receptive to undergo the powerful psilocybin experience. This ritualized reminder of the ancient origins of our treatment model, a powerful teaching handed to me and to others during our work with Ralph, appeared to have a positive impact on the course of the psychedelic treatment and, in my opinion, strongly contributed to the positive outcome of the study.

This was a reminder, however, that working with psychedelics is unlike conventional allopathic drug treatment. Psychedelics, as Ralph had learned over his vast sixty years of experience in the field, call for a highly specialized approach, which includes acknowledging and calling in the realm of the spirits.

Coming from a rather strict background of biological reductionism, this approach was rather antithetical to conventionally trained treatment providers like myself; nevertheless, it appeared to powerfully augment the intrinsic treatment process and affirm that when conducting this work, we are not necessarily alone. We have allies—if we ask for their aid respectfully. Through Ralph's teaching it was clear, at least to me, that asking for assistance and sustenance from the spirit world, including ancestor spirits, greatly facilitated the psychedelic treatment process and allowed for greater likelihood of efficacious and safe outcomes.

THE TORTOISE'S LESSON AND A NEW NAME

As accomplished a teacher as Ralph was, he was ever-vigilant for further lessons from his life experience. He also had a great capacity for humility, which made him an even more receptive student. I recall one day, back in the 1990s, we were hiking in the desert at the Joshua Tree National Monument in Southern California. During this hike Ralph spied a giant and venerable tortoise slowly crawling on the desert floor. Excited by the presence of this remarkable being, Ralph went over to the tortoise, picked it up by the shell, and explored its displayed underbelly, showing to those of us around him various facets of its unusual body structure. Then he gently placed the tortoise back on the ground and we continued on our way.

Within a few minutes, however, Ralph stumbled, fell, and severely injured his ankle. We helped Ralph down the hillside, back to one of our cars, and drove him to a local Urgent Care for an x-ray to make sure there was no fracture. We then drove Ralph and his now heavily bandaged ankle back to the house where we were staying. When we returned to our home base, Ralph exclaimed that he had learned a very important lesson from the experience, one of being more cognizant and respectful of other beings and life forms we may encounter in our day-to-day lives. I heard him describe this occurrence on a number of occasions over the years, reinforcing for us all this valuable lesson learned.

It has been almost two years since Ralph passed away in the spring of 2019. During this time I have reflected quite a bit on the value of my long friendship with him and the remarkable education I acquired through our association. While I have said my goodbyes to Ralph, I still sense his presence. Ralph had much to teach, and over the thirty years I knew him I had much to learn.

Once, during a rather harrowing trip to South America, as detailed in his book *Searching for the Philosophers' Stone*, Ralph described becoming very ill following a trek into the remote forest to take ayahuasca with local brujos. Following his recovery, and after some reflection, Ralph came to the conclusion that he had been the victim of an evil spell cast by a jealous *ayahuascero*. Though Ralph appeared to have been innocent of any wrongdoing, he was a bystander in a feud between two Indigenous practitioners.

After hearing his account, to my biologically reductionistic outlook his serious—albeit relatively brief—medical crisis appeared to have been caused by the venom of a spider's toxic bite. Ralph returned from this trip and life-threatening experience with a new name to be reserved for ritual settings: Raoul.

So, once again, I will say goodbye to my good friend and teacher, from whose association I benefited so much. He led a remarkable life, and he left behind an extraordinary body of work that still wisely instructs us on the optimal use of psychedelics. Whether by his given name, Ralph, or his received name, Raoul, he has contributed to a foundation of learning and knowledge that will allow for the field to which he devoted himself to flourish into the future, so long as we learn the lessons of the past.

So goodbye, old friend. You may be gone, but you are not forgotten. Your life's lessons and your teaching live on in those of us who had the great good fortune of being your friends and students.

Remembering Ralph:
Reminiscences on a Mentor and Friend
Dennis J. McKenna

Dennis McKenna, Ph.D., is an ethnopharmacologist. He is a founding board member of the Heffter Research Institute and founder of the McKenna Academy of Natural Philosophy. He was a key investigator on the Hoasca Project, the first biomedical investigation of ayahuasca. He is the younger brother of Terence McKenna and lives in Abbotsford, British Columbia.

Most people in the psychedelic community know the name Ralph Metzner. Many will remember him from his association with Timothy Leary and Richard Alpert at Harvard in the early '60s. They were the administrators of the Harvard Psilocybin Project, and Ralph was one of the founding board members, which also included David McClelland, Aldous Huxley, and Frank Barron.

■ Fig. 12. Dennis McKenna (Photo courtesy of Dennis McKenna)

Ralph was at the time a graduate student in clinical psychology. Started in 1960, the program ended in 1962 when accusations of improprieties were published in *The Harvard Crimson*. These accusations included, among other things, the giving of psilocybin to undergraduate students in contravention of the rules governing the administration of the program. Eventually these scandals triggered a public pillorying of Leary and Alpert and led to their departure from the Harvard faculty. Fortunately, Ralph had a somewhat less visible role in the program and largely escaped the public vilification that was directed at Leary and Alpert.

He was able to complete his doctorate in clinical psychology at Harvard in 1962 and moved on to work as staff psychologist at various medical institutions. He did not abandon his interest in psychedelics and expanded states of consciousness, however, and continued to collaborate with Leary and Alpert on various projects following their departure from Harvard. In addition to coauthoring *The Psychedelic Experience*, he was the editor of *The Psychedelic Review*, a journal started by the trio that was published from 1965 to 1967. He continued to teach and publish as well as work as a clinical psychologist while he pursued various professional affiliations.

This summary elides many milestones in Ralph's professional career as a thinker, author, psychologist, and, most importantly, a pioneer in the quest to understand the nature of consciousness and expanded states utilizing psychedelics and other tools of self-exploration. He is remembered and revered by his community, who respect him not only as a scientist who courageously pursued the frontiers of what was often regarded as forbidden knowledge, but also as a warm and kind human being, a mentor and role model to many.

It was in this context that I was fortunate to become acquainted with him in the early 1990s. Like so many significant events in my own life, my friendship with Ralph resulted from his connection with my brother, Terence McKenna. Terence and Ralph became close friends after he attended a lecture Terence gave at Arthur Young's Institute for the Study of Consciousness in Berkeley in the mid-1980s. The Arthur Young Institute was at the time a kind of salon that hosted lectures and symposia on a wide range of intellectually stimulating ideas and attracted an eclectic mix of luminaries and visionary thinkers.

Terence and Ralph recognized each other immediately as kindred spirits (Terence only having known of him previously from his public profile). They lost no time in pursuing that relationship, and following the meeting at the Arthur Young Institute, they continued to meet frequently at Terence's home in Sonoma County for lively conversations. At the time, Terence was just beginning to develop his own public profile, and I remember that he confided in me his delight at having made a connection with the iconic Ralph Metzner, and the warm personal friendship that flourished between them. At the time both were in important transitional junctures in their lives.

Terence was just beginning to come out in the public arena as an eloquent spokesman for psychedelics, after spending some increasingly nerve-wracking years under the radar as a purveyor of psilocybin mushrooms, while Ralph was still dealing, on some levels, with his Harvard experiences and the fallout from the trio's experimentations. While continuing to be interested in psychedelics, he was keeping these interests at arm's length and on the quiet.

Ralph was becoming uncomfortable with the cognitive dissonances engendered by this situation and was considering also stepping out to become more visible in his advocacy of psychedelics, both for exploration of consciousness and as healing medicines.

I think they shared this uncomfortable conundrum: how to find the courage to articulate their messages while at the same time avoiding denunciation as wild-eyed psychedelic fanatics in the public sphere, and, in Terence's case, the very real possibility of disastrous legal consequences.

I'm pretty sure that their eventual decision was reinforced by personal transformative experiences facilitated by Terence's high quality fungal products; whether those were shared experiences, I can't say. I do remember Terence confiding in me that, after many years of feeling ambiguous about psychedelics, Metzner had "rediscovered" them and had started speaking about them more frequently in public.

Although I may have had brief personal encounters with Ralph at some conference or other during the 1980s, our real connection did not happen until November 1995. We both attended a symposium in Rio de Janeiro that was organized by the União do Vegetal (UDV), the Brazilian religious sect that utilizes ayahuasca (which they called by its Portuguese transliteration "hoasca") as a sacrament.[6] This conference was a follow-up to an initial conference they had organized in 1991, at which leading researchers in the field were invited to help organize a biomedical study of ayahuasca in collaboration with the Health Studies section of the UDV.

That conference turned out to be the catalyst for the first biomedical investigation of ayahuasca that came to be known as the Hoasca Project. I undertook to participate in the study design and secured funding for the project from Botanical Dimensions and the nascent Heffter Research Institute. We conducted it with the encouragement of the UDV, at their Nucleo Caupari temple in Manaus, in 1993.[7]

The conference in Rio in 1995 was a follow-up to that project. As it turned out, this conference was the occasion for my closest personal connection with Ralph, when he introduced me, along with several others, to a very special substance: 5-methoxy-DMT. The circumstances were unusual—and far from ideal. It happened on the last day of the conference. As was customary with the UDV, they had arranged for an ayahuasca ceremony at the local temple in Rio to cap off the conference and send everyone home with a positive memory.

Ralph had lately been working with 5-MeO-DMT, which he called

---

6. J. C. Callaway, "A Report from the International Conference of Hoasca Studies, 11/2–4/95," *Newsletter of the Multidisciplinary Association for Psychedelic Studies* 6, no. 3 (Summer 1996).
7. See article on www.UDV.org.br. Find it under the Hoasca Tea tab, choose Scientific Research, then the Hoasca Project.

the "Jaguar Medicine," and with combinations of 5-MeO-DMT and DMT, which he referred to as the "Mayan Twins." I had heard about this but had yet to try either the combination or 5-MeO-DMT itself, except for a few attempts years before that were disappointing, due largely to the fact that I was terrified and afraid to take a big enough dose. (I was titrating my dose based on the Shulgin guidelines, which was not sufficient to elicit the full experience.)

That turned out not to be a problem in Rio! After the closing session of the conference, we all returned to our hotel (the venerable and newly renovated Hotel Gloria) to get ready for the ceremony later that evening. As will happen sometimes, a bunch of the conferees (about twenty or so) had gathered in one of the rooms to hang out and wait for the buses to arrive to take us to the temple.

Ralph Metzner was there, and he had the Jaguar Medicine with him—and offered to dose anyone who was interested. Well, I was interested, along with everyone else (I don't recall anyone abstaining) and so he began to fill his pipe and started dosing each one of us in succession. When it came round to my turn, Ralph dumped quite a dollop into the pipe; much more than I had ever attempted, and I was a little concerned. Ralph was not! He grinned and held the pipe out to me . . . I took one, two, three huge hits, and then fell back onto the bed, experiencing the "usual" total ego dissolution that is typical of this compound. I was not scared. There was no time for that, nor was there enough left of my ego to be concerned with that.

Internally, what I was experiencing was that I seemed to be reduced to a tiny droplet—a mote—of consciousness, that was somehow only one mote in a hyperdimensional "Oort cloud" of sentient consciousness, a kind of hive mind that (so I was assured) included all sentient minds that have ever existed, anywhere in the universe of time and space. And with that awareness came an incredible sadness, as I experienced all the suffering that sentience had ever experienced; I experienced it all, as a single mote, and as the entire hive mind. And then came redemption. An understanding that sentience, being alive, cannot be separated from suffering. Suffering is built into the bargain. But so is joy, and so is love. And somehow, I understood that all the suffering was worth it. It was okay; it had to be, and it was okay.

Gradually I came back into my body, a big smile on my face, and opened my eyes to Ralph's gentle gaze. There was not a lot to say, and I didn't, I only bathed in the afterglow of the experience. I was completely oblivious to anything that was happening in the external world while I was dissolved in the sentient Oort cloud. Ralph (and others) informed me that I had spent the whole time moaning softly, and repeating "holy moly, holy moly" over and over again. A typical enough reaction I suppose. The experience had quite an impact and I didn't rush to repeat it. Such an impact, in fact, that I didn't seek it out for another twenty-three years! Then I got a chance to try the "toad medicine" under very different but more ideal circumstances. It just confirmed what I had learned the first time around under Ralph's ministrations.

After Ralph completed his rounds, it was time to go to the lobby and catch the buses to the temple. We were all still resonating from our experience, and it was kind of a shock to step out of the elevator into a room packed with several hundred people, all excitedly jabbering away. I felt like our little group had experienced a visit to a very far and different place (which we had), and we weren't quite ready for reentry. But we adapted; we went to the temple, and I had one of the best ayahuasca experiences of my life.

Regretfully, following that 1995 conference in São Paulo, except for brief encounters at various conferences over the next nine years, I did not see much of Ralph, although we occasionally corresponded.

In March 2000, CIIS sponsored the first domestic conference on ayahuasca at the Cathedral Hotel in San Francisco.[8] Ralph was instrumental in organizing that historic conference, which remains as timely today as when the conference was presented more than twenty years ago. Ralph made memorable presentations with Jeremy Narby and Charles

8. Ayahuasca, Shamanism, Science, and Spirituality, March 17–20, 2000.

Grob, while I presented a report on the Hoasca Project together with my co-investigators, Charles Grob and Jace Callaway.

Most of the leading lights in the ayahuasca field at the time were represented, and many had been at the São Paulo conference in '95. The conference took place under a bit of a cloud. My brother, Terence McKenna, was in the last stages of terminal glioblastoma, which he had been suffering for nearly a year. The entire community and Terence's many fans and admirers, as well as his family and friends, felt profound sadness and helplessness as the inevitable end drew near. He passed away on April 3, just a couple of weeks after the conference. Though he could not attend, his presence was felt by the attendees.

In 2018, Ralph published his last book, *Searching for the Philosophers' Stone: Encounters with Mystics, Scientists, and Healers* (Park Street Press). His chapter on Terence and me in that book ("The Brothers Terence and Dennis McKenna") is one of the kindest, most empathetic, and accurate depictions of our unique fraternal bond and our shared obsessions that I have seen published anywhere. I will forever be grateful to Ralph for including this chapter; it provides a detailed and nonjudgmental unpacking of our relationship. He brought to bear the insights of a skilled clinical psychologist who could see below the surface to the inner dynamics, who knew both of us including our many warts, and yet loved and admired us greatly. Both Terence and I, of course, felt the same about Ralph. Much of the content of the chapter is derived from an extensive series of email exchanges that we had in 2011, while I was in the process of writing my memoir. These excerpts have not been published elsewhere to my knowledge, and they are well worth reading. It was lively exchange of ideas. I only regret that it could not have been in person, but it was rich, nonetheless.

Ralph Metzner was one of a kind. He was a good man, a courageous explorer of the frontiers of human experience, an exemplar of a life lived with clarity, curiosity, and compassion. He will always be remembered, and he will always be missed.

Courageous Explorer
Susan Homer

Susan Homer met Ralph Metzner in the spring of 1962 when she was twenty-one and he was twenty-five; they were married several months later. Although the marriage was short-lived, the psychedelic experiences that Susan shared with Ralph changed her life, confirming her interest in the nature of the mind and the possibilities for how one might experience it. She went on to study and practice the teachings of Gurdjieff and later became a practitioner of meditation in the tradition of Tibetan Buddhism. She has lived in New Mexico for more than fifty years.

When I remember Ralph, an image comes to my mind of him sitting at a typewriter, alone, on the veranda outside our room at the Hotel Catalina in Zihuatanejo. It is the summer of 1962. Ralph is barefoot, wearing rolled-up khakis and a loose-fitting striped jersey; he's grown his first beard. He stares at the typewriter with his hands poised over the keys. A hammock is hanging at the end of the veranda and beyond that, lush red hibiscus blooms. Down below, out of the frame, there is the beach and the idyllic circle of the bay set with the comforting sound of waves lapping ashore.

Who I see in this paradisiacal setting is someone having a wonderful time, thinking, writing, absorbed in his thought process. His inquisitiveness propelled an endless exploration of ideas and experiences about the world, inner and outer, about how the mind works, and about himself, and how his own mind works.

Ralph was a true and intrepid explorer. And while he was serious about his explorations, they were balanced with fun and excitement along the way. Ralph had both the heart and courage to follow his relentless curiosity. And it does take courage. You may find out things you'd rather not know; you may be led to ideas and beliefs that are beyond the pale, both within yourself or in your social surroundings. These collisions occurred more than once in Ralph's life.

■ Fig. 13. Wedding photo of Susan Homer and Ralph, 1962 (From the collection of Ralph Metzner)

There are other qualities that complement those of curiosity and courage—openness, humility, honesty, adventurousness, integrity—but for me, curiosity and fearlessness were Ralph's defining characteristics.

Palenque and Beyond
Tim Scherer

Tim Scherer is a Northern California–based real estate investor and author. He is a graduate of Brigham Young University, holds a master's certification from the Academy of Intuition Medicine, and happily guides shamanic journey–styled meditations as a community service.

I was in grade school in the late 1960s in San Francisco when my father, a conservative engineer, asked what I wanted to be for Halloween. "A hippie," was my response. He let me know we were going on a ride in our car, and soon we were driving down Haight Street on a post–Summer of Love, warm fall afternoon. The place was overcooked, and the freaks were out for sure. On the way home, he glanced at me in the rearview mirror and asked, "Oh, Timmy, what did you say you wanted to be for Halloween?" "A pirate," I replied.

Fast forward twenty years, and I had served a two-year mission for the Mormon Church in southern Spain, graduated from Brigham Young University, and had become one of the pirates in the financial district of San Francisco.

Then, a few years later, in the fall of 1994, I took my first mushrooms on the Cataract Trail on Mt. Tamalpais. The experience had left me so intrigued that a few days later I walked from my office to City Lights Bookstore where I stood at the counter in my suit and tie inquiring in hushed tones about books on mushrooms. I walked back to my office with three books written by Terence McKenna.

Shortly thereafter, my secretary handed me a very cryptic fax that Terence, Ralph Metzner, Paul Stamets, Jonathan Ott, and others would be presenting at a conference in Palenque, Mexico. I forwarded the flyer to my sailing friend, Fish, and notwithstanding our slight naiveté as to the nature of the event, we both signed up.

At dinner the first night in Palenque, under a giant palapa in the jungle, Fish and I felt starkly out of place in our yacht club polos and Topsiders (boat shoes) in what seemed to us a gathering of wizards. It was, in fact, a meeting of the world's foremost authorities on plant-based hallucinogens, which they were calling entheogens, a term coined by one of the presenters, Jonathan Ott, and roughly defined as something you ingest to give you the experience of God. Fish and I were fine with that, and we were excited to be there.

Having become fluent in Spanish as a missionary, I would learn from our taxi driver that mushrooms grew in the field directly across from the Palenque ruins and that if we were to hang out on a particular stone bridge after a morning rain, we might just see a toothless old man carrying a backpack, to whom we should query for "Ongos."

The next morning, Fish and I determined it had been raining, and we made our way to the stone bridge where we sat and waited for quite a while, until along came an old man carrying a backpack. We greeted him with the magic word, and he beamed the most radiant toothless grin. (And, I think he had already eaten a few and was well on his way.) We bought his entire morning harvest, dumped them into our cardboard box and headed back to the hotel where we just happened to bump into Paul Stamets who was happy to help us identify our haul. He reached in, grabbed one, and holding it up and noting the blue on the stem, he pronounced it *Stropharia cubensis* (also known by its current synonym *Psilocybe cubensis*).

We took our box of *Stropharia cubensis* back to our hotel room, washed off all the cow dung, and placed them on a white hotel room towel to dry. But they still smelled and tasted horrible, and so we drizzled them with the raw honey we had bought from some Maya kids on the side of the road the day before. At sunset, we ate a few of our honey-drizzled gems before heading out to catch the performance of a Balinese dance by Jonathan Ott's girlfriend. As Jonathan explained in great detail about the sacred nature of the dance, I had a vision of a seated light-being Buddha who descended to my left and greeted me with outstretched arms. I guess that being already knew the evening was going to be a truly sublime experience.

When Fish and I got back to our room, we ate our magic mushroom dinner, turned down the lights, and turned up our Deep Forest CD, which would run all night on replay. The minute I closed my eyes, I was hovering across the forest floor when I paused one foot above a frightening, fanged bat-like creature, lying on his back with his wings folded across his chest. Very anxious to move along, I came across a group of glowing celery-like beings who were standing in a circle and holding a glowing newborn human baby that they were infusing with their pure white light. That the rest of the mushrooms were sitting on the white towel just outside the bathroom made it a bit too convenient to eat just one more (several times) over the course of the evening, ensuring that our adventure would last until sunrise, at which time I had arrived at a place where I was one with all of creation.

The next night at dinner, Fish and I sat next to Ralph who was anxious to hear about our adventure. His first question was about the dosage. Fish and I glanced quizzically at one another and blankly back at him. "How many grams did you take?" he asked. Fish explained that we didn't have a scale. "Well, how many did you consume?" he asked. I had to confess we had lost track. Ralph persisted, "Yes, but how much did you eat?" "Until we were full . . . ?" Fish sheepishly suggested. I started laughing (and still do about that awkward moment).

We moved on to recount our visions to Ralph. Of the celery-like beings he said, "Oh, like a reverse photosynthesis, where they are giving their converted sunlight to the humans." When I told him about the bat-like creature, he commented that the Maya had anthropomorphic bat-like messenger beings and that this was probably a portal I had missed due to my fear. As I pondered that possibility, he followed with, "Why do you think they put gargoyles on the outside of the cathedrals? To frighten away the unworthy." Well, that was me, I thought. Little did Ralph know at the time that leaving the Mormon Church had left me spiritually adrift and struggling to integrate my newfound information into any kind of framework.

As we finished dinner, word was spreading that a bus would be arriving soon to take us to the Palenque ruins where the guards had been well-compensated to grant us exclusive access. A few hours later, we were standing in front of Pascal's pyramid, which was glowing in the light of the full moon, when Ralph asked if anyone would like to participate in a ritual. We followed him into the grassy courtyard of the Palace where we formed a circle and held hands. Ralph began, "Well, here we are in what the Maya referred to as the Navel of the World." Then, he acknowledged the spirits of the animals, plants, and our ancestors. As he did, my great-grandmother, Teresa, was suddenly standing right behind me.

Ralph eventually led us through the building and onto the steps facing Pascal's pyramid, where we all sat about halfway up while Ralph smudged us all with copal, a tree resin sacred to the Maya. This was how one was supposed to go about spiritual work, I thought. The foundation stone to my spiritual framework had been set.

Before leaving Palenque, I learned Ralph kept an office near my home, and I began to meet him there regularly upon my return. After a few months, he came to my little cottage in Mill Valley to guide me on a four-hour intensive. Upon his arrival, he asked if could put his lunch in my fridge, and I had to explain that I had tied it closed with an old halyard because it smelled after unplugging it. For all I know, he was wondering what the hell I was hiding in there. But, he smiled, casually placed his lunch on the counter and returned with a glass of water which he handed to me along with four capsules of ground San Pedro cactus, explaining they contained the same psychoactive substance used by the Native Americans in their vision quest work. As I was taking them, Ralph walked over to my fireplace mantle and began to observe my collection of crystals, beads, rattles, and candles. "This is how the hippies used to live," was his only comment. So I had found my hippie costume after all, at least in the evenings and on weekends at that point.

Ralph called in my ancestors, suggesting that one in particular would show up as a guide. This time it was my deceased grandfather on my mother's side. He was the grandson of Mormon pioneers, was of Welsh descent, and could be found every afternoon fly fishing on the Provo River in Utah. I recalled hiking into a canyon with him when I was a boy and climbing to a rock ledge where he taught me how to shoot his pistol. While he had suffered a miserable death due to complications of Alzheimer's disease just a few years ago, there he was dressed in buckskin, dancing in the dust and rattling, which evoked such a powerful feeling of reunion and reverence that it moved me to tears. I could not have asked for a more beautiful way to begin my journey.

When Ralph informed me it was time to see my most immediate past life, I felt it only fair to share with him that I wasn't sure about reincarnation. While for me it felt like I had just put my hand on the record player, Ralph was not deterred and asked if I was at least open to accepting reincarnation as a possibility. I was, and within a few minutes he was asking me to see my feet in that lifetime. He asked me to see where I lived, and I walked to my modest hut on stilts, located at the edge of the valley above the rice fields, where I lived with my wife and two children. Ralph asked how I died, and I saw a soldier with my same skin color, dressed in a gray uniform, standing in front of me and shooting me in the belly. "Well, that life didn't end so well, did it," Ralph commented.

Ralph began my birth regression that day asking me to see how my parents felt about one another when they first met. I saw my mother in junior high school recognizing the natural nobility of my father. I saw my mother pregnant in San Francisco not long after my father had taken his first job there. I could sense how concerned she was about finding a good doctor in Iowa when my father was transferred there. I could see that my mother had a made a soul commitment to expose me to her faith, even though she was not actively attending church at the time. I also knew it was important that I come into a family with a father who was of a different faith, as if I had designed my own eventual escape hatch from the Mormon Church.

Ralph walked me through some holotropic breathwork preparing me to see my birth. Once again, I was skeptical. "What does any child remember prior to the age of four?" I thought. But I had just seen my first past life, and so I went along with it. Then I was looking down into a room where my mother was lying in a hospital bed, as if I were having an out-of-body experience. I saw the black and white tiled floor, the bed angling into the room toward the window, and how the sun coming through that window told me it was late morning. My doctor was a short red-haired man who had two nuns attending him. I experienced the trauma of being stuck in the birth canal. Shortly after my birth, from the first-person perspective, as my mother held me while sitting in a chair on the lawn in our backyard, I was watching the muddy Mississippi River rolling toward me when a portal opened between me and the reeds on the riverbank, and an alligator lizard appeared greeting me with a "Hello, little boy!"

Before Ralph left that day, I asked him if these visions were possible without taking the San Pedro cactus. He responded that they were, that substances only helped to cleanse the windows of perception and that it was very much about doing the work in the proper mindset and setting.

After Ralph left that day, I phoned my mother and recounted the events of my birth. Her voice trembled and through her tears she confirmed everything I had seen, adding that the red-haired doctor had saved my life when I was coming out face first. It was grateful to be able to tell her I understood why she was so frustrated when I left the church, but that from my perspective she had fulfilled her soul commitment to introduce me to a spiritual practice.

My respect for Ralph grew immensely that day for having guided me into new realms I did not know were accessible. In the years following, I would do a lot of work with Ralph whose wise and insistent commitment kept me heading in the right direction as I built a new framework to contain the varieties of my spiritual experience.

After marrying and having children, I lost touch with Ralph for several years, but was happy to be invited to his eightieth birthday party, which was attended by many who had known him professionally over the years, including Ram Dass who Skyped in from Hawaii. Toward the end of the party, I was standing next to Ralph, when he turned toward

■ Fig. 14. Hiking buddies: Ralph and Tim Scherer on the Tennessee Valley Trail, Marin County, California, 2016 (Photo by Cathy Coleman)

me and said, "I just thought we would have spent more time together in this life." It broke my heart to hear that, and I wondered how I could have let that happen. I quickly determined that I had let my admiration and respect for him as my teacher get in the way of friendship. I flashed back to years earlier sitting at the kitchen table with him late at night after a medicine circle, when I shared that I had just seen a lifetime as a Knight Templar, upon which he reached across the table to shake my hand saying, "Ah, so that's what it is, my brother," before recounting his own visions of that life.

Before leaving his birthday party, I decided it was not too late to be friends and that we urgently needed to make up for lost time. So I found my way over to his wife, Cathy, who said he liked walking in nature, that he was not driving but that she would be happy to bring him down to meet me in Marin County.

A few weeks later, Cathy dropped Ralph at Tennessee Valley, just north of the Golden Gate Bridge, where he and I walked to the beach and back, talking nonstop about children, relationships, parents, and things confidential, as old friends do. It felt like a good beginning, and I vowed to reach out more often. Over the next few years, Ralph and I shared long lunches in the wine county and attended lectures together. It was important to be able to tell him how much he meant to me. I was happy to be able to tell him I had continued my education and learned to guide people into sacred space, without the use of substances, and that my mother had been a recent client, all of which seemed to complete the circle of work begun with Ralph so many years earlier.

The Many Faces of Ralph
Carla Detchon

Carla Detchon is a certified life coach. She helps clients access inner wisdom through guided meditations, integration practices, and energy work.

When I was thirty-four, my dear friend Tim Scherer and I took a weekend class with Michael Harner to learn about shamanism. During that class, we practiced doing shamanic journeys for ourselves and for other participants. At lunch, as we compared notes, I asked Tim why he was so much better at the journeying part than I was, and his answer was, "Because I've been working with this amazing man."

That man was, of course, Ralph Metzner. As Tim told me about his experiences working with Ralph, every fiber of my being said, "That's what I want." I remember that moment so clearly because it changed the course of my life.

■ Fig. 15. Carla Detchon (Photo courtesy of Carla Detchon)

I went on to work with Ralph for the next twenty-two years. He was absolutely my greatest—and my hardest—teacher. When I think about what I want to share about Ralph, what comes to me was his total commitment to the exploration of consciousness and psychedelics, as well as his abundant creativity with those two worlds. And we loved tripping along in the magical forays that he created.

THE MASTER MIXOLOGIST

Ralph excelled at matching various molecules to his mind maps. I remember a series of workshops he created to explore 5-MeO-DMT. Ralph quickly moved the groups from smoking that powerful substance to insufflating or snorting it, which provided a longer, more workable experience. He thought it was the perfect medicine to layer in Stan Grof's work focusing on the four stages of birth.

Another time, we explored the death realm—a topic he, Timothy Leary, and Richard Alpert wrote about in *The Psychedelic Experience: A Manual Based on the Tibetan Book of the Dead*. Ralph created a series of meditations that guided us through the bardos while on LSD. During the day, Ralph the Professor taught us about the Tibetan concept of the bardos, describing each of the six realms of the after-death states. That night, he used music, carefully crafted to invoke the spirit and energy of each realm. I remember thinking as the music started for the Asura realm (the realm of jealousy, fighting, control, and war), "Oh crap, this is going to be hard," but I learned to navigate through that dark, heavy energy, which is what he was ultimately trying to teach us.

RALPH THE MAGICIAN

Ralph was at his most magical during his six-day retreats where the work got deep, and that's where he really loved to play—in the depths. These retreats were master classes where his vast knowledge was on full display. Using the full six days, Ralph took us deeper and deeper into his map of consciousness.

When Ralph was on, he was transcendent. He told us full technicolor tales of Egyptian mythology that came to life under our eyeshades. He wove in Norse mythology where we journeyed to meet the three Norns, and, of course, he introduced us to Mimir and his Well of Remembrance. I have a deep relationship with these cosmic entities because of Ralph, along with a pantheon of other gods and goddesses.

He also taught us how to navigate the ethereal realms and connect with and respect our ancestors as well as creating relationships with animal, plant, and spirit guides. We learned to ask the names of these guides who showed up to help us. His map of consciousness was ever-expanding, and when we set off in our spirit raft to travel into the unknown wilds under his gentle guidance, we all felt like intrepid adventurers exploring the ever-expanding terrain of the past, present, and future together.

DJ RALPH—
SPINNER OF COSMIC TUNES

All of these experiences had their own perfectly curated musical score. Ralph was a cutting-edge musical maestro. Each morning, following our magical mystery tour evenings, Ralph would provide us with the names of the various CDs he had played the night before, and I could tell that our accolades for the music he had chosen brought him a lot of pleasure and pride. He had quite the ear for choosing just the right beats, tones, and rhythms, and his musical taste ran the gamut from jazz to Buddhist chanting to pop and soul. At the end of a long night of guiding us through transformational realms, Ralph would often relax and spin a few of his favorite songs, and they were always exceptional. Or he might ask us instead if we wanted to hear a story, and the answer was always a resounding yes, and then he would regale us with a highly entertaining personal tale or a mythical saga.

Ralph made these shared journeys exceptional and unique. His commitment to our learning, our growth, and to the Earth's evolution ran deep, and was a throughline in all the work he produced. Thank you, Ralph, for all that you gave us. You are deeply missed.

The Abbess and the Wandering Monk
Diane Haug

Diane Haug, M.A., L.P.C.C., is a licensed therapist living in northern New Mexico. She has staffed and taught Grof holotropic breathwork training modules internationally. She assisted Ralph with his vision circle work for many years.

I first met Ralph in 1990 at an International Transpersonal Association (ITA) Conference in Eugene, Oregon. Having already studied with Stan Grof[9] for some years, I had some sense of Ralph's place in the history of psychedelics and transpersonal psychology, but had never heard him lecture.

Although I can't quite remember the name of the talk, it had a strong ecopsychological focus. Ralph talked passionately about the need for a fundamental re-visioning of psychology—a "green psychology" that would bring the fullness of the natural environment into the theory and practice of psychotherapy. As a woman who, in her early forties, had chosen to take a five-year nature sabbatical in a remote corner of northeastern New Mexico, I found his ideas compelling.

Over tea, I asked Ralph if he would consider coming to lecture in Santa Fe, New Mexico. He happily accepted. And to my great delight he agreed to build into his visit an optional, experiential, land-based weekend in that same remote setting. Tempered by his own experiences with traditional Native American culture and his practice of the vision quest, Ralph understood the value of deepening one's intimacy with the natural world. He loved working in a wild landscape that was home to elk, bear, and large cats.

---

9. Stanislav "Stan" Grof is a Czech-born psychiatrist. Having lived and worked in the United States since the 1960s, Grof is one of the principal developers of transpersonal psychology. He researched nonordinary states of consciousness for purposes of exploring, healing, and obtaining growth and insights into the human psyche. He and his second wife, Christina, developed the holotropic breathwork process. He is a contributor to this volume of tributes.

■ Fig. 16. From left: Robert Weisz, Ralph, and Diane Haug
at Synergia Ranch, Santa Fe, New Mexico
(From the collection of Ralph Metzner)

Over the decades that followed, that particular potentiated land-based practice and our unique working relationship deepened and grew. In Ralph I had met not only a scholar and clinician—but an alchemist, magician, and Medicine Man. Indeed, a veritable contemporary Mystery School.

Ralph was a guide who acknowledged in the invisible world the realm of the unseen. His invocations were brilliant—always taking time to consciously honor life in all its myriad forms: the teachings of the four directions; the movement in the heavens; animal, plant, mineral helpers; our personal and collective ancestors—all recognized with gratitude. As an alchemist he understood the potency of the elements and the death/rebirth mystery as essential for any powerful and authentic transformational process. As we explored the life cycles of the human soul we honed our navigational skills.

■ Fig. 17. Ralph and Diane Haug at Synergia Ranch. This photo was
edited by Diane with the artistic software Prisma; Diane chose a filter
that offered a psychedelic effect (Photo courtesy of Diane Haug)

Ralph was my teacher, mentor, older brother, friend, colleague,
and co-conspirator. Confirming our soul connection, he would
occasionally refer to us as "The Abbess" (me) and "The Wandering
Monk" (he). I am incredibly grateful for the decades of exploring
inner landscapes together . . . of *remembering* where we came from
and where we are headed. Our relationship informed and enriched
my life.

Birth of a Psychedelic Culture
Gary Bravo

Gary Bravo, M.D., is a psychiatrist in Northern California and has written extensively on psychedelics, psychiatry, and transpersonal psychology. He was honored
to have been a friend, student, and colleague of Ralph Metzner's for more than
thirty years.

In 2004, Ralph Metzner proposed that I join him in a project—to
moderate a series of interviews with Ram Dass, with the purpose of
documenting an oral history of the psychedelic '60s, when he and Ram
Dass formed two-thirds of the infamous Harvard triumvirate (Timothy
Leary was the third). Of course I accepted, jumping at the chance to
work with two of my greatest teachers.

Ralph was concerned about Ram Dass, who had been quite ill earlier in the year with a kidney infection. At that point it had been seven
years since Ram Dass had suffered a stroke in February 1997. He was
paralyzed on his right side, was totally dependent on caregivers for his
daily activities and survival, and still suffered from expressive aphasia,
where he had trouble finding words and putting them together in full
sentences.

Ram Dass was up for the project. It was a time when he was still
living in the Bay Area just before he moved permanently to Maui. We
all met in a recording studio in Fairfax owned by an engineer who vol-
unteered his time for the project. The first session was quite disjointed,
as Ralph had pulled out his pipe filled with various herbs, of which
hashish was one component, and I had a difficult time keeping the conversation on track, eventually having to surrender to the stoned flow.
Of course Ralph was quite articulate and verbal. Ram Dass had to work
to get a word in edgewise, in addition to getting the words out.

Nonetheless, during the course of a series of conversations over the
next couple of weeks, Ralph and Ram Dass settled into a warm and

■ Fig. 18. Gary Bravo and Ram Dass working on
Birth of a Psychedelic Culture, 2007
(From the collection of Ralph Metzner)

intimate space, reminiscing about the days at Harvard, the experiments in Mexico and elsewhere, the Millbrook days, and ultimately the parting, when, after about six years together, they went their separate ways.

It was quite gratifying for me, having been too young to have participated in the '60s, to hear these two icons in dialogue as they attempted to recall the events, impressions, motivations, and meaning of those legendary times, so important in the history of consciousness, the counterculture, and psychedelia. Ralph, being the scholar he was, was interested in getting the history down as accurately and completely as possible. Ram Dass clearly was still somewhat depressed, having been hospitalized not too long before, still adjusting to being immobile and dependent, and also having had one of his greatest assets taken away from him—the gift of the gab. But during each session, as the conversations wore on, Ram Dass's affect brightened; he became less self-conscious and more fluent in his speech, and his trademark sense of humor became evident.

Ralph had another agenda for the talks. He told me beforehand that he thought Ram Dass might be ready to be open about his homosexuality in a public forum. It was true, even so many years distant from his psychedelic and holy man periods, Ram Dass confessed that he had always stayed in the closet because of shame about this aspect of his psyche, despite being so open and sharing of his human flaws and foibles while traveling the spiritual path. Typical of Ralph, he used the opportunity of recording history to do some (successful) therapy for his dear friend.

The conversations helped me to imagine the courage it took for Ralph Metzner, a brilliant but straightlaced grad student, attracted by Leary's theories of personality and social interaction (as well as his considerable charm and charisma), to volunteer for the Concord Prison Experiment, essentially agreeing to take psilocybin with convicts in jail. Leary had doubts that Ralph had what it took, but Ralph, after his initiatory psilocybin experience at Leary's Newton house, enthusiastically joined the Harvard Psilocybin Project as a loyal follower and major contributor to the subsequent direction of this movement.

Imagine Ralph, taking part in the legendary Good Friday Experiment[10] (he got the placebo), establishing a psychedelic-inspired communal house in Newton Center; setting up psychedelic "summer camps" in Zihuatanejo, Mexico; then expelled from Mexico, followed by subsequent failed attempts to establish bases in the West Indies. Finally, there was the serendipitous landing in Millbrook,[11]

---

10. The Good Friday Experiment occurred at Boston University's Marsh Chapel on Good Friday, 1962. Walter Pahnke, a graduate student in theology at Harvard Divinity School, designed the experiment under the supervision of Timothy Leary, Richard Alpert, and the Harvard Psilocybin Project—which, in addition to Leary and Alpert, included Aldous Huxley, David McClelland, Frank Barron, and Ralph Metzner. The experiment investigated whether psilocybin (the active principle in psilocybin mushrooms) would act as a reliable entheogen in religiously predisposed subjects.

11. Millbrook, New York, is the location of the Hitchcock Estate, which was the nexus of the psychedelic movement in the 1960s where Timothy Leary, Richard Alpert, and Ralph Metzner lived communally, along with numerous others, and where they conducted research and wrote The Psychedelic Experience. Millbrook is the name that refers to the psychedelic collective that lived there.

that cauldron of avant-garde creativity and experimental living.

Looming large over Ralph and Ram Dass's narrative was the figure of Timothy Leary. Though it had been forty years since they were a triumvirate, and Leary had passed on about eight years previously, Ralph and Ram Dass still seemed to be in awe of his charisma, vision, and intellect. Leary was clearly the alpha male. Ram Dass said his own contributions to the scene were cooking, cleaning, and taking care of the children. Ralph was the scholar and scribe.

As such, Ralph published and edited the *Psychedelic Review*, the first journal devoted to consciousness expansion. He worked closely with Leary on the groundbreaking and enormously influential book *The Psychedelic Experience: A Manual Based on the Tibetan Book of the Dead*, bringing the language and concepts of Eastern spirituality into the burgeoning counterculture. Following along this thread, Ralph was the first of the trio to travel to India in search of spiritual knowledge, later joined by Leary and his newlywed wife. These experiences consolidated into the seeds of the academic and healing field that combined psychology with spirituality, later labeled as "transpersonal psychology."[12]

Eventually the three went their separate ways. Richard Alpert famously went on his own journey to India. Leary went to prison. Ralph moved to California and gave up psychedelics while he was part of the metaphysical School of Actualism[13] in Southern California. Eventually, like many an old explorer, Ralph became a professor and passed on the distillation of his experiences and his encyclopedic knowledge to generations of students and disciples.

Following these conversations between Ralph and Ram Dass the project was expanded, and we solicited contributions from others who had "been there" during those wild and exhilarating times. These sto-

---

12. Originally coined by Abraham Maslow and Victor Frankl.
13. Actualism is the practice of Agni Yoga, or Light-Fire yoga, developed by Russell Paul Schofield. See the essay by Alan Levin titled "The Great Work" in this volume.

ries fleshed out the history and often provided surprisingly contrasting remembrances. Eventually, fostered along by enthusiastic publisher Deborah "Tango" Snyder of Synergetic Press, the book was published in 2010 as *Birth of a Psychedelic Culture: Conversations about Leary, the Harvard Experiments, Millbrook, and the Sixties.*

Neither Ralph nor Ram Dass seemed to have any regrets about their roles in the history of psychedelia. Some have blamed the Harvard triumvirate and their well-publicized escapades as a major factor in the government's shutdown of research and eventual criminalization of psychedelics. But it was clear to Ralph and Ram Dass that it couldn't have been any other way; they felt swept along by the set and setting of those heady times, fueled by psilocybin, LSD, DMT, and so forth, which they viewed as psychospiritual and evolutionary catalysts.

It turned out that Ram Dass went on to live another sixteen years, continuing his role as a humble and beloved spiritual teacher on the island paradise of Maui; and in one of those cosmic ironies, he actually outlived Ralph by almost a year. Ralph continued to explore, teach, and write prodigiously, working tirelessly for the Gaia vision, integrating East and West, psychology and spirituality, and cosmic and earthly wisdom. Both teachers had long since given up their fear of death, being stellar models for graceful aging and the setting aside of the corporeal self.

In the final session of the conversations with Ram Dass, Ralph, who was open to the idea of reincarnation, which he called "reincarnational echoes," stated that he identified strongly with the story of Marco Polo. Before one dismisses this comparison out of hand, there are some significant parallels.

Like Marco Polo, Ralph Metzner, accompanied by two companions, embarked on a metaphorical "Journey to the East"[14] to explore the terra incognita of the landscapes of consciousness. Like Polo,

---

14. *Journey to the East* references Herman Hesse's book of that name. See Timothy Leary and Ralph Metzner, "Hermann Hesse: Poet of the Interior Journey," in *The Psychedelic Reader*, ed. Gunther Weil, Timothy Leary, and Ralph Metzner (New Hyde Park, NY: University Books, 1965).

Ralph brought back tales of encounters with exotic beings and locales, and "more importantly, knowledge of the wonders of as yet undiscovered worlds."[15] Like Polo, Ralph wrote about his travels, even producing, through his extensive scholarship, an expanded cartography of consciousness.[16]

Eventually Ralph became an expedition leader, guiding groups and individuals into their own inner and outer universes, into the past and future, and navigating the multiple levels of reality. He always spoke of two main reasons for pursuing expanded states of consciousness: healing the past and visioning the future—and assimilating both into the present. His long and productive life exemplified this integration.

Steppenwolf's Magic Theater
Jack Silver

Jack Silver, J.D., is a public interest attorney specializing in environmental law. Jack was co-counsel in the Santo Daime case which was the first federal case granting a religious organization the right to use ayahuasca as a sacrament. Jack is a GTT-certified facilitator and practices aikido, Japanese tea ceremony, and calligraphy.

In 1968, when I was fourteen, I had my first psychedelic experience. We (a small group of stoners) had just finished reading *The Psychedelic Experience* and had the good fortune to have some Orange Sunshine available. At that time, I knew who Leary was, but I had no idea who Ralph was other than a coauthor of that book.

It was not until 1996, at the International Transpersonal Association (ITA) Conference in Manaus, that I had the pleasure of meeting Ralph in person. My youngest son and I attended his fiery talk on ecology. I

---

15. Ram Dass, Ralph Metzner, with Gary Bravo, *Birth of a Psychedelic Culture* (Santa Fe, NM: Synergetic Press, 2010), 227.
16. Ralph Metzner, *Maps of Consciousness* (New York: Collier-Macmillan, 1971).

■ Fig. 19. Jack Silver (Photo courtesy of Jack Silver)

was eager to meet him and was introduced by a mutual friend, Thomas Hines. Inspired by our meeting, I had a dream that night in which I saw a person looking over and guarding a river.

Soon after I returned from the Manaus conference, I started the group River Watch,[17] which is still going strong today. Ralph was one of the founding board members. Ralph also asked my wife Kate and me to serve on the board of his nonprofit Green Earth Foundation.

At times Ralph could be cantankerous, stubborn, and dogmatic; at other times, lighthearted, generous, and receptive. He was, after all,

---

17. California River Watch is a nonprofit organization whose mission is to strengthen the ability of citizens to protect water quality in rivers, tributary watersheds, oceans, bays, wetlands, and surface and groundwater in California.

human. It was no secret that Ralph had experienced great loss in his life. At one gathering I bemoaned the fact that a certain deep wounding I had in my life kept coming up in my sessions. "I just want to be over this," I said. Ralph looked at me with great kindness. He replied that for he and I such wounds do not heal; instead, they deepen our humanity. Although Ralph was a great teacher, it was his humanity I was drawn to more than his knowledge.

I recall at a Multidisciplinary Association of Psychedelic Studies (MAPS) conference Ralph, not one of the main speakers, was giving his talk in one of the smaller venues. The room was packed. When Ralph entered, he received a standing ovation. At first, he looked bemused—and then he smiled, accepting the adoration graciously. Unlike some of his contemporaries, who seem fixated on their legacy, Ralph always seemed to be more concerned that the listener focus on the message rather than messenger.

I attended numerous circles with Ralph. When Ralph was in his center, it was magical. He was an incredible storyteller and a talented spiritual guide and teacher. He often reminded me of Hesse's protagonist Harry Haller.

> And these men, for whom life has no repose, live at times in their rare moments of happiness with such strength and indescribable beauty, the spray of their moment's happiness is flung so high and dazzlingly over the wide sea of suffering, that the light of it, spreading its radiance, touches others too with its enchantment.[18]

At his circles Ralph was the Steppenwolf, inviting us into his magic theater.

---

18. Herman Hesse, *Steppenwolf* (New York: Henry Holt, 1929; first published in 1927 in German by S. Fischer Verlag A. G.), 44.

A Man to Remember
Uwe Doerken

Uwe Doerken is a business executive, management consultant, and entrepreneur who has lived in ten different countries in the course of his life, including Germany and the United States. He served as chairman and CEO of DHL Worldwide Express. He also served on the board of Green Earth Foundation for many years.

It was a cool winter evening, the kind that passes as "cold" in California, when the strange little guest house appeared out of the mist in the headlights of our car. Who had constructed an Alpine lodge in this distant corner of the Sierra Madre in Los Angeles?

It turned out that it was the Friends of Nature, a nineteenth-century Austrian hiking society who had built such guest houses all around the world for its members. Only much later did I realize the fitting metaphor: An old structure from the old world, repurposed for events most probably not imagined by its original builders. Little did I know what lay in store for me in this humble dwelling, and that I was about to experience one of the most foundational nights of my life.

The man I was about to meet was an old soul who came to play his part in birthing what he called the psychedelic culture that emerged in the United States, and particularly in California, in the second half of the twentieth century. He had the kind and unassuming manner of an experienced teacher and made you feel appreciated and immediately at the center of his attention. One of his fans called him the "Mr. Rogers Shaman," because he could explain his work in simple and easy to understand words, while remaining kind and understanding. Yet behind this humble and friendly face lived a radical and courageous mind that dared go places where others feared to tread.

In his customary scholarly way, Ralph made us all feel at home. He then proceeded to explain his methodology, what he would do with us during the rest of the evening, and the ground rules for our behavior.

Simple and effective ways that were battle-tested many times, and which gave structure to an experience that could otherwise become disorienting and even frightening. Together with my fellow travelers, some of them also new to Ralph's ways, I embarked on a life-changing journey.

During the next four hours, I reexperienced parts of my life that I did not think I had access to, and found out fundamental truths about my earliest weeks and months on Earth. I accessed visions of my future and impressions of what seemed to be past lives I had lived. I gained insights into new ways of thinking and of understanding my existence. When waking up the next morning, I literally felt that I had learned more about myself and the world in a single night than the preceding forty-some years.

This single night laid the foundation for my life-long deep appreciation of the shamanic practices that Ralph researched, wrote about, and so expertly practiced. It also was the beginning of a magical friendship with this fascinating man who will always have a big place in my heart.

I didn't immediately realize then what I know now: Ralph Metzner has afforded this incredible experience to thousands of people, and he has impacted every single one of them. The lives of many of us transformed in wonderful and unexpected ways.

This begs the questions "How did he do it? What made him stand out from so many others who were trying to plow the same field?" I believe it was because he developed so many different aspects in himself and integrated them into the sparkling and multifaceted person that he was.

The Scholar

Ralph approached life as a scholar, always open-minded and full of curiosity. He never stopped learning, and he entered conversations with genuine interest in the other and what she might have to add to his understanding. His openness to new ideas drew him to the most varied and sometimes unusual theories and concepts. Because he dared to go beyond generally held beliefs, he discovered correlations and made connections that others did not.

The Author

Like all good scholars, Ralph made sure to structure, organize, and document his findings, and to publish them from ever-new perspectives. In a field that includes many practitioners who work in a more chaotic way, he served as a reliable and authoritative guide, applying intellectual rigor at every opportunity.

Early on, he and his fellow researchers at Harvard discovered the power of ancient texts in decoding the mysteries of life and death; for example, the Tibetan Book of the Dead or the various divination oracles employed in different cultures around the world.

He connected balanced personal development with humanity's need for sustainable coexistence with Earth and creation, and he gave recommendations and practical insights on both subjects. He described and systematized reports on experiences with entheogenic allies and described how best to design and create them.

Ralph's later books contain an amazing distillation and succinct documentation of all he learned throughout his life. He examined a vast body of material from the perspective of the scholar, as witness of the birth of a new culture, then as the humble individual who lived through life like we all do.

The Alchemist

Building on Jung's interest in the subject, Ralph was a committed student of alchemy as an instrument to understand psychological transformational processes. He studied the ancient methods these inventors of chemistry and medicine had employed to discover new principles of transformation, which then served him as a communication device for describing the shifts in consciousness he wanted to help us achieve.

More impressive is how he then took this material and made it part of his practice. He connected practices like Agni Yoga with alchemical operations and left us with truly original and powerful meditation techniques with which to navigate our consciousness.

It was apt that at one time he called his seminar work "MAD"— for Metzner Alchemical Divination (tongue in cheek, as usual). In applying these ancient methods of material transformation to the psyche of groups and individuals, Ralph became a true alchemist of subtle energies in the inner worlds in which he traveled.

The Shaman

Ralph's starting point into his work was his abiding fascination for the ancient ways of shamanic healing. He traveled to faraway places to experience them himself, and he always learned something new.

His open mind led him to receive and assimilate knowledge from spiritual energies and beings. He showed a reverence for nature and its healing and guiding forces. Rarely have I seen a scholarly attitude go hand-in-hand with complete receptiveness of shamanic ways like it came together in Ralph.

Like many good shamanic practitioners, he gathered insights from the natural world, kept what he liked, and distilled them down to his own perfected method of doing his work. The essence of a shaman is pragmatism, the ability to gain authentic insights from chaos and limited resources. Ralph was a master practitioner, and a great teacher, a shaman in his own right.

The New Age Thinker

Ralph was nothing if not a radical thinker, cloaked in a quiet and balanced demeanor. He was both careful, yet also willing to take measured risks, and unafraid to take unusual positions at conferences and conventions in both the United States and Europe. As he said himself, work with entheogens was present in most human civilizations throughout history, but usually as the pursuit of a minority, not the mainstream. In this vein, Ralph incorporated selected practices into his daily life.

He integrated quite a few original and unusual concepts into his mental construct of the world. Some of them bordered on conspiracy theories. But as the fearless pioneer and thinker he was, he defended these with the same zeal in intellectual discussion as the rest of his thinking.

The Artist

Ralph had his artistic side. He loved poetry, and he translated many poems between German and English. He penned his own and regularly brought poignant poems to his group sessions to underline or strengthen a message.

In his later years, he took up piano playing, songwriting, and singing, and succeeded in publishing a CD of his own songs. Who of us could ever forget the "Bardo Blues," his lighthearted song about the deep issues of death and rebirth as discussed in the Tibetan Book of the Dead. He even invented a sort of simple yet effective group dance with it. We fondly sang and danced this song at Ralph's memorial in San Francisco in 2019.

The Human

While accomplishing so much in his chosen field, Ralph was of course just another mortal like the rest of us. He was not shy to share his struggles and triumphs, his challenges and his gifts. It was as if even his own life became a subject of study for everybody, with the valuable lessons from which all could learn.

Ralph could take us many places, including heaven and hell, but as he made clear when we traveled the six realms of Tibetan Buddhism, it is the human realm in which we feel most at home, and in which we should aspire to spend most of our time. It is here where we have the freedom of choice in each moment, where we can build a life and legacy. He was a shining example of this.

The Friend

Ralph took friendship seriously. He maintained numerous relationships with collaborators and allies around the world. He looked out for friends in need, as I witnessed for myself when one of us went through an existential crisis.

Ralph delighted in bringing people together and exchanging ideas. As he had such wide-ranging interests and such a vast network, he could

■ Fig. 20. Ralph and Uwe Doerken, 2017
(Photo courtesy of Uwe Doerken)

connect some unusual matches indeed. I thoroughly enjoyed having him as my friend ever since that first time I met him in that quaint Alpine lodge at the edge of Los Angeles.

Ralph had so much impact on us because he was all these personas, each lived to the fullest and in his own special way, wrapped into one unique and irreplaceable sparkling diamond.

Many traditions have taught me that death is just another shift of consciousness in our existence, and not to be feared. Ralph helped me *experience* this eternal truth. This has made me a calmer, more centered, and more empathic person. It makes me think that Ralph is in a good place now, hopefully benefiting from some of the good karma he has accumulated. No bardo blues for this busy soul.

Thank you, Ralph, for all you gifted us while you were with us in this life!

Healing with *Salvia divinorum* and Ralph's Helping Hand

Friedrich Rehrnbeck

Friedrich Rehrnbeck, D.O., C.N., is a practitioner for complementary and alternative medicine (*Heilpraktiker*) in Germany, trained in applied kinesiology and psychokinesiology as well as in hypno- and trancetherapy. He is an instructor for the Metzner Alchemical Divination training in Europe. Friedrich prompted the idea for this book.

It was in January 2006 when I was thirty-nine that we first met. I was invited to a shamanic ritual circle by a friend of mine. I was a rookie in the psychedelic realms. Excited, anxious, and in a blue funk, I was willing to learn more about me, my existence, my traumas, and how to heal myself and become a better person.

I hadn't read any more of Ralph than his *Green Psychology* book that, at the time, I honestly did not quite understand. When I told my ex-wife that we were invited to a circle with Ralph Metzner she became wildly excited. She had been a fan of Ralph's for ages.

I remember having a soul-touching experience during this memorable event in January 2006, a journey in the setting with music selected by Mark Seelig[19] and Lisa Gerrard, that opened the "doors of perception" to me and marked the beginning of my path as a psychonaut.

I saw Ralph again the same year at the celebratory event of Albert Hofmann's one hundredth birthday in Basel. He invited me to a place near the Swiss-Italian border where I subsequently spent a week with him every year. I followed his inspiring teachings regularly until his last visit to Europe in 2015.

Because I wanted to be reinvited to these mind-thrilling Circles

---

19. Mark Seelig is a contributor to this collection of essays.

■ Fig. 21. Friedrich Rehrnbeck and Ralph Metzner, 2015
(Photo courtesy of Friedrich Rehrnbeck)

every year, I did as he suggested and took part in the alchemical divination program he offered in Europe. It turned out to be one of my most remarkable decisions. Since I completed the course, I not only used alchemical divination as a profound technique in my psychotherapeutic practice with my patients, but I also teach this method successfully to the many participants in my workshops.

I felt a deeper personal connection to Ralph when I found out that he was almost as old as my father, and that his son, Ari, was born the same year as me. When Ralph uttered the essential sentence, "If any of your parents or relatives is not able to be a useful counterpart, take an elective affinity instead," he instantly became my surrogate father.

For this Gedenkschrift, I thought about the most touching moment for which I will remember him for the rest of my life. It happened in the very last week of our Shamanic Ritual Circles in the wonderful Italian palazzo where we met. All of the participants were close friends and traveling companions for years. The energy level that we had created during the first days of our one-week journey was ecstatic. And so we came to the point when Ralph asked us to locate a trauma in our life that we had not yet even thought of to be a trauma. We would have the help of a medicine called *Salvia divinorum*.

About twenty minutes after we had ingested the medicine, which tasted awful, as shamanic medicines often do, I started thinking about my relationship with my father that I had worked with for a period of more than six years during these sessions in my therapy. His appearance puzzled me because I thought I was through with my mother/father issues.

There was still one occurrence that I had always thought of as a trivial, inherited error. That was when my father punched me when I was a child. Before this point in my life, I always joked about that act of violence by saying: "I have only been beaten by him three times. That's not so much. I survived it!" As I found out later on, this point of view was not true.

During this remarkable *Salvia divinorum* journey, when we sat in the Outer Room to discuss the traumas that we all had encountered, I felt totally separated from all my other friends in the room. I even felt separated from Ralph, and disconnected from myself and my whole life. I was emotionally totally dissociated. And suddenly I remembered that this was the same feeling that I had had when my father beat me. Suddenly it occurred to me that when he beat me *I dissociated to withstand this humiliating violation.*

I shared my feelings about the trauma and told the story about being a child about seven years old on the way to Yugoslavia with my parents to spend our holidays there. We were on our journey for the whole night coming down from Vienna to the south of Yugoslavia. Meanwhile, it was afternoon and my mom parked the car in a garage so that we could go on the ferryboat to an island where we planned to spend the next two weeks. I was tired and sat down on one of the red suitcases that we had brought along. My father had told me several times not to sit on the suitcase. I was so tired, and I did not want to sit in the street, so I sat down on the red case again—and "Bam!" my father slapped me in the face so hard that I had a headache for more than two days.

Until this very moment I always thought I deserved this punishment, but when Ralph heard my story he turned to me and said, "Your father was a jerk in this case! I cannot imagine any good reason for hitting you so hard!" I turned pale, and instantly I felt that Ralph was right, and out of my emotional numbness I felt this painful wound in my heart.

The next evening, we prepared for a long, profound psychedelic medicine journey, and as soon as we started processing from the Outer Room through the door into the Inner Room it became clear to me that this was going to be a hard ride. I felt insecure, shaken, vulnerable, and sad. Ralph, as the captain, usually sat at the head end of the room. His journey partner was the tillerman (*Steuermann*) on the door end. We as the ship's crew laid down on our mattresses on both of the long sides. This arrangement we called our Spirit Canoe, or in German, *Geisterkanu.*

The onset of the medicine was strong. I had laid down at Ralph's right side with my head toward him, as usual. I always tried to get this place because being close to him prevented me from doing mischief with my mind and helped me to concentrate and stay with my intentions and questions. Immediately after the onset I was sucked through a big, colorful visionary tube right into the relationship with my father. I went through all the hard times we had but also the beautiful ones. I stopped at a point in my puberty where I became an adult young man when my father shifted from the intimate relationship we had and became more of a rival, as if we were two grown-up primates. I was seventeen and we had an argument about literally nothing and, all of a sudden, he raised his hand and was about to hit me and I stood there smiling at him saying, "Come on, hit me, but be aware of the backlash because this time I'm going to hit you too!"

This was the very moment when something between us broke that was never mended. I lost my father. All of a sudden, I came out of my vision and found myself in the Inner Room. I was drowning in tears and as my consciousness faded again back into my inner realm, my heart felt like bursting to pieces. I shouted out inwardly, "Father, why did you abandon me?"

I felt lost in the middle of nowhere as all my concepts of love and faith broke down at once. My masks were torn off and my self-apperception faded. I felt lonely in this universe like I never felt before. Just in this moment I felt a warm soft hand touching my forehead as I was sobbing spasmodically. It was Ralph's hand. During leading and guiding the group with his words, he was able to comfort me in my pain. He answered my prayers just by putting his hand on my forehead.

All of a sudden, I realized our relationship to the full extent. He was my elder, a stand-in for my father, a healer for my pain, a teacher who could not have been better, a therapist, a friend, and, as he later called it, a shamanic brother. At this moment he was all of that to me at the same time, and to this day and forever I am grateful for that experience.

Ralph always said, "When I die, I'm only dead! I'm not gone." I still communicate with him, not only in good times, but also when times get rough. He still calms my restless mind with his infinite wisdom. And sometimes when I lie down tired and worn out from my work with my patients and frustrated by all the ignorance that exists in this beautiful, mind-blowing world, I still can feel his warm loving hand caress my head as if he wanted to say, "It will all turn out to be all right in the end. You will see!"

The Clear Bead at the Center
Dorothy Fadiman

Dorothy Fadiman, M.A., has been producing documentary films for more than forty years. Her book *Producing with Passion: Making Films that Change the World* describes her journey.

Many years ago, I had an experience with the psychedelic known as Ecstasy that I will remember forever. Ralph had offered to guide me on an inner journey, and I accepted. Ralph measured out what he felt was the right dose for me and I took it without hesitation. I had heard that he was an excellent guide, and I trusted him as a friend.

As I lay quietly exploring and experiencing the vast darkness of the universe, at some point I found myself entering a space of existential grief as I let myself see and feel, with no images . . . only blackness . . . the pain and suffering of human souls on Earth, the suffering of the Earth itself, and a vast field of hopelessness. All black. All grim. All without relief.

And suddenly, in the furthest reaches of my inner world, I saw a pinprick of light—a tiny opening, a gateway for a ray of light, barely visible, peeping through that hole. I described this to Ralph. I told him I had spotted a pinprick of light in a sea of darkness. He responded by saying something to me that changed my life that day and my experience of existence forever. He quoted the first line of a poem by Rumi, and then read the rest of the poem to me:

> *The clear bead at the center changes everything.*
> *There are no edges to my loving now.*
> *I've heard it said there's a window that opens*
> *from one mind to another,*
> *But if there's no wall, there's no need*
> *for fitting the window, or the latch.*
>
> JALAL AD-DIN MUHAMMED RUMI

That line—"The clear bead at the center changes everything"[20]—has, ever since that day, given me a key to move through what at first may appear to be impenetrable darkness.

The Broken Lineage
David Lukoff

David Lukoff, Ph.D., is an emeritus professor of psychology of the Institute of Transpersonal Psychology in Palo Alto, California, author of eighty articles and chapters on spirituality and psychology, and a licensed psychologist in California. He is a coauthor of the *DSM-IV* and *DSM-5* category Religious or Spiritual Problem, which includes problems related to psychedelic substance experiences, and is the founder of the Spiritual Competency Academy that offers programs on psychedelic substances and other topics related to spirituality.

> *Becoming conscious of ancestral memories is like sweeping our hearth, clearing the ash so that the fire can burn well. When a hearth is choked with ash and buried memories, it is difficult to sustain fire. We sweep the hearth with our acceptance and understanding of what has been passed on to us from our ancestors. We do this for our ourselves, our family, and for the future.*
>
> ANNE SCOTT, *SERVING FIRE*
> (BERKELEY, CA: CELESTIAL ARTS, 1994)

It was through my work in ceremonies with Ralph that I recovered my ancestors. Prior psychedelic experiences had opened me to the "long view": I had connected with my reptilian self, my monkey self, my single-celled self, even experienced my origins in ancient star dust. Yet while this sense of connection extended back billions of years, I have always felt

---

20. John Moyne and Coleman Barks, translators, *Open Secret: Versions of Rumi* (Putney, Vermont: Threshold Books, 1984), 10. Used with permission.

a gap, a disconnection and puzzlement over my direct human ancestors.

My grandparents were part of the wave of millions of Jews who escaped persecution in Russia and Eastern Europe around the turn of the twentieth century. Contact with the old country was severed, partly by their choice and partly by governmental restrictions. The result was that I grew up knowing virtually nothing about my family beyond my grandparents. In contrast, my wife, who is German (and not Jewish), can trace her family back to the eleventh century.

I decided to explore my ancestral background in a session with ibogaine. I knew that ibogaine was used by peoples in equatorial Africa such as the Bwiti (formerly called pygmies in the Western literature) in rituals to commune with their ancestors, and I hoped that it would enable me to make contact with mine. In preparation, I read a few pieces on Jewish history and life. I also asked my parents what they knew about our ancestors (not a topic of much conversation during my upbringing). I videotaped these discussions so that whatever they knew about our family tree could be passed on. Unfortunately, it wasn't much.

My father's grandfather, I learned, was an alcoholic who even attempted to steal my grandfather's (his son's) money that the family had saved long and hard for passage to America. I learned that another relative had been one of the first Jewish graduates of a Russian university—but, unable to find any employment, he spent his days reading books while his wife supported the family. And of course, I heard about the horrific pogroms, murderous unprovoked attacks by Cossacks, that Jews had endured for hundreds of years in Russia.

The ibogaine I took was part of a group ritual vision quest. Everyone, except Ralph and the two assistant guides, was working on his own issues, and we had shared our intentions with each other at the beginning of the group. This sharing had created a sense of camaraderie and support for our separate voyages of discovery. I took the ibogaine (my first time with this plant medicine) at about 6:00 p.m. I set my mind to my intention by trying to imagine ancient settings such as Jerusalem (based on photos and drawings). My mind wandered and floated; the music was energizing my imaginal faculties, and images came more readily than usual for me.

I wasn't sure what to expect, but I wanted to *meet* my ancestors. Were they butchers? Tailors? Did I come from a line of rabbis or Talmudic scholars? (My mother's father was a rabbi.)

Images of my two grandfathers came into my mind. I did not know either very well. My father's father had come to this country at the age of twelve—by himself. He had the name of a cousin to contact, who helped him get a job sewing. He saved and acquired his own sewing machine, saved and brought over his family from the Ukraine, saved and opened numerous businesses. He was quite successful for thirty years before going bankrupt in the early 1950s.

My mother's father was born in New York and raised in a family that also knew poverty. My mother tells a story about her father being sent to the market without any money so that the neighbors would not know that they didn't have any food. He was able to win fellowships to obtain a Ph.D. in Greek and Latin at NYU, but since academic jobs were virtually closed to Jews, he also went to rabbinical school. His first job, which he held for the rest of his life, was leading a congregation in El Paso, Texas. His Ph.D. was not in vain as it garnered him a faculty position at a local university that needed four Ph.D.s to gain accreditation.

Since my personal contact with my grandfathers, as well as the pictures I'd seen of them, were limited to their adult years, I always remembered them as older men. But now I was viewing them as *children*. It was shocking at first to see these venerable figures as kids. I immediately sensed that their childhoods were not happy. Poverty had taken a toll on their ability to engage in pleasant childhood pursuits: trips to the beach, vacations, the freedom to explore nature. Huck Finns, or even Tom Sawyers, they were not.

As I started to feel a twang of sadness come over me, their attention suddenly seemed directed at me. Whereas I had been observing them as children, now they were looking back directly at me. No words were exchanged between us, but they started communicating with me. They were letting me know that a major part of their life's work had been to secure what had been missing in their lives for their children, their children's children, and for my children as well. And just as I as a parent partake in my six- and eight-year-olds' games and share their joy, my grandparents had been, and still are, sharing the joys of all of our childhoods.

This proud legacy of a life without the threat of starvation or pogroms, of opportunity to "advance" in the society, is a well-documented part of the Jewish immigrant experience (e.g., *World of Our Fathers* by Irving Howe). But now it was an experiential reality for me that I shared together with my own grandparents.

As powerful as this transgenerational interaction was, these were relatives about whom I already knew something. What about my more distant ancestors? I tried to move further back, but found myself mainly pushing and feeling frustrated that I was losing the momentum of my quest. I decided to take a booster, another dose of ibogaine, to propel me through the wall between me and my ancestors. After ingesting another dose, I once again relaxed into the trip, letting the music take over my consciousness, and sometimes invoking ancient images of Masada or the Exodus from Egypt.

I was observing a scene with a group of Orthodox Jewish men in caftans standing together on a street corner; a scene from an Eastern European shtetl perhaps 500 years ago, maybe 1,500 years ago. Then I realized that they were aware of my presence, but were avoiding me. I had expected that once I made contact with my ancestors, they would welcome me. But, no, they were seeming to reject me. My heart raced. I didn't know if I was angry or fearful. What was going on? Why were they ostracizing me?

Then the momentousness of my marrying a person outside the Jewish faith hit me. In my view, the division into religious groups was a relatively recent phenomenon in human evolution. I was quite happy with my decision to find the person I most wanted to share my life with, a soul mate, without regard to religious or ethnic considerations.

I initiated a conversation with these men, explaining that I wanted to meet my elders. I wasn't bringing my wife or children (who by Jewish law are not Jewish). They were listening. I continued that I was a Jew (although I did not mention that my spiritual life draws on many other traditions as well). Then I asked them point blank to show me something about my ancestors.

At this point, the journey speeded up as they took me off to many places. I became part of a tribe crossing a desert. I was building a temple. I was running through the streets being chased by soldiers on a drunken pogrom. My family and I were pulling a cart with all of our possessions together with all the other Jews ordered to leave the country. I was dancing at an all-night wedding celebration. It was an awesome experiential recapitulation of Jewish life over the millennia.

At the end, the Jewish men in caftans were still there. They had done their job for a *Landtsman*.[21] But the feeling of an abyss between us remained, and I was surprised at this after what they had just done for me. Spontaneously, I invited them to come on a visit to see the life that I had built from the foundation provided by them and my other ancestors. They looked at each other, and then one with a particularly long beard nodded an assent, so off we went.

We were now in my house, a one-hundred-year-old Victorian in a small town in Sonoma County. Jews were forbidden to own land in many places and times, and often were restricted to living in the less desirable areas. As we walked onto the deck and looked over the terraced gardens in the backyard, it must have seemed like a sign of wealth to be living in such a house. But it also signified an era of freedom to live where and how one wanted. I communicated my satisfaction at putting down roots in this community, not a ghetto but a town that not only included a Jewish temple but was home to people of many faiths. As my wife and children could be seen walking along the rose bushes cutting flowers, I shared my appreciation for being able to freely select a life partner, to obtain an education, and work in an occupation—all

---

21. Someone who comes from the same or nearby hometown, especially if one or both of you no longer lives there and all the more so if one or both now live far away from home.

without restrictions. I know that there's a cost to this freedom, ecologically and spiritually as well. But I was celebrating the choices afforded by these freedoms that were unknown to most Jews in the past whose survival depended on an interdependent community that dictated conformities in most areas of life. I could see that this was eye-opening, but also unsettling and even a bit overwhelming for them.

There were no hugs at our parting, no "See you later," no blessings. But now these men seemed to radiate a sense of goodwill toward me. The connection with my ancestors that I had sought was now established.

I realize that I have passed along to my "half-Jewish" children a karmic situation that they will need to resolve in their own lives. And when the time is right, I know a medicine that might help them on their ancestor quest.

P.S. In the midst of writing this account, I went to say goodnight to my eight-year-old son. After I tucked him in, he turned to me and said, "I loved you three thousand years ago."

Extraordinary Things Happened When I Was with Ralph
Christian Rätsch

Christian Rätsch, Ph.D. (1957–2022), was a freelance scientist, author, and lecturer in Hamburg, Germany. He was a renowned anthropologist and ethnopharmacologist who specializes in the shamanic uses of plants. He did fieldwork and research in Chiapas (Mexico), Thailand, Bali, the Seychelles, and an eighteen-year study on shamanism in Nepal. He is the author of numerous articles and more than forty books, including in English *Marijuana Medicine*, *The Dictionary of Sacred Plants*, and the *Encyclopedia of Psychoactive Plants*.

This essay was translated from German into English by John Baker, Ph.D., and Uwe Doerken.

Ralph and I shared numerous psychedelic experiences of the highest caliber, especially in the realms of the mighty tryptamines. During a conference at Esalen Institute in Big Sur, California, Ralph offered me his infamous "Jaguar Twins." The effects knocked me right out of my socks! I had an all-encompassing experience that revealed the very nature of being. It was an absolutely indescribable experience, the pinnacle of bliss, but also extremely frightening. It has taken me many years to process this mystical experience. In doing so, his wisdom always proved helpful. For that, and for so many other experiences, I thank him.

Ralph and I spent some intense times together at the end of a canyon near his home in Fairfax, Northern California, in the mid-1980s. We spoke at great length about Germanic mythology, which I had learned about as a child through the marvelous tales that my father told me (we were free spirits with no traditional religion but a deep veneration for nature). One evening, Rupert Sheldrake[22] came by for a visit, and we had an inspired and jovial time together. On another evening, Ralph and I enjoyed a television broadcast of Wagner's *Tristan and Isolde*. On another evening, we climbed into the hot tub in Ralph's garden. We were captivated by the beauty of the night, and by a sky filled with stars that seemed close enough to touch. Out of the blue, Ralph asked if I would like to smoke some toad foam. Of course I would!

Ralph filled a small pipe, handed it to me, and lit it. I inhaled as deeply as I could. Leaning my head back, I peered into the magical night. Suddenly, I was overwhelmed by mindboggling sensations. I looked up and watched as the stars flowed together into an immense form. An enormous female came down from the firmament, embraced me tightly, and kissed me. A torrent of divine love poured forth from her mouth. We merged together into one another. Tears of joy were flowing from my eyes. I was pure love and happiness. I thanked the Toad Goddess, and looked at Ralph's delighted face. All we could do was laugh!

---

22. Rupert Sheldrake is an English biologist, parapsychology researcher, and author of over ninety scientific papers and nine books. He is best known for his theory of morphic resonance.

■ Fig. 22. Christian Rätsch, Ralph Metzner, and Stan Grof in Solothurn, Switzerland, in September 2014, at the thirtieth anniversary of the Swiss publisher Nachtschatten Verlag (Photo by Claudia Müller-Ebeling)

Years later we had another opportunity to smoke toad foam together. This time we were in a Bavarian castle, in the chambers of a foundation that had generously financed a symposium I had organized on the topics of nature and the healing arts. The symposium was reserved for a select circle of psychonauts[23] and researchers. Among the participants I had invited was Albert Hofmann.[24]

One evening Ralph, Albert, and I were sitting comfortably together around a glowing fire in one of the magnificent rooms of the castle. As

---

23. A psychonaut is person who explores altered states of consciousness through the use of psychoactive medicines.
24. Albert Hofmann was a Swiss chemist known as the discoverer in 1943 of lysergic acid diethylamide (LSD).

Ralph was describing some of his adventures with toad foam, we could see Albert's interest growing. Suddenly Ralph asked Albert if he would like to try some. Indeed, he would! We quickly constructed a pipe out of aluminum foil. This we filled with damiana leaves, over which Ralph crumbled a good amount of crystallized toad foam. As Albert sat in his grand chair, Ralph and I knelt by his feet. Ralph held the pipe up to Albert's mouth, and I lit it. Albert inhaled deeply, and quickly sank back into his seat. His face radiated joy as he gazed blissfully into the infinite. As the effects were wearing off, Albert sat up and exclaimed with delight, "I was entirely one with nature—just like the time in the forest when I was a child! How extraordinary!"

Enchantments
Claudia Müller-Ebeling

Claudia Müller-Ebeling, Ph.D., is a freelance scientist, lecturer, and author in Hamburg, Germany. She studied art history and cultural anthropology in Freiburg, Hamburg, Paris, and Florence. She is a co-organizer of several international conferences in Europe on altered states of consciousness. Claudia is an author and coauthor (with Christian Rätsch and others) of several books, including *Shamanism and Tantra in the Himalayas* and *Witchcraft Medicine*.
    This essay was translated from German by John Baker.

In 1971, Barth Verlag, a small publishing house in Weilheim, Germany, published a German edition of *The Psychedelic Experience: A Manual Based on the Tibetan Book of the Dead*, by Timothy Leary, Ralph Metzner, and Richard Alpert. My pirated copy had a psychedelic cover, and it went with me wherever and whenever I moved, first out of my parents' house and into various student quarters, from Freiburg to Paris, and finally to Hamburg. Ever since my first reading of the now dog-eared copy, I have claimed Ralph Metzner as my favorite author.

My first personal encounter with Ralph occurred in the 1980s. "New Age" was a hot new trend from hippie California. A psychotherapist in Freiburg, Germany, had invited Ralph to give a lecture and lead a ritual in a luxuriously renovated Jugendstil house. Shortly before, Ralph and the German *berserker* ("wildman") Christian Rätsch, my husband, had gotten to know one another at a psychedelic conference at Esalen. As a result, Ralph personally invited the two of us—what an honor!— to this illuminating private gathering.

Ralph's insights into the hidden domains of the psyche, Germanic mythology, and the German language thrilled and inspired me in lasting ways. At the time of our first meeting, he was regaining his proficiency in the German language of his childhood. His insights were both enlightening and humorous: "In German, you give (*schenken*) a person your attention; in English, you *pay* attention to them."

In 1990, Ralph and Cathy invited us to their home in Sonoma, California. Together, we visited the Botanical Preservation Corps, cofounded by Rob Montgomery and his wife. This was a kind of Noah's ark for sustaining the plants of the gods and was also the first mail-order nursery for psychoactive plants. Years later, Rob (together with Terence McKenna, Jonathan Ott, and Ken Symington) organized a number of week-long ethnobotanical seminars in Palenque, Mexico, and we participated as teachers together with Ralph on several occasions. At one of them, Christian Rätsch introduced Ralph to "his" group of Lacandon Maya that he had been spending time in the rainforest, an encounter that left a lasting impression on Ralph.

In California, Ralph arranged an enchanted meeting with a pagan commune living out in the country. The group, which had been officially recognized as a religious community, shared their living room with an owl, while a python hung over the shower and white-haired unicorns lazed in the meadow! The proud breeder, Oberon Zell, had learned how to twist the two horns of young goats together so that they would grow into one.

A Worlds of Consciousness conference without Ralph Metzner would have been unthinkable. No matter where they took place or who

■ Fig. 23. Claudia Müller-Ebeling and Ralph on a boat ride on the Aare River, Switzerland, 2014 (From the collection of Ralph Metzner)

it was that organized these events, each offered us an opportunity to reconnect and to carry on our professional and private exchanges. We met in San Francisco, near Vancouver, Heidelberg, and Amsterdam (when Ralph accepted our invitation to the "Psychoactivity" conference), and in Basel in January 2006, on the occasion of the epic and now legendary conference held to honor Albert Hofmann on the occasion of his one hundredth birthday.

In early September 2014, a celebration marking the thirtieth anniversary of the founding of the publishing house Nachtschatten Verlag was held in Solothurn, Switzerland, featuring Stan Grof and Ralph. This was the last time we saw Ralph (see photo on page 114).

Now it is time to talk *about* Ralph, and to pay tribute to his life and influence. A person may be esteemed and admired for his deeds, talents, achievements, and discoveries. He may be honored for the insights and knowledge he shared. If that person was able to overcome his own painful experiences with compassion, humanity, and wisdom, we might find ourselves opening our hearts to him. And if one has the privilege of sharing many important experiences with such a person, then he would almost certainly become a friend. All of this was true of my relationship (as well as Christian Rätsch's) with Ralph Metzner.

Stars only come out at night. Visions reveal themselves only in the dark. Ralph Metzner spent his life exploring the ways these people ritually, and respectfully, used their plants of the gods. *He worked to preserve their wisdom, expand our consciousness, and promote a more responsible approach to the environment.*

Remembering My Amigo
Luis Eduardo Luna

Luis Eduardo Luna, Ph.D., director of Wasiwaska, was born in the Colombian Amazon region in Florencia. He has over forty years of experience with ayahuasca in various contexts: as an anthropologist with Indigenous groups in Peru, Colombia, and Brazil that use ayahuasca as a sacrament. He has authored several books, including one with Pablo Amaringo, *Ayahuasca Visions: The Religious Iconography of a Peruvian Shaman.*

"*Amigo*, do we have any issues?" We had not seen each for some years. "Not at all, Ralph," I said. He was perhaps determined to resolve any problems that remained with other people. I noticed the change in his clothing, which had gradually become more colorful. He always wore some kind of hat. On one occasion, I was happy to see him wearing a necklace I had given him decades before.

Ralph was my friend and mentor. He was among the most important people in my intellectual and spiritual development. When Ralph died, I felt I was totally on my own. I no longer had that older mentor I could ask for advice regarding matters of the soul.

I first met Ralph in the early eighties while visiting Terence McKenna in his home in Sebastopol, California. "He looks like a clerk,"

■ Fig. 24. Luis Eduardo Luna and Ralph, wearing the ceremonial necklace that Luis Eduardo gave him (Photo courtesy of Luis Eduardo Luna)

said Terry. "Nobody would suspect his adventures of the mind." At that time, I went to California often, especially after the publication of my study *Vegetalismo: Shamanism Among the Mestizo Population of the Peruvian Amazon* (1986). Ralph was among the first to receive a copy of the book.

One of my memories of that time with Ralph took place in Esalen, by the Pacific Ocean, where Terence, his brother Dennis, Ralph, and I participated in a seminar. I had just returned from a trip in the Peruvian Andes, where I had guided a group of Scandinavians doing the Inca Trail down to Machu Picchu. Terence had asked me whether I could possibly find and bring a living specimen of *Desfontainia spinosa* for Botanical Dimensions, the ethnobotanical garden that he and Kat Harrison had created in Hawaii. Richard Evans Schultes had reported that this plant was used in Chile as a hallucinogen. I succeeded in finding the plant along the trail, but it took too many days before I could reach California to bring the plant alive. I was only able to deliver some dry specimens that were passed eagerly from hand to hand during the seminar.

We stayed a few days at Esalen. One night, Ralph invited us to try what he called "The Maya Twins," a combination of DMT and

5-MeO-DMT. I was at that time thoroughly intoxicated by Terence's ideas about the "DMT signal," a sound the two brothers said they had heard during their Experiment at La Chorrera in 1971.[25]

At the end of that year, Terence, Erica Nietfeld (his partner at that time), and I had spent two months together in Villa Gloria, a wooden house my parents had near Florencia, in the Colombian Amazon, where we took *yajé* for the first time. By this time, many years later, I had additional experience with yajé and ayahuasca while doing field work among mestizo *vegetalistas* of the Peruvian Amazon, and I was interested to see how these chemicals, found in so many plants, would work in isolation.

As he handed me the pipe, Ralph told me: "Most people fall back on the bed after inhaling." I was young and proud, and preferred to remain seated. I filled my lungs, only one hit. I heard—or thought I heard—the DMT signal, and as Terence told me they had done back in La Chorrera, I imitated the sound with my voice, louder and louder, like a siren. Ralph calmed me down. My voice was probably heard from quite a distance from the room where we were staying, and people might have been concerned. "You're not going to jump from the cliff, are you?" Ralph asked. "Of course, not," I replied. I was shaken, but still in one piece.

In 1995, in a hotel room while attending a conference in the company of prominent friends who shall remain anonymous, I had my sec-

---

25. Brothers Terence and Dennis McKenna and three friends traveled to La Chorrera in the Colombian Amazon in search of *oo-koo-he*, a plant preparation containing dimethyltryptamine (DMT). Instead of they found fields full of gigantic *Psilocybe cubensis* mushrooms, which became the new focus of the expedition. Terence was the subject of a psychedelic experiment in which they attempted to bond harmine with their own neural DNA through the use of a set specific vocal techniques. They hypothesized this would give them access to collective memory. Terence claimed the experiment put him in contact with an informative, divine voice he believed was universal to visionary religious experience. He often referred to the voice as "the mushroom." The experiment is described fully at the McKenna Academy website, https://mckenna.academy.

ond experience with 5-MeO-DMT, also provided by Ralph. Once more, I filled my lungs. I had not even fully exhaled when I felt my mind accelerate from zero to infinity. No time for reasoning. I disappeared into brightly vibrating ovoidal geometrical patterns.

Coming back was not so simple. I recovered the sense of being myself while traveling at high speed through hyperspace, like changing TV channels rapidly, suddenly recognizing for an instant the world to which I belonged, but then being engulfed again by the visionary maelstrom.

"They are losing me," I thought. I heard Ralph's voice: "You're breathing too fast. Breathe slowly." I found myself on my knees, my hands on the floor, my mouth fully open and hyperventilating. The jaguar, Ralph told me later. He had probably seen it many times, and this was the way he would later name this medicine. I had barely managed to slow my breathing when we heard a knock at the door. It was a female colleague of ours, totally unaware as to what was going on. I sat quickly on a sofa, and we all pretended we were just chatting. "Hello D.," I said, as if nothing had happened. Some hours later, it was my turn to speak at the conference. I was well prepared, and fully energized. I got a standing ovation, or perhaps I just imagined I did. My friends said I did well.

Ralph and I met again many times through the years. I have memories of being with him in a UDV (União do Vegetal) ritual in Brazil. Ralph was astonished that only men could access the highest rung of the ladder of the hierarchy of this religious organization.

In April 2004 we conducted two ten-day seminars together. Ralph's sessions were highly structured, with an hour preparation, guided meditations, and deep integration the day after—what he called hybrid therapeutic-shamanic circle rituals.

In one of the sessions, Ralph told us to examine the lineage of both of our parents. I discovered how much I had neglected my father's side, the Indigenous one, as my mother and her family were not only white but proud of it. I realized how, especially during my childhood and teen years, I was ashamed of being partially Indian. I remember being called *indio*, which in Colombia, at least at that time, was an insult. Even though through my meetings with Don Apolinar and taking yajé with him I had discovered Amerindian epistemologies, the work with Ralph was more than an intellectual exercise, it elicited a deeply felt sense of belonging to that Indigenous world as well.

On the other hand, Ralph also had an opportunity to engage with his own issues, about which he humbly told us. He said that it was like peeling away the layers of an onion. He realized that sometimes instead of going deep into his own process, he found himself thinking about what he was going to say or writing about it in order to escape from it, like a cognitive addiction. He found himself moaning and groaning, and then he dove into his discomfort, seeking the source of it:

"Then I got it, for the first time, what it was. When I was a child . . . you know . . . I was born in 1936. In 1945 we were living in Berlin. We lived a bourgeois existence, we had no direct experience of the war until the end of the war. The end of the war is like total collapse of society, ruined houses, occupying armies, deprivation, starvation. I lived in a children's home in northern Germany. I was nine. There is a defining memory I have. I was so hungry. I picked up a piece of bread and the woman at the other side of the bed started to nod. I remember an old Nazi woman who was running this home, they used to corral the food for themselves. We children could see them after bedtime stuffing themselves with bread, while they gave us a kind of gruel . . . When my mother found this out she took us out of there, and we lived for a while, three kids and my mother, in one room, in the upper floor of a house, for several months. So there was a prolonged period of extreme deprivation. And I realized the consequence of that was starvation. I started to think of starvation, starving children. One of the thoughts I had was that a starving child does not need empathy. Later, I had the food and plenty of nourishment. But it is important to see how to heal that layer. I was working with empathy for the child, and also for the intestinal system, which has its own consciousness. I could see how my intestinal system developed patterns after that: eating unconsciously, and eating food that was not particularly good for me, but always because there is a layer of survival panic. I remember later on, in my twenties and thirties, sometimes my income was low, and I was not sure whether I would have enough to eat the next day, and that put me in survival panic. That gave me a lot of empathy for people in lots of parts of the world. But I still felt I had to heal the pattern of this deeper layer. I needed to stay with it, and not escape into thinking about it, not escape into talking about it. Cosmic visions might be interesting and useful, but they do not do the healing."

In May 2012, Ralph and a group of friends and researchers interested in sacred plants and substances spent a week in Tuscany. We rented a villa and spent the days walking along the roads and visiting Etruscan sites, and the evenings learning from each other—an extraordinary opportunity I will always cherish. When we next met five years later at the Exploring Entheogenic Entity Encounter Conference, in marvelous Tyringham Hall, in England, Ralph was already quite frail. He told us this was going to be his last trip to Europe. I was afraid, as it so happened, that this was going to be the last time I would be able to see him in person.

Now I console myself with his books and recordings, a treasure trove where I always discover something new. I was recently rereading his *Green Psychology*, a deep and prophetic work, in which he urges us to transform our relationship with the Earth and all its nonhuman persons. As Thomas Berry, one of Ralph's mentors, wrote: "Our relationship with the earth involves something more than pragmatic use, academic understanding, or aesthetic appreciation. A truly human intimacy with the earth and with the entire natural world is needed.[26]"

---

26. Thomas Berry, *The Dream of the Earth* (San Francisco: Sierra Club, 1988; reprint Berkeley, CA: Counterpoint, 2015).

■ Fig. 25. Amigos in Santa Catarina, Brazil
(Photo courtesy of Luis Eduardo Luna)

Independently of our ethnic origin, we have to recover the animism of our ancestors, the real First World. As Ralph points out, if we could go back in time, the worldview of, for example, the pre-Christian Lithuanians, as shown by Marija Gimbutas (another of Ralph's great friends and mentors), was similar to Amazonian beliefs: the sun, moon, stars, forests, lakes and mountains, plants and animals, are all sentient beings with whom we share this planet.

When Ralph came for a visit to our home on the Brazilian island of Santa Catarina, he was wearing the flowery shirt his daughter gave him for the occasion. I have a photograph with him on one of the walls of my office. He really was my amigo.

Treasured Time with Ralph
David Jay Brown

David Jay Brown is the author of *Dreaming Wide Awake: Lucid Dreaming, The New Science of Psychedelics: At the Nexus of Culture, Consciousness, and Spirituality*, and fourteen other books about the frontiers of science, art, and consciousness.

When I was growing up, Ralph Metzner appeared almost mythic to me in his accomplishments. He was a truly legendary figure, an intellectual giant, whom I initially got to know through his books and other writings. I was deeply influenced by his work during my early development as a writer, and throughout my career he's been an essential teacher of mine. I've been especially intrigued by his thoughts about the relationship between alchemy, ecology, and psychedelic states of consciousness, and I found his ideas about the psychological implications of past lives in psychotherapy practice to be particularly powerful and life-changing.

■ Fig. 26. David Jay Brown and Ralph
(Photo by Sara Huntley, courtesy of David Jay Brown)

I first learned of Ralph's work as a sixteen-year-old teenager when I came upon a copy of *The Psychedelic Experience: A Manual Based on the Tibetan Book of the Dead*, which he coauthored with Timothy Leary and Richard Alpert (later Ram Dass). This was a book that I read aloud during some of my early LSD trips, and the words "O nobly born" send a chill up my spine to this day. I later discovered a copy of Ralph's book *The Ecstatic Adventure* in my college library when I was nineteen, and devoured it with immense interest. I read Ralph's book *Maps of Consciousness* next, and this is where I became convinced to take ancient divination systems—like the I Ching, the tarot, astrology, and alchemy—seriously. Ralph's refreshing outlook and beaming intelligence on these matters encouraged me to see beyond conditioned ways of looking at them—and at the world.

Ralph's unique form of brilliance expressed itself as a rare mix of scholarly discipline and radical open-mindedness, a respect for the mystical secrets of ancient teachings and a passion for the frontiers of scientific exploration. Guided by a powerful sense of intuition, Ralph was a master at synthesizing different systems for both healing the mind and expanding consciousness. As one of the early psychedelic drug researchers he was clearly decades ahead of his time, and the world is just starting to catch up, with a global psychedelic renaissance in full swing.

So you can only imagine what a delight it was that Ralph and I became friends and colleagues later in my life. I first met him through our mutual friend Nina Graboi back in the early 1990s. I encountered him at numerous gatherings, parties, and conferences.

I felt honored when Ralph invited me to write promotional quotes for some of his books, and I was thrilled that he wrote such wonderfully articulate quotes for some of mine. I particularly enjoyed reviewing the manuscripts for *Searching for the Philosophers' Stone: Encounters with Mystics, Scientists, and Healers* and *Ecology of Consciousness: The Alchemy of Personal, Collective, and Planetary Transformation*.

I interviewed Ralph several times, and I worked with him when I edited the special themed MAPS Bulletins from 2007–2012, as he was a regular contributor to the publication. One of my extensive interviews with Ralph appears in my book *Frontiers of Psychedelic Consciousness*.

Ralph had a charming way of blending his scholarly aristocratic presence with a warmly approachable personality, and he was always thought-provoking, insightful, and inspiring. He also had an extremely kind heart.

During one of my interviews with him, in 2013, I asked Ralph what he thought happened to consciousness after we die. After summarizing some of the compelling research that has been done around near-death experiences (NDEs), he said:

> Of course, we have no way of knowing to what extent these accounts of NDEs describe the typical dying process of those who don't return to life, but we have no reason to assume otherwise. The most striking aspect, to my mind, is the universally positive, even ecstatic and blissful, nature of the afterlife, once the physical release has happened. This is such a contrast from the huge cloud of unknowing anxiety that surrounds the idea and prospect of death. And here is the reason for the tremendous healing benefit that could come for people who are able to use psychedelics, and, of course, also meditation, to prepare themselves for a dying that is already in their imminent prognosis.[27]

I also asked Ralph if he could "summarize the basic message" of his life. He replied:

> In my book *The Six Pathways of Destiny*, I describe six major paths in which we express our creative energies in our communities and in our world. Three of these have been the primary fields to which I have devoted most of my time and energy; three others have been paths I've also pursued and practiced, but more intermittently. My

---

27. David Jay Brown, "Alchemy, Ecology, and Psychedelics: An Interview with Ralph Metzner," *Frontiers of Psychedelic Consciousness: Conversations with Albert Hofmann, Stanislav Grof, Rick Strassman, Jeremy Narby, Simon Posford, and Others* (Rochester, VT: Inner Traditions, 2015), 94–95.

three principles are: one, explorer, scientist, seeker, and pioneer; two, teacher, historian, social scientist, journalist; and three, healer, shaman, therapist, peacemaker. The three secondary pathways, to which I've devoted less time and energy, are four, artist, storyteller, musician, poet; five, warrior, guardian, reformer, activist; and six, builder, organizer, producer, engineer. I expect to change the relative emphasis on one or another of these pathways as my days and years lengthen. To summarize most succinctly, I could quote Mahatma Gandhi, who said, "My life is my message."[28]

I miss Ralph. I miss his brilliant mind and sparkling spirit. We can all be thankful that Ralph recorded his songs, as well as his bounty of inspiring thoughts, provocative ideas, groundbreaking research, extraordinary encounters, and life-transforming insights for us to reflect on and cherish.

Life-Changing Work with Sacred Medicine Circles
Mark Seelig

Mark Seelig, Ph.D., is a clinical psychotherapist, musician, teacher, and disciple of experiential shamanism. He is employed as lead therapist trainer by Usona Institute.

This article was originally written over twenty years ago.

INTRODUCTION

I want to tell you about extraordinary things, including observing the processes of the maturing of individuals, the healing, the teachings

---

28. David Jay Brown, "Alchemy, Ecology, and Psychedelics: An Interview with Ralph Metzner," *Frontiers of Psychedelic Consciousness: Conversations with Albert Hofmann, Stanislav Grof, Rick Strassman, Jeremy Narby, Simon Posford, and Others* (Rochester, VT: Inner Traditions, 2015), 91.

about life and death that we received from the spirit of the medicines, as well as the many stories that deserve to be told. Through all of this I honor the wise women and men who have gone before us who preserved the sacred art of holding shamanic ceremony so that we may now be able to step into the field they created and find our own ways to cultivate contemporary formats for these rituals.

One such person, an eminent researcher, fearless explorer of consciousness, carrier of the native peace pipe, and beloved teacher who played a pivotal role in my life, was Ralph Metzner.

PERSONAL HISTORY—A LIFE THREAD

This story, which led to the creation of sacred medicine circles over two decades ago, started in a small town in the middle of Germany, and from there it spread out across several countries in Europe, and then across the United States. It is both a personal account and a report on ritual work with sacraments with individuals, couples, and groups.[29] A strange confluence of events kept moving my life's path in a direction that, in retrospect, could never have been predicted. Yet there is a definite thread that feels like a kind of "spiritual logic" that led me to where I stand now. Today I am inclined to call it guidance by Spirit.

I have always taken great interest in the multitude of spiritual traditions. Over the course of various academic and therapeutic trainings I increasingly focused on the disciplines of Buddhist meditation (*zazen*) and breath (rebirthing and holotropic breathwork) for my personal development and transformation. I had begun experimenting with LSD and other medicines at the age of eleven but did not understand their potential and relevance.

At the age of eighteen I stopped using these substances after a huge dose of LSD that, due to my uninformed use and serious neglect

---

29. By *medicines* and/or *sacraments* I am referring to consciousness-expanding plants and substances, mostly called entheogens, psychedelics, hallucinogens, and empathogens.

of creating a positive set and setting, scared me to death. I remember celebrating New Year's Eve in Germany, partying with all my friends, lighting firecrackers, drinking lots of alcohol, and feeling deeply frustrated about not having a partner nor a sense of what my life was all about. The LSD journey was bound to be the nightmare where I ended up in a hospital with an injection of a good amount of Valium. It took me a week to recover. I knew I was never going to touch any of these "drugs" again.

Well, Spirit had a different plan. I was being led onto a path that would heal this traumatic event many years later and then guide me to discover that the shamanic wisdom plants would be my future teachers.

Born in Berlin, Germany, I spent part of my childhood and youth living and going to school in California, returning to Germany frequently, and then living in South Dakota for some time, studying psychology at a tribal college. In 1996, at the age of thirty-eight, I began reconnecting to the Californian part of my roots. Through a number of circumstances and with the help of good friends I dared to venture into healing my horrifying LSD experience from twenty-one years earlier by using a small amount of LSD in a ritual setting under the guidance of a trusted and experienced friend. The journey turned out to be a deeply spiritual and meditative reconnection to an inner space I had often experienced sitting at the feet of an Indian spiritual master in the early '80s. It was obvious: I had to continue on this path. Just what that was going to imply, though, I did not have the faintest notion until a dangerous heavy metal poisoning episode compelled me to move into nontraditional medicine work on a regular basis in order to heal.

BEING CALLED— THE VOICE OF THE GODDESS

After several sessions with LSD I started reading more and more about shamanic traditions, particularly about Amazonian *ayahuasceros*,

Mestizo *curanderismo*, and everything else I could get my hands on. Having been a mycophile (a lover of mushrooms) all my life, I started dreaming of magic mushrooms—no wonder, after all the books I had devoured on the subject.

Eventually I started cultivating the species *Stropharia cubensis*, which went successfully, but a frightening circumstance kept me from trying my mushrooms: I had returned to California once again and a week after my arrival—sitting at my friend's desk in his San Francisco home doing my email—I got hit by what felt like a stroke. I thought I was going to fall off the chair and pass out. I did not. Instead, I found that I had suddenly acquired a fairly severe dizziness. This dizziness continued with me for six years. I had my body and brain checked in the United States and in Germany; no diagnosis. "You are perfectly healthy" is what I heard again and again, but I felt sick to death. An M.D. friend of mine then found the probable cause: mercury poisoning. I had brief seizures with very high blood pressure, felt extremely fatigued, irritable, depressed, and generally like a very old man. My friend explained to me that I would have to undergo a chelation process.[30]

I started the chelation but the dizziness was not alleviated. I learned that mercury accumulates in the brain stem from which it can hardly be removed. I felt condemned to having to live under the spell of dizziness for the rest of my life. At that point a friend from Florida, well-trained in the use of entheogenic medicines, came to visit. We had planned to see the Indian sage Mother Meera who lives

---

30. The biggest problem during this process is the fact that the chelating agents are generally not capable of penetrating the blood-brain barrier. Therefore, they cannot remove residual toxins from brain tissue. They can only clear out organs and the body in general. This circumstance presented a very serious challenge to the effectiveness of healing the symptoms I was facing as they appeared to precisely result from the residue in the brain stem and cerebral tissue. I obviously was at a loss of what to do. The newly emerging field of neurogenesis has produced evidence suggesting the enabling of new neuronal connections by ingesting spirit plants. That would explain many people's healing, including my own.

in Germany and holds regular *satsangs*, ritual gatherings during which she gives shaktipat,[31] a direct way of transmitting her blessing. When we drove home my friend became increasingly curious about my basement cultivation project and could not believe that I had not tried any of my little friends. I explained to him that I was too scared due to the dizziness.

He happened to have some MDMA with him and suggested to start working on my fears with the help of this medicine and to consider moving over to some mushrooms later in the session if I felt comfortable. After all, Mother Meera had done some "repair work" already, so he thought I was ready to continue the process. He offered to sit for me through the night. I had great trust in him, knowing that he had worked with medicines for many years. So, since there were no known neurological contraindications, I decided to jump. There was nothing to lose. My life was crazy anyway.

What was to unfold during that night can only be described as a calling or an invitation by Spirit. I experienced one of the deepest spiritual and physical healing processes of my life. About half an hour after ingesting the MDMA I found myself in a good, solid, and fearless space. There was no dizziness. I enjoyed this relief, and after about two hours I decided to take a high dose of my mushrooms as suggested and weighed out by my friend. Without fear, I felt how the content of the journey became more visionary. I was attacked by demons and monsters eating my flesh, and a herd of huge ants crawled over my remaining bones, cleaning up the rest.

Somehow I knew that all this was a cleansing process. I breathed deeply and told myself to relax my body. The more I did, the more the monsters faded and a feeling of bliss began to emerge. I started hearing a voice. I was invited into the heavenly palace of a goddess, which

---

31. *Shaktipat* in Hinduism refers to the transmission (or conferring) of spiritual energy upon one person by another. It is a Sanskrit term from *shakti* ("psychic energy") and *pata* ("to fall").

unfolded in front of my inner eye. There, this Goddess told me she is the feminine creative force of the universe and that she would show me where to go in my life from now on.

She said I was to come back to her as often as I pleased and that I was to study with her. She spoke to me with the deepest compassion and love and now has been doing so in all subsequent mushroom journeys. In each and every one of my sessions she came and instructed me for hours how to move into my brain and strip the little black crystals that I saw in my visions off of the dendrites in my brain, where they sat impeding the free flow of neurotransmitters.[32] Repeatedly, I had to go through extreme death fears and many difficult journeys, but she kept supporting me with her loving guidance, instructing me to fully trust her and the process.

After about two years of continuous work with the mushrooms, my condition improved progressively and substantially. I would have several dizzy-free days in my everyday state of consciousness and would feel resilience and stamina coming back. I gradually felt an increasing optimism. The content of the sessions and the instructions given by what I now regularly called "The Goddess," or the "Cosmic Voice," started shifting over to teaching me how to work with my clients. At that point in time, I had already been working as a psychotherapist with people for some ten years—it was time to take a new step.

The Goddess began telling me that I should consider offering medicine work to particular individuals, and that I should also think about creating a ritual group setting for holding medicine ceremonies. I remember feeling both shocked and honored, but mainly caught up in immediate self-doubt, questioning how far I should go in trusting

---

32. Several neurotransmitters have molecular structures similar or even almost identical to psychoactive compounds; see Rick Strassman, *DMT: The Spirit Molecule* (Rochester, VT: Park Street Press, 2001), 32–37. Depressive moods and disorders—a condition that I certainly found myself in—are almost always directly related to a dis-balanced neurotransmitter profile. It is therefore well possible, particularly in the case of psilocybin, that it would temporarily enhance or alleviate the compromised neurotransmitter balance.

that inner voice. Regarding all other issues that she spoke to me about, I had no hesitation to take her word, but this suggestion . . . I was completely ready to immediately prioritize my distrust and deny the possibility of expanding my work into this dimension, obviously more of a reaction than a thoughtful decision.

I began asking myself many questions: How could someone like me, who had never studied under the tutelage of an Indigenous shaman, dare to work with such powerful medicine?

I kept asking her how I was supposed to do this. Her answers were always very simple: "Trust your knowledge, expertise, and experience and hand the rest over to me; I will guide you and you will feel the guidance in your heart and spirit. Also, I will put you in touch with teachers who are very experienced in my work; seek them out and study with them." I decided to surrender, to stop letting my doubts take the first priority. The search for a teacher was the next step before I would begin to mention the new perspective of the work to some of my clients.

FINDING RALPH METZNER— GATHERING COURAGE

Over the course of my readings I had come across several books and articles by a man whom I felt I could openly relate my experiences to. This man was Ralph Metzner.

Ralph strongly supported me in trusting what I had experienced and invited me to come study with him in his training formats. I remember leaving his office realizing that I had just made a pivotally important decision. I knew, before even thinking any further, that I had found what the Goddess predicted, and it was clear that I would enroll in Ralph's trainings. I was more than thrilled about this development. In addition to my personal work at home I would now be able to collect more guidance, which felt like a good basis to manifest what the Goddess had encouraged me to begin: medicine work with some of the clients who had been working with me for a long time, and the creation of a ritual circle.

The training format Ralph offered was a rather intense process during which various medicines were used to support a guided process of healing and self-exploration. Typically, the format would begin with an empathogen the first night of process work and continue with a different medicine every night, including various tryptamine-containing plants. Plants that contain tryptamine include psilocybin mushrooms, ayahuasca, and certain Amazonian snuffs. The mushrooms used in the ceremonies contain psilocybin/psilocin as the major psychoactive compounds; they do not contain DMT. However, due to the molecular structure psilocybin/psilocin belongs to the larger family of tryptamines; they are also forms of DMT, namely 4-phosphoryloxy-DMT (psilocybin) and 4-hydroxy-DMT (psilocin).[33] This is of crucial importance because, as most readers are probably aware, there is a decisive difference between empathogens like MDMA, a psychedelic such as LSD or other semisynthetic substances, on the one hand, and the tryptamines (e.g., psilocybin, DMT, 5-MeO-DMT) on the other: Under the influence of the latter, particularly DMT and psilocybin/psilocin, people frequently report having I–Thou experiences of a dialogical nature with an intelligent "other," a cosmic entity endowed with a perspective on existence that is much vaster than our human understanding. The encounter with this entity usually happens in the form of hearing a voice, being instructed in various ways, being "scanned" in a physical and energetic sense as if to become aware of energy blockages, or having visions of, and encounters with, "alien beings." Best known examples of these phenomena are the voice the shamaness Maria Sabina had come through her, the icaros (sacred songs) brought to ayahuasceros by the spirit of the vine, the visions of the brothers McKenna, and so on.[34] The tryptamines always gave me the strongest experiences in that

---

33. See Rick Strassman, *DMT: The Spirit Molecule* (Rochester, VT: Park Street Press, 2001), 36.

34. See, for example, Howard Beach, "Listening for the Logos: A Study of Reports of Audible Voices at High Doses of Psilocybin," *MAPS: Bulletin of the Multidisciplinary Association for Psychedelic Studies* 7, no. 1 (1996–97), 12–17; Jaya Bear, *Amazon Magic—The Life Story of Ayahuascero and Shaman Don Agustin Rivas Vasquez* (cont'd.)

they put me in touch with what I now just called the Goddess. Regardless of whether it was ayahuasca or mushrooms, I found myself inevitably but gladly immersed into a Divine realm of being privileged to study, listen to, and receive instructions on the incredible magnitude of consciousness, the meaning of life in general, and insights into deeply personal issues.

In the training format with Ralph, the sacred atmosphere in the circles provided a setting in which even very difficult and challenging experiences were dealt with in a positive manner so that participants generally came forth feeling enriched and having gained insight into important matters regarding their personal and spiritual life.

Frequently during these ceremonies, I thought to myself: If only I could have had this kind of guidance during my early LSD experiences . . . not only would I have had a much more profitable outcome but I would probably have continued studying medicines starting right back then. I realized fairly soon, though, that such musings are born out of my ego and my ideas of "progress," as opposed to a true surrender to the mysterious paths of Spirit.

Returning home after these gatherings I would feel that another important step had been taken in the direction of becoming a more aware, compassionate, and loving human being. This was felt in such small things as changes in my language and gestures, and also concerning bigger issues such as making decisions about changing how and where to work.

(Taos, NM: Colibri Publishing, 2000); Cesar Calvo, *The Three Halves of Ino Moxo: Teachings of the Wizard of the Upper Amazon* (Rochester, VT: Inner Traditions International, 1995); Peter Gorman, "Journeys with Ayahuasca, the Vine of the Little Death," *Shaman's Drum* 29 (1992): 49–58; Peter Gorman, "When Ayahuasca Speaks: Initiations in Shamanic Healing," *Shaman's Drum* 47 (1997–98): 30–39; Bruce F. Lamb, *Wizard of the Upper Amazon: The Story of Manuel Cordova-Rios* (Berkeley, CA: North Atlantic Books, 1974); Bruce F. Lamb, *Rio Tigre and Beyond: The Amazon Jungle Medicine of Manuel Cordova* (Berkeley, CA: North Atlantic Books, 1985); Terence McKenna, *True Hallucinations* (San Francisco: Harper, 1993); Henry Munn, "The Mushroom of Language," in Michael Harner, *Hallucinogens and Shamanism* (London: Oxford University Press, 1973).

BEGINNING THE WORK—
PRACTICAL ISSUES

In the summer of 1998 I held my first medicine circle. I planned to use my mushrooms (*Stropharia cubensis*). I burned incense in preparation, said prayers over the medicine, blessed everyone in the room, and chanted sacred *bhajan*s and *mantra*s (devotional songs), which I accompanied on the guitar. Then I passed out a threshold dose for each person. Five people were present and four of them had never taken any entheogens or psychedelics. I determined the threshold dose according to my personal experience with the mushrooms to be at 1.25 grams. Since I am an extremely sensitive person I knew that this dose might actually have been a little too small for the participants, but I decided to make sure that they would not be overwhelmed by the experience. I wanted them to get a taste, and maybe leave feeling they could have gone deeper instead of going home bewildered and frightened. The entry dose proved to be just right, leaving everybody impressed with, but not scared by, the spirit of the mushrooms. At the same time, it became obvious that it would soon be possible to move deeper.

Continuing the medicine circles on a monthly basis I found myself collecting valuable experience and gaining increasing trust in the format of the rituals. Typically, we would gather on a Saturday afternoon, begin with a sharing round, and then ingest the medicine. After two hours I would offer a booster, something I did not do in the first year of the work, and somewhere between 10 p.m. and midnight I would formally close the circle. I would then have light meals brought in and celebrate the return to everyday consciousness with food and conversation. The first circles were four-hour events without a booster, and people went home after they had fully come back. A year later, the format had developed into a four-day, sometimes six-day, residential event with three to five continuous nights of ritual work.

Mysteriously, things began falling into place more and more and I was able to acquire most of the well-known medicines from sources that I knew were reliable concerning the purity of the semisynthetic materials and potency of the plants.[35] In addition, I also introduced less-known compounds that were still legal and partly even available through the internet. It was quite uncanny at times how all these materials somehow seemed to be coming within our reach as if asking to be tested for incorporation into our toolbox.

HEALING ENERGIES— A WEEKLONG MEDICINE CIRCLE

A little over three years after the initial small workshops I announced my first weeklong medicine ceremony.

Space does not permit me to relate the content of the entire week of working with various medicines. I will simply relate our work with what Ralph nicknamed the "Jaguar," which is similar in effect to plants used by South American shamans.[36] Containing 5-MeO-DMT, the Jaguar is used as a snuff in very small amounts: 10 mg is a threshold dose for many people, while 20 mg can be on the edge for some. It requires a sensitive scale to make sure of the precise dosage.

The third day of our weeklong ceremony everyone was well into their process. A deep level of trust had built up among the members of the group. The first shamanic inquiry had been completed with many valuable insights, and it was now time to probe deeper. The Jaguar works well in between longer journeys because, in spite of its force, it is short acting:

---

35. Particularly in the case of MDMA it is important—as most readers will know—for the health of the consumers and for the results of the sessions to be sure about the quality of the medicine. See, for example, Julie Holland, *Ecstasy: The Complete Guide* (Rochester, VT: Park Street Press, 2001); Nicholas Saunders, with Rick Doblin, *Ecstasy—Dance, Trance & Transformation* (Oakland, CA: Quick American Archives, 1996); Bruce Eisner, *Ecstasy: The MDMA Story* (Berkeley, CA: Ronin Publishing, 1994, 2000); and the numerous studies on MDMA published by MAPS in their quarterly bulletin over the past years, available on their website www.maps.org.

36. The reader will remember *The Emerald Forest*, a movie showing a scene where a shaman blows snuff up a tribesman's nose. Various snuffs are also described in Mark J. Plotkin, *Tales of a Shaman's Apprentice* (New York: Penguin Books, 1993).

the journey lasts about sixty minutes. There are no ill aftereffects so that the person snuffing it fully returns to baseline after one hour, with a completely clear head, feeling renewed, energetically cleansed, and alert.

I arranged the group setting into dyads, assigning a sitter to each experiencer. During the trainings with Ralph this had proven to be a good idea since Jaguar journeys can be rather dynamic, frequently carrying people to the perinatal realms and exposing them to the dynamic forces at work during the birthing process.[37] Fifteen minutes into the session I was glad that I had followed Ralph's advice. Two of those who went first were well familiar with higher dosages and decided to snuff 25 mg of the medicine, which is an amount definitely not recommended for beginners. The two were well into a deep regression at the twenty-minute mark. The movements of their bodies seemed to mirror birthing experiences. They started babbling, rolling around on the floor, drooling saliva, and one woman uncontrollably vomited and urinated. While all this might seem like something that should be avoided, it is well-known from perinatal psychology that reasonably facilitated regression into perinatal realms can have an immense healing effect,[38] as was the case with this woman. She emerged from the session fresh, clear, and relieved, and ready to sit for the next person ninety minutes after she had snuffed the Jaguar.

Everyone was exhausted after the day of the Jaguar. We wanted to give the next working day a slightly more analytical focus and had decided to use LSD. The dosages chosen were midrange (i.e., between 200 to 300 mcg). I had actually planned on combining a smaller amount of this medicine with the sacred cactus San Pedro, but unfortunately the package I had ordered was lost in the mail so I decided to use the LSD only. The day was surprisingly uneventful, but nobody objected to that.

---

37. The term *perinatal* is a combination of two Greek words: *peri* meaning "around" or "pertinent to," and *natal* meaning "the birth." The theory of perinatal psychology is elaborated on by Stanislav Grof; see, for example, *LSD Psychotherapy* (Pomona, CA: Hunter House Publishers, 1980).
38. This insight is along the lines of Stan Grof's research and the training format he offers, called Grof Transpersonal Training (see www.breathwork.com for details).

We closed the week by giving thanks to all the helping spirits, to our ancestors, teachers, the animal kingdom, our power animals, plants, and to the one great Spirit working through everything that is alive. Everyone removed their sacred objects from the altar and we held ritual closure by bowing in gratitude to the Buddha nature within all of us and by the group thanking each person for their presence. Lunch before departure was peaceful and quiet while an occasional remark about an extension for an additional week was heard. I inwardly passed that on to Spirit, feeling that the greater forces would certainly guide us all to where we were supposed to be in the future.

THE AWAKENING OF
COSMIC CONSCIOUSNESS—
THE BLESSINGS OF SACRED MEDICINES

Looking at what has happened to me over the years, and realizing what depth of healing I have personally experienced, I am actually at a loss how to communicate the blessings and relevance of the work with sacred medicines. Others such as Ralph in his many publications do a much better job at this than I.[39] I want to reiterate the explicit point, though, of gratitude to the Indigenous peoples of this Earth, particularly to the North and South American shamanesses and shamans who have preserved the wisdom that we all partake of today and who have so freely passed their knowledge on to us. We will forever remain their disciples.

Having witnessed many times how healing and gratifying this kind of ritual work can be for others who begin or continue on this path, I

---

39. See, for example, Ralph Metzner, "Hallucinogenic Drugs and Plants in Psychotherapy and Shamanism," *Journal of Psychoactive Drugs* 30, no. 4 (1998): 333–42; and Ralph Metzner, ed., *Ayahuasca—Hallucinogens, Consciousness and the Spirit of Nature* (New York: Thunder's Mouth Press, 1999). In addition, see these valuable works by others: Jim DeKorne, with David Aardvark and K. Trout, *Ayahuasca Analogues and Plant Based Tryptamines (The Best of The Entheogen Review 1992–1999)*, ER monograph series, no. 1. 2nd edition (Sacramento, CA: The Entheogen Review, 2002); Lester Grinspoon, with James B. Bakalar, *Psychedelic Drugs Reconsidered* (New York City: The Lindesmith Center, 1997).

am certain that there is a greater collective force at work, a force that seemingly counteracts the destructive tendencies threatening the very survival of the planet and of all living beings. *I do not have the slightest doubt that sacred medicines, if used in ritual settings, have the capacity to teach us how to live in harmony with all sentient beings and with our abode, planet Earth.*

Having appreciated a wide variety of religious and spiritual traditions, I have never been able to favor one discipline or doctrine only. I can say, however, that the blessings I have received through the work with sacred medicines, specifically with the teaching plants, have been the deepest of my life, and to me they are comparable only to sitting at the feet of an enlightened spiritual master. In fact, one of the questions brought to the Goddess during one of my journeys was about the role of these masters, to which she replied: "They are my channel."

What I see is that the collective revival of sacred medicine rituals is a great hope for the awakening of a level of consciousness that might well be called "cosmic" in the original sense of the Greek word. Cosmic, because it puts things and beings in order, realigning our lives with the natural rhythms and teaching us respect for the sacred.

I pray for the voice of the Goddess to speak in healing ways to us all. May all sentient beings be relieved from suffering.

Thank you, dear Ralph. You live in my heart and spirit eternally!

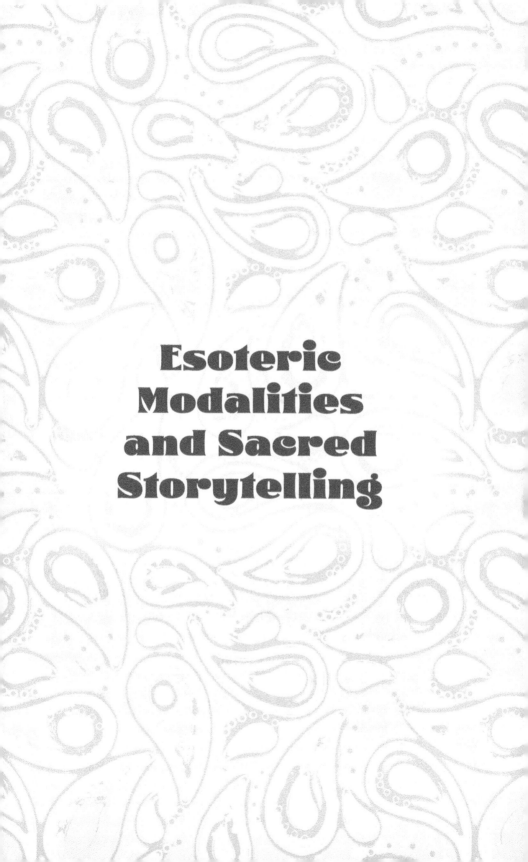

Esoteric Modalities and Sacred Storytelling

The Great Work
Alan Levin

Alan Levin, LMFT, is a psychotherapist, meditation teacher, and author in Nyack, New York. Alan joined Ralph in the study and practice of Agni Yoga with the School of Actualism. He continued to work with Ralph and assist in many of the ceremonial retreats.

• • •

The Great Work is a term used in Hermeticism and other occult traditions to represent the attainment of enlightenment following a spiritual quest or the freeing of the human soul from confining unconscious forces. The process of the Great Work brings the unconscious into the conscious awareness so it can be integrated into the self.

In 1969 I was living in a hippie commune in San Francisco's Haight-Ashbury and saw a small notice in one of the underground papers about a retreat with Ralph Metzner. I'd only heard of Ralph as the third member of the notorious Harvard group that had written *The Psychedelic Experience: A Manual Based on the Tibetan Book of the Dead*. I'd seen Tim Leary speak in Berkeley and Richard Alpert (Ram Dass) in San Francisco after his return from India. I wanted to see what jewels of far-out wisdom Ralph Metzner could share.

I was motivated also by the topic of the weekend retreat, "Maps of Consciousness"—I Ching, tarot, astrology, and numerology, things I was *into*. I went with a good friend who shared my interests in what Metzner would share about these esoteric teachings.

The workshop took place at a small, rural retreat center outside of Fresno called Sweetsmill. Here is a description of my first encounter as I wrote about it in *Crossing the Boundary: Stories of Jewish Leaders of Other Spiritual Paths*.

When I first met Dr. Metzner, I was so unimpressed that I nearly left. Clean shaven, short hair, looking like the archetypal straight guy, he spoke in a dry, mostly humorless tone, with just a slight edge of irony. He seemed to bristle when my friend and I lit up a joint.

After a day or so at the retreat, I decided to take a small amount of LSD before the next session in the series. It had become my way to "really check something out" . . . As I started to feel the acid come on, I heard him say that he was changing the plan for the session. Instead of it being about numerology, astrology or whatever, he would introduce us to something called "Agni Yoga," a kind of meditation teaching he'd been exploring. I right away became disappointed because I wasn't interested in yoga and never could meditate.

Then it started to happen. I began *seeing* that Ralph wasn't just speaking words to convey information. He was somehow emanating the teaching he was offering. He transformed into a wizard, a magician, a trickster, surrounded by the very light he was talking about and radiating throughout the room . . . His physical presence changed and instead of seeming dry and hollow, he was extremely alive, filled with energy and seemingly aware of everyone in the room. He now had my full attention. I followed his direction to focus on a light above my head and experience a shower of this energy down through my body. It actually seemed REAL.

Immediately after the group session, I walked up to him. I wanted more and right away. When I asked him how to experience more of this teaching, he closed his eyes and his body seemed to dematerialize. Part of him went up and up in stages and then slowly came back down. (Many who knew Ralph will recognize this silent pause before responding to a question.) When he came back down, he told me to follow him to his cabin and led me through an experience in which I felt all the negativity, doubt, fear, shame and pain that I'd been carrying for my whole life cleansed from my body, cell by cell, cleansed by a stream of white light. I felt clearer than I'd ever felt, confident and certain that this was the path for me to follow. Ralph had initiated me into the spiritual

lineage of Agni Yoga and what would be a forty-five-year relationship with him as well as a meditation practice I use to this day.[1]

I went home to my commune in the Haight and told everyone,
including my wife, that I was going to Valley Center in northern San
Diego County to study Agni Yoga at the School of Actualism. I took
leave from my wife and two babies and set out hitchhiking down West
Coast Highway 1 with a backpack and lots of acid and pot. Everyone
who picked me up would get a hit from a joint and a dose of the Light-
Fire technique I'd just learned and felt free to share.

The School of Actualism was described by Ralph as a Western esoteric school of transformation. It taught meditative practices of tapping
sources of inner Light-Fire to bring the divine aspects of our higher consciousness to our mind, our earth-body, and all dimensions of the world
for healing and awakening. Russell Schofield, the School's founder,
summed these teachings up with the core intention of "earthing."[2]

When I arrived at the school, I found that Ralph was living in a
bakery truck parked outside the Schofield's home, the school's center.
With Russell, Ralph was working closely on completing his book *Maps
of Consciousness*, the subject of the retreat I'd attended. Both *Maps
of Consciousness* and the book that followed, *Know Your Type*, were
written, at least in part, with the intention of drawing people toward
Actualism. In each book, there was a final chapter describing Actualism
as the teaching that provided methods for truly experiencing the meaning of the maps of consciousness or identity for spiritual transformation.

For a while, Ralph lived with a small group of Actualism students
in a Victorian house in Escondido. In need of income, he took a job
as chief psychologist at Fairview State Hospital in Costa Mesa. He

---

1. Alan Levin, *Crossing the Boundary: Stories of Jewish Leaders of Other Spiritual Paths*
(Berkeley, CA: Regent Press, 2015), 13–15.
2. *Earthing* is opening to the many aspects of the inner light of formless/form, divine
presence, and letting that be channeled into and through the earth elements of one's
mind and body and out into the world.

worked with a wide range of patients with intellectual disabilities and also supervised staff counselors. With the psychologist position as his day job, he continued offering the maps of consciousness workshops throughout the region. The workshops recruited folks to come to his home and be introduced to the beginning teachings of Actualism. In these sessions, he would briefly introduce the techniques, and then he would play recordings of tapes of Schofield's guided meditations.

Actualism taught that the techniques themselves should be kept secret until one could be initiated into the experience of them directly. This had to be done with someone trained to work with you on the inner planes while you were hearing the recorded method for the first time. Otherwise, we were taught, the experience would be worthless, or even dangerous if a person's energy was not properly prepared and supported to receive what the method was transmitting. So while the tapes of Russell's words were playing, Ralph was doing inner work to "hold the Light steady and amplify the experience for the initiates." The teacher training program aimed to teach the teachers how to do this inner work and amplify the experience of the students.

During this period Ralph was a dutiful disciple of Russell's and adhered quite strictly to the protocols of the school. He showed great respect and deference to Russell. I believe from talks with Ralph that he saw Russell as a clear channel of wisdom and light, a clairvoyant who could read the Akashic record and help others accelerate their spiritual growth. Ralph became the primary emissary of Actualism, offering workshops on astrology, the I Ching, or maps of consciousness, and was always introducing people to the Agni Yoga experience. He was dedicated to recruiting new students for the school and eventually helped establish outposts or "Star Centers" in Costa Mesa, San Francisco, Dallas, and New York, as well as San Diego.

It was during his time in Costa Mesa that he lived with his young son, Ari. Living close by, I was always honored to assist at the workshops and sessions in his home and my son Brent was a close friend to Ari.

Through some of his personal connections, Ralph became aware of an alternative high school in rural Mountain Center, near Idyllwild, California. The land was owned by Glenn Yarborough and was used during the summers as a Jewish camp. The residential school was having financial trouble and an arrangement was made for the School of Actualism to take over the land. We then created our own version of an alternative school, Star Mountain School. With Ralph as director, Star Mountain School strived to be a residential high school offering an academic curriculum where all subjects had a focus on consciousness, including training in the Agni Yoga work.

Ralph developed a luminous advisory board that included Alan Watts, Ram Dass, and John Lilly. The latter two paid quite interesting visits to our school during which Ralph and others sought to enlighten them with Agni Yoga. Alan Watts, in a congratulatory note, offered a personal warning about "isms." I recall Ralph rolling his eyes and shrugging it off at the time, though he most likely felt differently ten years later when he broke from Actual*ism*.

Interestingly, being in the San Jacinto Mountains, Star Mountain School was near the communal home of the League for Spiritual Discovery. The L.S.D. was a group connected with Tim Leary who was still in prison or on the lam at the time. From conversations, I knew that Ralph was uncomfortable with their presence as we were trying to put a serious, more or less *straight*, face to our work that would reach into the mainstream world.

It was the case that in the very early days, Actualism was one of the few spiritual schools that allowed psychotropic drugs to be used as amplifiers of the practices. There were several instances where Ralph would suggest or offer such amplifiers when we were together. That changed during the Star Mountain years and all students were told to no longer use these substances if they wanted to advance in the school or teach. As far as I know, Ralph adhered to this.

It seems fitting here to include some of the basic teachings of Actualism. I believe these had a profound influence on Ralph. He continued to develop beliefs and practices and to share them for the rest of his life. The teachings were transmitted to us through Schofield via recordings, but the advanced students and teachers would have live sessions with him. They were embraced by Ralph during that time and continued to be part of his practice and teaching throughout the rest of his life, even after leaving the school.

Russell often said that "we live in a sea of energy." That is, the *Beings of Light that we are*, the Immortal Ones, our true nature, manifest as Light-Fire energy. That energy makes up not only the physical world but multiple levels of reality. These energies are structured into forms that make up our bodies at the different levels (physical, perceptual, emotional, and mental) and the feelings and thoughts in our field of consciousness. In addition, higher dimensions exist with energy fields that correspond to souls, angels, and the archangels.

Actualism taught that our multidimensional bodies have an anatomy that includes a central axis along which are numerous centers (equivalent to chakras) from above the head to below the feet and an energy field that extends many feet all around and throughout our bodies. All the levels of energy are actually emanations from the formless-form of pure Spirit that is infinite and omnipresent.

Our ability to see or know all this directly increases as we clear away the obstructions that have formed through conditioning in this life or karmically. We learn to direct inner Light-Fire to dissolve and clear these obstructions. It was always emphasized that we did not need faith or blind belief, but we could experience all of this through the techniques we learned in the school's very elaborate system of step-by-step lessons and hands-on bodywork. In those sessions, we learned to work with a series of different Light-Fire energies, each a color frequency that has one or another quality needed in life. Among these are creativity, wisdom, healing, warrior-strength, regeneration, and so on. All these basic ideas were elaborated somewhat in Ralph's early books *Maps of Consciousness* and *Know Your Type*. What was never shared in public talks or writings were the specific methods, which, as stated above, could only be shared in a session with a trained teacher.

THE GREAT WORK

Beyond the practices, there was a general sense of agreement that *we were doing the Great Work:* the same Work or Opus of the Western esoteric traditions of Alice Bailey, Helena Blavatsky, and the Theosophical Society; the Russian mystic teacher, Gurdjieff; the writings of various channels of higher beings, such as the Seth book series by Jane Roberts; and Edgar Cayce; and contributions to the general emergence of the New Age before it became the "New Age."

Ralph often would meet with Russell for private interviews and writing sessions. Out of this came a series of monographs, never published, that sought to articulate Russell's unique take on various ancient myths, fairy tales, and sacred texts. Russell interpreted these stories as coded messages that pointed toward the yogic, alchemical inner work of transformation and transmutation of consciousness that we were doing with the Agni Yoga methods. Years later, Ralph's guided "divinations," both with and without the amplification of entheogens, further developed these understandings into experiential teachings.

The efforts at Star Mountain School, under Ralph's direction, aimed to integrate the practices and belief systems of Actualism into the regular curriculum of high school English, math, and history. It was a noble idea, far more difficult to actually do with a group of mostly unreceptive teenagers than we had envisioned. After a year, with the high school floundering financially and in other ways, Star Mountain School closed. We all packed up and moved to various locations, many of us establishing different communal living situations that supported the practice and teachings of Agni Yoga.

Some advanced students who were in the teacher training program were asked to set up centers for the School of Actualism in several cities. Meanwhile, Ralph moved back to Valley Center to live with Ari and his then partner, Jan. He also lived close to Russell and his wife, Carol Anne Schofield, again. He continued his travels, spreading the Actualism teachings and working on his writing in collaboration with

Russell. In October 1974 Ralph's son Ari, at age eight, was killed in a bicycle accident, an event that Ralph described as the greatest tragedy of his life.

Ralph began to focus on developing a growing group in San Francisco and would travel back and forth to Valley Center. It was during that time that he met and formed his relationship with Angeles Arrien, a wise Basque woman who became a profound wisdom teacher. He moved to San Francisco and established an Actualism center there. He began teaching at the California Institute of Asian Studies[3] in 1975.

During this period, what were smoldering differences between Ralph and Russell's wife, Carol Anne, became fierce. Carol Anne was the executive head of the School of Actualism and for a variety of reasons would often be in conflict with Ralph and his ways. There were intense sessions in which Ralph would be confronted about one or another way in which he was not adhering to the strict guidelines of the school. Ralph submitted to this, I believe, out of respect for Russell. After a while, it all became untenable.

Given the group's sense of mission as bringers of Light to the world, the conflicts became interpreted as a mythic battle of good versus evil. Everyone close to the situation experienced some of the trauma of the events. Eventually, Ralph could only choose to terminate his relationship with the school.

When I met up with Ralph back in the Bay Area (after departing from Actualism myself), he shared with me about the healing work that enabled him to resolve it all for himself. He had strong connections with people outside the Actualism community who could offer a reality check. When we spoke, he was able to relate to the whole experience with good humor and no resentment or ill will. He felt he was able to distinguish the immensely valuable teachings from the personal and

---

3. California Institute of Asian Studies (CIAS) was renamed in 1980 as California Institute of Integral Studies (CIIS).

cultural issues of the school. In fact, ironically, it was the Agni Yoga practices that helped him to heal and integrate the whole experience.

Ralph moved on with his life, and years later he initiated and coordinated a conference on ayahuasca at CIIS. One of the speakers, Alex Polari, a leader of the Brazilian Church of Santo Daime, shared his understanding that religions throughout the ages had distorted or lost the purity of the original spiritual insights that were their origins. He noted how institutions tend to rigidify and bureaucratize. But, he added, "due to the critical destructive trajectory of humanity at this time, it was worth the 'risk of institutionalization' to bring the Spirit of Ayahuasca to the world." Several times in later gatherings, I heard Ralph reflect on this statement, no doubt resonating with his experience with Actualism.

As mentioned before, Ralph continued to use the tools and tech-

■ Fig. 27. From left: Ralph, Alan's wife Ginny Brooke, and Alan
at Ralph and Cathy's home in Sonoma, California, 2003
(From the collection of Ralph Metzner)

niques of Agni Yoga, the primary teaching of Russell Schofield and the School of Actualism, for the rest of his life. They were an integral part of all the teachings, the ceremonies and rituals he guided, and they influenced his numerous writings and talks. While he continued to explore with boundless curiosity the many traditions and lineages of consciousness and spirituality, he always integrated them with Agni Yoga, the Great Work, the light-work of personal and global transformation.

A final personal note: I'm thinking of one of Ralph's guiding spiritual teachers, Gurdjieff, and his book, *Meetings with Remarkable Men*. On my life journey, Ralph was the most remarkable human being I have had the privilege to know and walk with. I know that the work of earthing, to which he dedicated his life, expanded over time and found expression in his deep commitment to Mother Earth and helping humanity to find a way through the political and ecological crises of our time. May we all open to his continued presence and guidance in our lives.

All Turned Out for the Good
Ralph Abraham

Ralph Abraham, Ph.D., is a mathematician who held teaching positions at the University of California, Santa Cruz; UC Berkeley; Columbia University; and Princeton University. He founded the Visual Math Institute in 1975 and has been involved in the development of dynamic systems theory. He met Ralph Metzner while studying Actualism, and they remained friends through numerous pathways.

Ralph Metzner and I were close friends from fall 1969 until fall 1970. We rekindled our friendship years later and it continued throughout his life. In the summer of 1970 we shared a house in Escondido, California, while studying Actualism with the founder, Russell Schofield.

I will begin with a brief summary of the psychedelic events leading up to our meeting in 1969.

■ Fig. 28. Ralph Abraham (Photo by Ralph Metzner)

RALPH FROM HARVARD
TO MILLBROOK, 1959–1967

Ralph met Tim Leary in the fall of 1959 while a graduate student at Harvard. At the end of that school year, the Harvard Psilocybin Project was created by Tim Leary, Frank Barron, and Richard Alpert. Ralph had his first psilocybin trip at Tim's home on March 13, 1961. About a year later he finished his Ph.D. Shortly after that he had his first LSD trip in Zihuatanejo with Tim. In the fall of 1962, he returned to Harvard on a National Institute of Mental Health (NIMH) postdoc. In the spring, *The Psychedelic Review* journal was launched, edited by Ralph, Paul Lee, and Rolf von Eckartsberg. Then the axe fell on Tim and Richard, and they all left Harvard for Millbrook.

At Millbrook, among many other fabulous meetings and creations, Ralph worked with Gerd Stern and his group of multimedia artists, USCO,[4] in the fall of 1964 to create the Psychedelic Theater, a set

---

4. Founded by Gerd Stern, Michael Callahan, Steve Durkee, Judi Stern, and Barbara Durkee in New York in the 1960s, USCO was an American media art collective. Its name is an acronym for "us company" or "the company of us."

of performances for theaters in New York City. Ralph and USCO, along with Tim and Michael Hollingshead, created Psychedelic Explorations, a show presented at the New Theater at 154 East Fifty-Fourth Street in New York City on Monday evenings beginning June 14, 1965.

These shows featured psychedelic light shows with transparent liquids by Richard Aldcroft. They were presented around the East Coast during fall 1965 and winter 1966. In the summer of 1966, new shows were presented at the Village Theater on Second Avenue. The idea of these shows was to give some indication of a psychedelic experience.

I attended one of the shows in New York City. This was a crucial influence in my decision to experiment with marijuana (fall 1966) and LSD (fall 1967), with the help of my Princeton undergraduate friends. This led directly to my move to Santa Cruz in the summer of 1968. Santa Cruz was a center of the Hip culture.[5] It was full of hippies, and it had nightly Acid Test events[6] with light shows at a venue called the Barn. Santa Cruz is where I later met Tim Leary, Ram Dass, and Ralph.

In the spring 1967, Millbrook dispersed.

I have a journal from August 1969 on, which has survived intact and serves to recall relevant events.

---

5. The "Hip culture" refers to the counterculture of the 1960s, originally a youth movement that began in the United States during the mid-1960s and spread around the world. The word *hippie* came to describe those members of this social movement, particularly in New York City's Greenwich Village, San Francisco's Haight-Ashbury district, and Chicago's Old Town. Hippies created their own communities, embraced the sexual revolution, and many used drugs such as marijuana and LSD to explore altered states of consciousness. Santa Cruz had a strong Hip culture, as described in Ralph Abraham's edited book *Hip Santa Cruz: First-Person Accounts of the Hip Culture of Santa Cruz, California in the 1960s* (Rhinebeck, NY: Epigraph, 2016).

6. The name "Acid Test" was coined by author Ken Kesey after the term *acid tests* used by gold miners in the 1850s. The Acid Tests were a series of parties held by Kesey primarily in the San Francisco Bay Area during the mid-1960s, which were centered on the use of and advocacy for LSD, the psychedelic drug commonly known as "acid." LSD was not made illegal in California until October 6, 1966.

ACTUALISM, SUMMER 1970

Ralph found an excellent house in Escondido, near the Actualism center in Valley Center. It was large enough for the community of eleven who wanted to live together for the summer experiment with Actualism. It included me, Caroline, and our sons Peter and John; Ralph and his son Ari; Lori Williams and her son Eran; Emelia Hazelip and her daughter Selenia; and Winston Nelson.

We passed the summer weeks with stoned lessons in Actualism, taking the children to swimming lessons, and exploring the surrounding desert. Arguments developed about the children eating ice cream and watching TV.

As fall approached, I began to plan my return to UCSC to teach, while Caroline decided to stay with the Actualism community.

Arguments over the plans for our children to return to school escalated into a major contention. I did not want the children to be brought up in a cult. I understood that Ralph intended to create a school for the Actualism community.

So the family split apart. Caroline, Peter, and John would stay in Escondido, while Emelia, Selenia, and I would return to Santa Cruz. Thus, the family separated in early September 1970.

AFTER LEAVING THE SCHOOL OF ACTUALISM
The Off-ramp: Santa Cruz, 1970–71

Back in Santa Cruz, the house on California Street was rented out to a group of students, while Emelia, Selenia, and I moved into a house with an old orchard on Ocean Street Extension.

Caroline, supported by Ralph and Schofield, decided to proceed with a legal divorce process. This made life in Santa Cruz very difficult for me. The divorce trial was in San Diego. The School of Actualism was represented by Schofield, Ralph, and several members of the group.

The children came for occasional weekend visits. This ended on my birthday, July 4, 1971. I was devastated. Also, the lawyers had seized all of my UCSC salary. I decided to go to Europe until things cooled down.

....

Europe and India, 1971–72

I spent the academic year 1971–72 teaching at the University of Amsterdam. In the summer of 1972, I went to India for a brief holiday, but I ended up staying until January 1973.

The conflict in Escondido led Ralph and me to go in different directions. Ralph left Actualism in the mid-1970s and relocated to Northern California, taking a job at the California Institute of Integral Studies in 1975.

In 1984 Russell Schofield fell asleep at the wheel of his car, hit a tree, and died. Following this tragedy, the entire Actualism community dissolved. Many members moved on to other spiritual traditions. Ralph had become a therapist again in private practice in Northern California, giving crucial help to other grieving members of the group. Ralph and I resumed our friendship. We enjoyed occasional visits to each other's homes, which were close enough for day trips.

EPILOGUE 2019

After a long time, my second wife, Ray, and I planned a visit to Ralph and his wife, Cathy Coleman. On February 18, 2019, we arrived for dinner and were joined by DeLee Lantz, our mutual friend of long standing. After we sat down for dinner it became clear that Ralph was having a hard time breathing. He told us he did not have long to live. By the time dessert was on the table, Ralph came around to the subject of our remote past in Escondido and its aftermath, my divorce from Caroline. He expressed a sincere apology for his role in that, and referred to Actualism as a cult. I was greatly relieved by this, and I believe he was also.[7]

---

7. Cathy noted that Ralph expressed several times afterward what an important clearing our exchange on that evening was for him.

Less than a month later, Ralph had died. He had two crucial influences on my life: the introduction to LSD and the divorce. All turned out much for the good, so I am deeply in his debt.

At the Well of Remembrance
Monika Wikman

Monika Wikman, Ph.D., is a Jungian analyst, astrologer, and author of *Pregnant Darkness: Alchemy and the Rebirth of Consciousness*. She hosts a nonprofit project under Earthways.com, the Center for Alchemical Studies. Podcasts with Monika on various topics can be found at Shrinkrapradio.com, Chasingconsciousness.com, and SpeakingofJung.com.

The following reflections are drawn from the eulogy that I gave at Ralph Metzner's memorial service. Not long after, his wife, Cathy Coleman, invited his friends, colleagues, and students to send in written offerings for this collection of essays in memoriam, and this dream came:

I see Ralph's clear and simple presence in dreamtime, he is standing in an open field, holding into himself with both arms a bouquet of flowers that Cathy has gathered for him, which in spirit is shown to be the collection of essays or offerings she is assembling.

And so it is.

"THE FOUR-FOLD SPHERE OF FIRE THAT GOVERNS THE WORK"

I begin with an alchemical image, "The Four-fold Sphere of Fire that Governs The Work."[8] Ralph used to meditate on the Four Spheres of Fire in his Agni Yoga practice. It was the work of fire in the Imagination, brought into the body.

---

8. "The Four-fold Sphere of Fire Governs The Work," originally from Michael Maier, *Atalanta fugiens*, Oppenheim, 1618. Also collected in *Alchemy and Mysticism* by Alexander Roob (Cologne, Germany: Taschen, 2014), 279.

■ Fig. 29. "The Four-fold Sphere of Fire that Governs the Work"
(from *Atalanta Fugiens* by Michael Maier, 1618)

HONORING RALPH'S IMPRINT UPON US

I have had the good fortune of knowing Ralph and Cathy in multidimensional ways from about 1992. My relationship began through studying with Ralph in small shamanic circles in potentiated and non-potentiated states, and eventually becoming good friends with both of them. I am also deeply blessed to have found some of my dearest lifelong friends from those beginnings.

I am honored to have been among those supporting Ralph and his family in his last two years of life, with moments that will always remain close to my heart. I owe more to Ralph for the ways he impacted

my life and work than I can ever say. I will bring out a few images here
to illustrate some of his attributes.

Ralph's passing leaves us with his genius and humanity. A strong
light lives on through the trail of all his creative enterprises, which is a
bit daunting as a whole: his books, songs, audio and video recordings,
teachings, and more.

He impacted our worldviews and many dimensions of the psyche
and of reality. His influence includes living in closer daily relationship
to the Source via the great Imagination.[9] I imagine ongoing private
offerings will be subtly prompted from within us, when we least expect
it, welling up from our depths in honor of Ralph and the greater total-
ity of his being. I imagine it is here we will most naturally find Ralph,
for he served the depths with all he had.

Ralph manifested the archetypal patterns of the wounded healer
and the explorer. I would like to offer glimpses into some of these patterns via selected astrological symbols and their mythic elements that
seemed to be present in Ralph's life. And then in closing, I would like
to honor the imprint Ralph leaves with us around conscious dying.

SERVING THE DEPTHS:
CHIRON, ODIN, AND THE
VESSEL OF RECONCILIATION

The story of Chiron comes from Greek mythology and is also represented by the comet of the same name. Being a centaur—half horse,
half male god—Chiron aims his bow to the stars. Metaphorical, psychological, and cosmological resonances and parallels appear in this
image. Chiron symbolizes an active archetypal force in the psyche that
bridges Earth and sky, matter and spirit, and works these dimensions
into harmonious relationship with one another in various ways. *That is
Ralph's dynamism.*

---

9. "Imagination" in the Blakean sense, the *perennial philosophy*, and as identified in
Aldous Huxley's "mystical universalism."

Chiron is an orphan; he becomes the foster son of Apollo, who raises him to be an archer, hunter, healer, and a musician. Chiron's healing apothecary brings about ever new gifts that emerge from the bridging of worlds. The fruit of these worlds results from continual fresh penetration into the mysteries of spirit and matter.

Chiron is credited with the discovery of botany and pharmacy as well as the science of herbs and medicine. He was the beloved teacher of many significant well-known Greek gods in the arts of archery, healing, the hunt, music, medicine, and more.

The placement of Jupiter in Sagittarius, conjunct the Galactic Center, in Ralph's chart indicates the gift of a teacher who accesses greater regions of psyche and develops relationships with the presences encountered. Jupiter's prominent placement at the ascendant of Ralph's horoscope further accentuates his gifts as a teacher of wisdom. The Sagittarius archetype of the healer-teacher-archer was at the base of Ralph's work. This healing axis emerged most clearly in his depth teachings as he became a prominent forerunner in ecopsychology, and also in his shamanic practices.

Ralph also had a strong energetic constellation in his birth chart around the entrance to his seventh house of relationship with Chiron, Mercury, and Mars conjunct (the wounded healer, Hermes the communicator, and the warrior) all in the sign of the sacred twins, Gemini.[10] He taught others (seventh house) patterns of initiation, imagination, and healing. Ralph exhibited an articulate teaching, healing, warrior energy, symbolic of the dual sign. This combination of archetypes and celestial energy was present in the way he played with opposites with levity, and how he directed his mental energy.

---

10. Cathy Coleman's essay in this book discusses how her and Ralph's relationship began when she discovered Chiron and Ralph was experiencing his Chiron return. Cathy brought that material to Ralph at their beginning. They followed this archetype in their horoscopes, which expanded their understanding of their love bond as well.

THE WOUNDED HEALER:
HEALER, HEAL THYSELF

Chiron's wound in Greek mythology occurs when he, as the leader of the centaurs, trots out of his cave responding to a commotion happening among the rowdier centaurs. A stray arrow from Hercules' bow lands in Chiron's thigh (sometimes seen as his foot) and no one can help him get it out or heal it, neither the deities nor the great shamans. So he crawls back to his cave alone to connect with the invisible realms in search of healing.

In some versions of the myth, the poison in the arrow is impossible to heal and Chiron finds that the transformation required is to become human, accept his fate, and die.[11] In terrible pain he prays to the gods to allow him to die and they, in gratitude for his teachings, grant him mortality, which is a gift of mercy. After his death the gods grant him life in the night sky as one of the eternal ones.

He has traded his immortality for mortality (exchanging fates with Prometheus who then is no longer being punished for bringing fire to human beings) and becomes a varied constellation in the sky.[12]

In some extrapolations of the myth Chiron is seen emerging from his cave bearing numerous healing arts that he has learned from tending his own wound, and he shares these with the world.

---

11. Becoming mortal and then immortal translates in the eternal in the symbol of a star. In this way Chiron has become fully human and offers this as part of his archetypal pattern, which one could think of as underscoring the value of human beings working with this archetypal field via healing states. The goal is to work with the wound, and accept one's humanity and death itself. Tolkien, in the *Silmarillion*, has a being from another dimension tell a human being, "The greatest gift the gods have for humans is mortality." And in alchemy all of transformation depends upon our relationship to death, for awakening, dying off to old selves, old constellations, and old identities. The Chiron myth parallels this reality.

12. This part of the myth is provocative, for we are now in the Promethean era collectively, Prometheus/Uranus being the ruler of the Aquarian Age. And with the shadow of this new age, we know the Promethean problem and question looms over humankind. Will humans be able to grow sufficiently in consciousness to handle the fire of creation and destruction, and not destroy the natural embodied world?

The dictum "healer, heal thyself and thus the world" belongs to the archetypal story of Chiron and to all of us who are touched by it. The healing is the medicine that flows through the person and into the world in the form of the sharing of new consciousness, healing modalities, creative awakening, love, insight, and more.

HONORING RALPH'S INITIATION AS A WOUNDED HEALER

In his last days, close to death and reflecting back on his childhood, Ralph reported experiencing, in a surprising new way, a fresh dimension and experience of love for the alienated, challenged teenaged boy he once was. This dimension was palpable; love and wisdom were maturing in him, giving him a more tender relationship to his own soul and a renewed appreciation of the depths of the "impossible" darkness that marked his boyhood.

Ralph's psychological wound with WWII ran extraordinarily deep. His young psyche was immersed and tangled in it. Ralph subsequently wrote about the insights around this trauma in several places in his books.

From age fourteen, Ralph, having again left his home in Germany, attended Gordonstoun Boarding School in North Scotland. Ralph writes about this time:

> At this school, my schoolmates lost no opportunity as schoolboys do, to tease and taunt me about my German origin. I was the "dirty kraut," the "enemy" of not so long ago. I experienced the shame and humiliation that Jewish children experience in anti-Semitic cultures or African American children experience in many parts of the U.S.
>
> . . . I remember realizing that I hated every German I knew or knew of. Only much later, through my studies of depth psychology and through psychotherapy, did I appreciate how this hate

programming had created a "shadow" self, filled with shame and self-loathing.[13]

During these years at the boys' boarding school, Ralph said that he could not connect with anyone. He was wildly alone. He also experienced the shadow of the Holocaust: thinking about it, dreaming about it, he nearly drowned in his feelings of guilt as a young half-German boy.

While he was still at Gordonstoun, Ralph had a series of dreams and visions from the invisible realms where angels were imparting energetic transmissions of light and pattern onto the Earth in front of him, through him, and all around him. The sense of peace and belonging from these dreams and visions were a balm to young Ralph. And, although he did not know what to make of the visions at the time, he knew he was not as alone as he had been feeling. He had the sense that his life had purpose, and that he had a destiny.

Driven into deep aloneness socially, he turned toward books and the library, nurturing his formidable skills, avidly reading, studying, and writing. The scholarly side of himself blossomed. He carried his wound the best that he could.

And from here, academic development, ambition, and drive led him to Oxford. There he focused mightily on the study of the Holocaust. In his searching, Ralph found that his personal shadow was tied to the malignant darkness of the collective shadow of the times.

Ralph had to learn how to disentangle the personal and collective energies of the psyche. Working with one's wound is part of the archetypal pattern of Chiron. Chiron. the dwarf planet, sits in the gateway to the outer planets. Chiron's glyph symbol is the skeleton key, the "opener of the way." The key in part symbolically correlates to what lies at the root of wounding.[14]

---

13. Ralph Metzner, *The Well of Remembrance: Rediscovering the Earth Wisdom Myths of Northern Europe* (Boston: Shambhala Publications, 1994), 270.
14. See the similar mythic pattern with Sedna: in Inuit mythology when encountering her at the bottom of the sea, you must bring a comb and comb out of her tangled hair

Ralph followed his strong inner knowing, which was brought out by his interests in Agni Yoga, shamanism, psychedelics, alchemy, dreams, mythology, and music. Like Chiron the archer targeting the transpersonal that lives beyond the personal dimensions of the psyche, Ralph's life from the beginning had this aim: to connect with healing, reconciliation, communion, and insight.

Something new was happening between the old man and the young boy, a new recognition, a new embrace, a renewed field of Ralph's own wholeness drew these stages into greater integration of himself. It was mysterious to witness this union in him in the weeks before he died, and it is what prompted me to peer into the portion of the Chiron and Odin mysteries that his life embodied.

One of Ralph's tools for meditation and awakening was to draw a mandala with one's youth on the east, and one's old self on the west, and the transcendent and higher dimensions on the vertical axis, above and below. The explosion of insight transforming Ralph at the end of his life seemed like that work in the mandala, of the old and young embracing as one. In these moments, Ralph's greater awareness was seeing into his life's journey, honoring and loving his early harrowing experiences. The younger self was receiving love from the greater Self, and also in turn from Ralph the old man.

RALPH'S CHIRONIC APOTHECARY

Ralph lived creatively and generatively, following his curiosity and interests, including fearless forays into the wild, the fresh, and everything "out of the box"! He employed mythic content and imagery, meditation, legendary storytelling, yogic techniques, koans, jokes, depth psychological principles, music, teachings from alchemy, UFO phenomena, and more to stimulate and give form to the expansion of consciousness.

---

and madness the part that is your own. The more humans meet her at the bottom of the sea in this way, the more her healing increases so she can swim the oceans emanating healing songs and her long, beautiful braids flowing instead of being trapped in madness.

He brilliantly developed effective tools for working with groups. Harnessing his apothecary as a Chiron figure and his explorer spirit bringing along the teachings in hand, Ralph, as a creative, grounded guide, led people to engage with the substantive depths of their psyches.

I recall the week just after 9/11, when I was attending a shamanic retreat with Ralph. The shattering crisis in New York City was with all of us, and the collective trauma body was activated with all of the alarm of the unknown that surrounded those first days. I had assumed we would dive deeply into serene states of being as antidotes and was stunned when, in guided meditation, Ralph asked us to see ourselves into the scene and attend to the reality unfolding in New York City and in the psyche. He wanted us to envision this horrible reality and see what wisdom would come.

I recall feeling a deep sigh of anguish. Sitting next to Ralph who could hear my sigh, I caught the strength he provided to the vessel that carried our work. His Taurus sun carried solidity. He stuck to his form and intention even after a good number of deep sighs were registered in the room. We ventured into the Imagination as Ralph helped us create, with the presences from the visionary world, a field of healing of the trauma body for ourselves and others through a process of courageous, compassionate, visionary attunement.

I was surprised at how Ralph confronted the collective level of darkness and helped each individual to not only unravel and heal from the influences in the collective, but to turn around and be part of the visionary work, to see into, address, and help heal the cataclysm at a collective level.

This is just an illustration of how Ralph's intelligence was focused toward helping people get more from their lives. He wanted substantive progress and new creations to come out of our work. He worked for the greater *coniunctio*, the union of worlds.

Ralph's intention and goal remained true, to expand into the archetypal depths and heights, and to bring home and into human life the boon of the journey, the relationship with the imaginal. *This was his aim.* And as with the ancient alchemists, the goal was to bring the *albedo*, the ecstatic transcendent objective, into the *rubedo*, the blood red world of human life.

ODIN

In addition to the wounded healer archetype, Ralph also embodied the spirit and mind of the explorer. Together, his spirit and mind combined with his Great Imagination to inform his work.

In *The Well of Remembrance*, Ralph invites readers to open connections among the past, present, and future that the Norse gods represent. "Following the guidance of the one-eyed god, we may drink from the Well of Remembrance in order to know once again our primordial origin, our present becoming, and our ultimate destiny."[15]

Ralph emulates Odin: opening the way to the source, and helping others discover it. The explorer's thirst for knowledge and wisdom bring to life a living shamanic connection that is both ancient and also freshly happening every minute.

ODIN'S ARCHETYPAL PATTERN
REVEALED IN THREE MYTHIC PARTS

Ralph delineates from the myths of Odin three parts that illuminate this pattern of awakening; namely, the Norns, the Eye of Sacrifice, and the Vessel of Reconciliation.

The Norns

In one myth, he hangs upside down on the root of the World Tree, while the three Norns, the seers, the fates—Past, Present, and Future (Skuld, Urd, and Verdandi)—oversee his hanged position. Beneath the

---

15. Ralph Metzner, *The Well of Remembrance: Rediscovering the Earth Wisdom Myths of Northern Europe* (Boston: Shambhala Publications, 1994), 13.

hanging god, the Norns bring up the Runes from the depths of the well of Urd, held by the roots of the Tree. The Runes are among the early symbols that communicate and mediate the divine and human worlds.

The Eye of Sacrifice

Another myth tells of Odin drinking from the Well of Mimir at the foot of the great Tree of Worlds. This is the Well of Remembrance,[16] which affords knowledge of ancestral and evolutionary origins. In this myth Mimir tells Odin that in order to drink the holy water from the great Well of Mimir held by a root at the base of the World Tree, Odin will have to sacrifice one of his eyes. Odin gouges out his right eye and drops it into the Well of Mimir. Mimir, seeing Odin had made the necessary sacrifice, dips his horn into the well and offers the now one-eyed god a drink of the holy water. Odin lives the rest of his life connected with the infinite source of knowledge.

This voluntary sacrifice of one eye results in Odin being able to see in both worlds. He gains the capacity to see into the patterns of nature, and the symbolic and transcendent reality of all life.

Ralph states that "We too, must learn to read the inner spiritual meaning of natural phenomena in order to hear the dissociation from nature produced by mechanistic scientism." Dreams and the work with the Imagination help us gain this insight.

The Vessel of Reconciliation

In this story, the warring gods Aesir and Vanir make peace and hold a ritual of reconciliation. Ralph was partial to this myth. If the warring gods could make a vessel to hold their warring, *then we humans too could create a ritual and a Vessel of Reconciliation that could bring peace.*

---

16. "The Well of Remembrance is an exercise in ancestral remembrance—the kind of re-membering that is the healing antidote to dis-membering. In German, to remember is *erinnern*, which literally means 'interiorize,' to know with inner knowing." Ralph Metzner, *The Well of Remembrance* (Boston: Shambhala, 1994), 13.

This myth tells of the path to Knowledge through the *coincidentia oppositorum* (coincidence of opposites), through love and through the reconciliation of previously conflicting opposites. Ralph was deeply committed to promoting the process of reconciliation.

RALPH'S INTEGRAL RELATIONSHIP WITH DEATH AND DYING

As my teacher, colleague, and deep soul-friend, Ralph left an indelible imprint. He inspired me with his work with the Imagination in the context of his teachings on death and dying and also witnessing his process leading up to his own death. It was an honor to share time in reflection with Ralph regularly in his last year of life with his progressive breathing difficulties due to idiopathic pulmonary fibrosis (IPF). With this work he was putting in order important pieces in his life, and readying himself and those closest to him for his departure.

Ralph had a relationship to the land of the dead, to the spirit world, and to guides and allies that allowed him to walk an alchemical path of life with awareness and value. He taught of being present with the end of our lives by imagining into and relating to the reality of our deaths. And Ralph's own accepting departure was a quiet, subtle confirmation of his wisdom on that.

I sensed the impeccable warrior attitude in Ralph arise in his relationship with death in the final months and weeks. He was clear-minded and would align and realign with the process as necessary, actively participating in it.

Ralph knew the key for living and for dying was to release any entanglements with other people. Up to the evening he died, he was actively tuning into all his relationships and practicing the Hawaiian Ho'oponopono mantra: "I love you; I am sorry; please forgive me; thank you."

Four days before he died, while I was making breakfast, the phone rang. It was Ralph. "Good morning, Monika, I am calling to say goodbye." Stirring scrambled eggs, I stopped in my tracks as I heard his voice on the line telling me that we would not be meeting again in this lifetime. This phone call was to be our last moment in time together. His voice was clear, present, and warm, though not sentimental in any way. I felt the open-minded, openhearted warrior poised in the present, a moment of pure presence, care, and completion.

Ralph, true to form in that moment, stunned me. He wanted me to know, among other things, that there was no obligation to writing projects we had played with through the years. So we mutually released any obligation. Then came the new agreement that, without obligation, we would look forward to any collaborations in the future that we might do, with Ralph participating from the other side of the veil. Then came our shared laugh.

The memory of his phone call still brings tears. The sheer beauty of Ralph, so very true to his essence with integrity to his philosophy and real-life practices in these last days of life was awe-inspiring.

When I hung up from this phone call, a sea breeze came in across the windowsill of my kitchen, playing in the house. In this moment a dream from the night before returned. Just hours prior to this surprising call, I dreamt that I was standing in the kitchen and, reaching above myself into the sky, I and my male partner draw down with our hands a golden amber chrysalis with a new type of honeybee being born inside. This new honeybee required both the yin and yang hands to reach into the other dimension and draw it down into the everyday life of the kitchen.

During these days and weeks, I had also been continuously checking in on a live camera feed of an eagle's nest in the wilds. The eagle parents flew in and out to brood over their delicate eggs. Day by day, moment by moment, I saw the spring storms ruffle their feathers, the days turning to darkness and again to dawn. I enjoyed that attentive witnessing. It felt as if the warm gaze from eager witnesses like me was part of the field of incubation of these baby eaglets, warming their pending birth into this world.

Four days after Ralph's phone call to say goodbye, Cathy let me know that Ralph had died peacefully in his sleep. My immediate feeling was one of joy and happiness for Ralph; he had died the good death he had envisioned, and I breathed deep sighs of relief for Ralph and for his family and his community as well. Suddenly, I felt the active ritual of attuning to the eagles' nest as a mirror of Ralph's own hatching out of this life and into the mystery of the beyond. The felt sense of Ralph's eagle egg hatching remains ever present when I muse over his own death, a signature of Ralph and his attention to dignity and divinity in dying.

I imagine whenever the depths rise up we will feel Ralph. He helped initiate people into their own relationships with the depths. At times I have felt a sense of Ralph's essence so near. His sudden shifts in perspective and wry humor were balanced with challenging objectivity. He welcomed other forms of connection and communion across the membrane between time and space and the land of the dead.

I will close these reflections in honor of Ralph with a few lines from the poem "Vacillation" by W. B. Yeats.

■ Fig. 30. From left: Diane Haug, Ralph, and Monika Wikman
at Synergia Ranch in Santa Fe, 2015
(Photo by George Goldsmith, courtesy of Monika Wikman)

> *Begin the preparation for your death*
> *And from the fortieth winter by that thought*
> *Test every work of intellect or faith,*
> *And everything that your own hands have wrought*
> *And call those works extravagance of breath*
> *That are not suited for such men as come*
> *proud, open-eyed and laughing to the tomb.*

So here is my offering, Ralph, to add to the bouquet of offerings Cathy called forth from the community of souls you have touched. And I look forward to further collaborations.

Ralph's Ultimate Magical Mystery Tour
Leo Figgs

Leo D. Figgs, D.O., is a recently retired osteopathic physician, ophthalmologist, and eye surgeon. He is coauthor of *The Survival Papers*.[17]

When I first heard about this project of people sharing memories and reflections on Ralph's contribution to their lives, I asked myself, what could I offer? Acknowledging how grateful I am to have known Ralph, I started to review my own experiences, pondering what I appreciated most about our relationship.

What struck me first was Ralph's storytelling. He was a master storyteller with an encyclopedic collection of tales—mythological, psychological, historical, anthropological, and transpersonal. He was truly fascinated with inner landscapes, unpredictable archeology, genealogy,

---

17. *The Survival Papers* was a finalist in 2012 for the Montaigne Medal from the Eric Hoffer Book Award for the most thought-provoking book. Leo's path includes a near-death drowning experience at age thirteen, studying with Indigenous healers, and surviving his son's suicide. These events influence his perspective when helping others deal with catastrophic loss.

and cultural lineages. Leading groups of spiritual entheogenic explorers allowed his vast knowledge and experience to cultivate the fertile depths of our individual and collective conscious and unconscious natures. By guiding us with integrity, clarity, and intention, he would weave through his storytelling hidden gems, connections, and insights that would enlighten the circle with an illumination as bright and as joyful as a traditional Christmas tree lighting festival.

Magical moments would occur during these sessions. When storytelling, sometimes his mind would connect various pieces of information into a new gestalt and he would burst into gleeful, wide-eyed laughter that instantly awakened everyone present, drawing us all into a hilarious perception of his new insights and revelations of metaphors and ironies. In these moments, he transcended any classical professorial or shamanic leadership role, reveling in the excitement of a discovery and with childlike exuberance. His cadence would accelerate in order to keep up, as rapidly cascading connections revealed themselves to him in novel and as yet unexplored ways. He would break out laughing at whatever was stirring within, thrilled with the excitement of new understandings, coincidences, synchronicities, and appreciations for the magnificent revelations that erupted during those psychonautical voyages.

These are my favorite images of Ralph, his shining spirit spontaneously celebrating with all present the glory of an entheogenically enhanced Spirit Canoe or a transdimensional spaceship journey. His unabashed ear to ear grin, with tears converging in the corners of his twinkling eyes, affirmed my sense of being in the presence of a true teacher, a master storyteller, a wisdom bearer, a shaman, an alchemist, a healer, and a German-Scottish bodhisattva. We who have shared these moments have been blessed beyond our ability to imagine.

RALPH'S ULTIMATE MAGICAL
MYSTERY TOUR FALL 2003

Ralph arranged and offered a guided tour to Egypt in the fall of 2003, a fortuitous time because I had the professional freedom necessary to

■ Fig. 31. Ralph, tour guide, 2003
(Photo by Leo Figgs)

travel for several weeks. My wife Jennifer and I were excited to join him on his Egyptian tour he had christened: "The Ultimate Magical Mystery Tour."

Our trip to Egypt was truly an unimaginably magical tour. A small group of fifteen of us gathered in New York and then flew to London and on to Cairo. In Cairo we joined up with another group led by Nicki Skully, a shamanic healer, teacher, and leader of spiritual pilgrimages to Egypt. Ralph had toured with her the previous year. Our two groups were about the same size and we all got along really well. We collaborated easily as our groups traveled together to the various sites. Once there we would typically separate with Ralph and Nicki leading their respective groups.

As a young woman, Nicki was the dancing skeleton opening concerts for the Grateful Dead. When the Dead came to Cairo for three days of concerts at the Great Pyramids in 1978, they were assigned to a young Egyptian man, Mohamed, who handled their trip. Mohamed became the owner of one of the largest tour companies in Egypt, and we were honored to have him as our head tour guide. His chief assistant handled our entire trip and arranged our amazing journey.

■ Fig. 32. Tour guides Nicki
Scully and Ralph
(Photo by Leo Figgs)

In this crowded tourist season, sometimes there would be twenty or more tour buses waiting. We were amazed at how the gatekeepers, guards, shopkeepers, and other guides deferred to our guide who seemed to know everyone.

An outstanding example of our good fortune was our visit to the Great Pyramid of Giza. Ralph's group was to go in first and would go down into the Lower Chamber, the "Pit."

We had not gone very far onto the pyramid, maybe thirty yards, when we came to an intersection with two tunnels. The option on the left had a locked metal gate like a jail cell, while the hallway on the right led to the Queen's Chamber and up to the King's Chamber. As the guard unlocked the gate, he told us that this passageway to the lower chamber was closed to the public. He advised us that the passage got very short and narrow with barely room to turn around if needed. He turned on a light switch that dimly illuminated the tunnel with pale yellow bulbs that were strung up along the upper corner. Then he left and we never saw another guard until we exited the pyramid over two hours later.

We started down the passageway single file with Ralph eagerly leading the way. The tunnel descended at a surprisingly steep angle, tapering until you could no longer stand up and you had to stoop, squat, or crawl. This uncomfortable passageway seemed to last forever, as we crawled on the hard rock squeezing in on all sides, the light dimming more and more, and my claustrophobia increasing. After crawling over 370 feet down the descending passageway, we gratefully arrived at the subterranean chamber, the Pit.

When our group of fifteen finally all emerged from their crawl, we gratefully found places to stretch and sit while Ralph reviewed his understanding of this chamber. He pointed out that we were actually sitting on top of the rocky plateau that supported the incredible mass of the pyramid. The lights were turned off and we sat in silence. I was reminded of a phrase in *God's Trombones* by James Weldon Johnson where he described the darkness as "blacker than a hundred midnights down in a cypress swamp." As we enjoyed the silence, some of us sensed a deep hum or a pressure from the immense weight that was above and around us. When the time came to move on to the next chamber, we were rested and ready, if dreading the long achy ascent back up the tunnel toward the other chambers. The stairway continued up past a horizontal corridor to the Queen's Chamber and then opened into the Grand Gallery that ascends to the King's Chamber.

In the Queen's Chamber, Ralph continued to share with us what he knew of the history, stories, and speculations about the pyramid. The Queen's Chamber is apparently misnamed because there is no evidence that anyone was entombed there; it most likely contained a statue of the Pharaoh Khufu, who built the Great Pyramid in about 2550 BCE.

Our group came out of the Queen's Chamber and ascended the stairs just as Nicki's group descended from the King's Chamber. As we noticed this convergence on the stairway, both groups spontaneously broke out singing "As I went down in the river to pray." The song echoed beautifully within the gallery as we slowly passed each other while singing. It was an unimaginably special Spirit-generated moment that I continue to treasure. I still get chills and goose bumps when I recall it.

As we entered the King's Chamber, we circled around the massive red stone sarcophagus. We joined hands and Ralph led us in prayer. We then took turns lying in the sarcophagus while the group intoned and chanted. As we laid in the sarcophagus some of us heard the deep resonance generated by hitting the side walls with our fists.

We had deeply embraced the mystery and majesty of the last remaining of the seven wonders of the ancient world. The bus ride back to the hotel was surprisingly quiet as it seemed that we were all processing the awe of our experience.

We visited the Sphinx, and the pyramid complex, the Citadel, to experience a Sufi Zikr, traditional music and dance. We toured the Khan El Khalili Bazaar, the Saqqara necropolis, the step-pyramid of Djoser. Ralph also elaborated and deconstructed the symbol of the *djed* pillar, its meaning and uses as an amulet and psychic tool, in its many manifestations throughout Egypt.

We then flew from Cairo to Aswan and boarded the cruise ship Sonesta Nile Goddess, our home for the next four days as we sailed down the Nile to Luxor, exploring the various temples and sites along the river. The first morning we were up well before dawn as our group was bused to the docks where two feluccas sailed us to the island of Philae.

As we arrived at the island, unoccupied except for a few temple guards, we went to the beautiful Temple of Isis in the Garden of Osiris where we had meditation and rituals. There Ralph shared his knowledge of Isis, the "Earth Mother Goddess of life, nurturance, and healing." We sat in awe as the sun rose in the east emerging between the pillars of the temple. Ralph described the moment as witnessing "Nut birthing the sun out of the womb of space." He pointed out the sculpted images of people bringing gifts and offerings to the goddess who used the "ankh, another symbol and magical tool," to give life.

We traveled downstream from Aswan, north toward Cairo for an afternoon sail to Kom Ombo. There we toured the temple, half of which honors Horus, the "warrior-god of clarity and light," and half of which honors Sobek, "the crocodile-headed god of the instinctual nature." Ralph shared stories about the "ancient, reptilian, evolutionary heritage of human life." We then sailed on to Edfu where we docked. We were advised to eat and rest since later that night, about 9:00 p.m., we would be visiting the Temple of the Falcon-Headed Horus. Much to our surprise, instead of traveling in several tour buses, about twenty horse-drawn carriages pulled up and took all of us to the temple. It was a clear night with the stars spangled across the equatorial sky.

The temple is one of the largest and best preserved in Egypt. Worshipped as the child of Isis and Osiris, Horus is depicted as a falcon god and was the ruler of the skies and the deity of the pharaohs. The walls and passageways are carved with many amazing battle scenes.

Ralph told us that Horus is the "archetypal visionary warrior, struggling against the forces of separation and darkness, personified by Set and Sobek." The scenes symbolically are "wars of light against darkness," or, "historical records of actual battles between the Anunnaki 'gods' Horus and Set, and their respective followers."

I can still see Ralph's face glowing as he delved deeper into this esoterically fertile garden of delight. One of my favorite images of Ralph is standing by him as he marveled at some of the breathtakingly beautiful bas-relief sculptures. Witnessing the spontaneous marriage of years of Ralph's scholarship combined with the magic of adventurous discovery is a moment of inspiration more than powerful enough to last several lifetimes. Even so, this image is not the first one that comes to mind when I recall our trip to the Temple of Horus. That's because I was able to witness similar moments several times as we journeyed, and as Ralph allowed himself to be drawn into and captivated by the images as they revealed themselves.

On one of the last nights we were in Egypt, we were invited to have dinner with Mohamed and we gathered at a rooftop restaurant for a final meal together. I had noticed that Mohamed always wore a western-cut suit and cowboy boots. He also typically wore a cowboy hat when covering his head. I thought it was rather unusual. He stood out from the crowd and certainly drew people's attention.

His arrival at dinner with his wife really took the cake. His wife was a beautiful blue-eyed blond ex–Texas Cowboys cheerleader. We had a wonderful evening together. Ralph and I laughed about that several times and it was appreciated as an example of the ironies in our ever-changing world.

RESPECT AND GRATITUDE

I view Ralph as mentor, father figure, peer, friend, and fellow journeyer on the spiritual quest. We shared the heartbreaking loss of our sons and

■ Fig. 33. Leo Figgs and his wife, Jennifer Cunningham, standing next to her painting,[18] titled *Icarus Reborn* (Photo by Ralph Metzner)

---

18. Jennifer Cunningham created this collage/painting of a journey-vision of a dream image of a soul coronation on Venus for Isaac, their son, after his death. The knowing was that all souls have this coronation after death. In the vision he was surrounded by a multitude of others who had gone before him and who also wore elegant headdresses and robes. This painting is pictured in their book *The Survival Papers*.

the heart-healing reclamation of their gifts and wisdom during their life and afterlife. His loss occurred years before ours, yet there were times with Jennifer and me that the thinly healed wounds would open and the deep pains and his emotions bubbled to the surface. We all dipped our cups deeply into the pure waters of empathy and compassion.

We were a balanced tripod, each and all sharing equally in providing support, understanding, strength, and solace. We were peers in the ever-present pain of parents seemingly separated from their children forever. We were also partners in the reassuring and affirming experience of sharing an enduring conscious communication with them from beyond the veil. These moments of shared synchronicities united the three of us and when they occurred, we all recognized how precious and connected we were with each other.

Times of self-revealed openheartedness continue, even still, in the form of after-death communications, dreams, voices, intuitions, memories, synchronicities, and totems. Our shared journey in the Spirit Canoe continues, and I savor each new stroke that brings us closer and closer to the event horizon of manifest unity.

Inspiration for New Dimensions Radio
Justine Willis Toms

Justine Willis Toms is the cofounder, creative producer, and host of New Dimensions Radio, which delivers "uncommon wisdom for unconventional times." Since 1973, New Dimensions has hosted numerous luminaries, including Ralph Metzner. Justine is the coauthor with Michael Toms of *True Work: Doing What You Love and Loving What You Do* and the author of *Small Pleasures: Finding Grace in a Chaotic World*.

In the early '70s, the San Francisco Bay Area was a consciousness candy store, filled with the sweetness of the wisdom of so many spiritual leaders flooding in from all over the world. Scores of new organizations were thriving, such as the *est* trainings founded by Werner Erhard; the establishment of the California Institute of Asian Studies, founded by Dr. Haridas Chaudhuri, later known as the California Institute for Integral Studies; and the Stanford Research Institute (SRI), where Willis Harman, Ph.D., was senior social scientist. Ram Dass was giving talks to eager practitioners. Tibetan lamas were teaching meditation. Swamis were arriving from India—Swami Satchidananda, Sri Muktananda, and many others.

To say I was a newbie in this burgeoning field in 1973 would be an enormous understatement. In the previous year I had been knocking on doors and passing out literature created by Watch Tower Bible and Tract Society of Jehovah's Witnesses.

All my life I've had an innate spiritual enthusiasm, and I was quite happy to feel I had finally arrived at the way, the truth, and the light. However, my life took a decisive turn in March of 1972 when I met and fell in love with Michael Toms. What I didn't anticipate was my spiritual path would be split wide open by him. We were married in December 1972. I knew I had to reconcile my current spiritual affiliation with the Jehovah's Witnesses and I grappled with him over biblical scripture. I recall that every time I read certain verses and explained my interpretation of them, Michael didn't negate my view but gave me a wider and deeper one by saying, "Yes, and you might look at it like this." It took me years to understand that my spiritual pursuit was not about embracing dogma. Rather it was about going for the biggest and most trustworthy truth I could stand on.

There are two special people, Ralph Metzner and Charles Tart, who were part of the origin story of the work that I have been doing for the past forty-eight years. It was March 4, 1973, when radio station KPFA held a fundraising event at Zellerbach Auditorium in Berkeley. The speakers were Henry Puharich, Ralph Metzner, Ken Johnson, Charles Tart, Ramamurti S. Mishra, and Shafica Karagulla. The event was entitled "Parapsychology, Frontiers of Consciousness."

It was Ralph Metzner who imprinted my soul when he led us in his Agni Yoga Light-Fire practice. The impact of that visualization was amplified by the two thousand souls having the same experience in the same moment. I was totally transformed. It worked like magic in a most visceral way. Ralph's ability to take us all to a new level of consciousness allowed me to transcend my own materialistic understanding of the world. It was a cleansing of the lens of my perception and my view was widened. I was launched into a new landscape from which I would never again retreat. In this life-changing moment, Ralph not only embodied the Light, he was able to radiate it throughout the room. My spiritual quest moved from my head to my heart. It can be likened to a door being opened, and even though there are occasions in my life when I want to close that door and turn away from the responsibilities of this new seeing, that door would never again be closed completely. The light continues to seep in through the cracks even forty-eight years later. I'm always grateful that it does.

The very next day Michael and I were inspired to conceive of New Dimensions Foundation as a nonprofit organization. By Tuesday, with a lawyer, the articles of incorporation were drafted and within five months it became a radio program series on KQED. New Dimensions

■ Fig. 34. Justine Willis Toms
(Photo courtesy of Justine Toms)

has been broadcasting ever since on public radio stations around the United States, inspired by Ralph and Charles Tart that Sunday in 1973. The theme of New Dimensions' mission statement remains:

> It is only through a change in human consciousness that the world will be transformed. The personal and the planetary are connected. As we expand our awareness of mind, body, psyche, and spirit and bring that awareness actively into the world, so also will the world be changed. This is our quest as we explore New Dimensions.

A Rich Strand of Jewels
Paul Müller

Paul Müller has a strong interest in politics and psychology. He was born in Basel, Switzerland, one year after Albert Hofmann's "Bicycle Day."
This essay was translated using www.Deepl.com and with the help of Uwe Doerken and Cathy Coleman.

Ralph Metzner spoke about alchemical divination at the turn of the century at a conference at the Gaia Media Forum near my workplace. At the end, Ralph took out a rattle, started rattling, and guided some sixty people on a divination journey—and the magic of that moment was the beginning of a long journey that still continues.

With the sound of the rattle, I left "listening mode," and the mood in the room changed as well. That's when I wanted to know more.

Since I had only started working with psychedelic substances shortly before, I approached him and asked if there was a possibility to join one of his circles. He responded with an invitation to the Metzner Alchemical Divination (MAD) training, a three-part non-substance program that was being offered in several different workshops he was starting in Europe and the United States.

Through the divination training workshops, Ralph wove a rich strand of jewels that included his knowledge of shamanism, Agni Yoga, mythology, and alchemical wisdom. The MAD workshop had three parts, starting with Janus, the Roman god; then Hermes, the Greek messenger god; and concluding with Mimir, the Nordic giant who activates secret knowledge or memories. For me, these workshops were an opening into new realms. I experienced much more than learning a useful technique—it was an expansion of consciousness.

Later I was invited to participate in a "circle ritual" (*Kreisritual* in German). It went on for several days, with ceremonies that introduced me to states of nonordinary consciousness. It was a "total work of art." In the ceremonies I entered into realms not easily accessed on one's own. Psychedelic substance combined with a sacred atmosphere, extraordinary music, and Ralph's teachings formed what Ralph called a Spirit Canoe. As a group we met from time to time.

Below I will share several gems of the necklace that Ralph strung together in his teachings.

Gem of Ritual: Each ceremony began with a ritual, including calling in the four cardinal directions. Once the circle was opened, everyone shared their intention. The circle ended with giving thanks.

Each year we met in Northern or Central Europe and each participant journeyed under Ralph's guidance; his knowledgeable comments contributed to the magic.

Gem of *Genius Loci* (Spirit of Place): We invoked one or more places with their own genius loci.

I lived mostly in Basel and learned during my stay in nonordinary consciousness that the journey is influenced by the history of the place, in my case, the Celts and Germanic tribes.

The setting that Ralph created assisted the traveler in nonordinary consciousness to get to places in the psyche that are hard to reach. His invocations link the journey to the *genius loci*: plants, mushrooms, animals, seasons, ancestors and sages, human relationships, light beings, and the inner Creator.

Gem of the World Tree: Known in many traditions, the World Tree symbolizes growth from the roots to the top, a journey through the Web of Life, even arising into new worlds and new perspectives.

Through the exploration of the World Tree, there is support, context, and inspiration in the inward journey to other worlds.

Gem of the Circle: Coming together in a circle for vision, connecting the group and strengthening the individual experience.

Ralph used many methods, including music, images, and poems in his workshops and classes, so I was looking for a symbol that would represent the circles he drew. I imagine a circle like a *charivari*, where many meet in costumes of their own choosing, and someone acts as music director, bringing them together.

To honor Ralph is not to simply continue his work, because that is not possible. But rather to use his books, divinations, and one's own knowledge to help others travel to expanded states of consciousness, supplemented with contributions of the knowledge of mystics, poets, and wisdom teachings. Honoring also includes working to clarify one's own path, as Ralph's intention was always to open new and individual paths.

My wish is that many people are able to participate in circles, guided by the gems of Ralph's teachings, and thus approach the state that the mystic William Blake poetically describes as increasing one's awareness of the Web of Life:

Auguries of Innocence
To see a World in a Grain of Sand
And a Heaven in a Wild Flower
Hold Infinity in the palm of your hand
And Eternity in an hour

WILLIAM BLAKE

Reverend Ralph
Gail Colombo

Gail Colombo is a practitioner of Metzner Alchemical Divination, a clinical aroma therapist, and an anthroposophic aesthetician. She is a cat-loving environmentalist, supporting the best life for feline companions through her business, Cat Faeries.

Ralph's influence in my personal life and my business life was vast. Rather than elaborate on his many influences, I will tell two stories, one about Ralph who loved animals, and one about Reverend Ralph, my friend.

RALPH WHO LOVED ANIMALS

Once a month or so Ralph and I would have lunch near his psychotherapy office in Northern California (San Rafael). It was usually up to me to find someplace new and different. One day I told Ralph to bring his lunch and that we were going somewhere special. He did not know that less than five minutes from his office was a magical animal shelter called WildCare that takes in injured wildlife. Among their services for animals are operations, rehabilitation, and training for in-home foster care. When the animal patients are ready, they are released back into nature near where they were found.

Unfortunately, many of the patients are injured so severely that they cannot be released because their injuries prevent hunting, flying, or seeing. The permanently injured animals become "ambassadors" and live in comfy species-specific enclosures or at a pool outside of the hospital. Here you could visit Vladimir the flirtatious turkey vulture, Sequoia the northern spotted owl, Mohave the desert tortoise, and many more, all while munching on lunch at the picnic table.

Ralph loved that he could get within feet, and in some cases inches, of animals and birds that one would normally only see from afar. He was overjoyed to discover that such an endearing and important place was so near his office. We became frequent visitors to WildCare to see our animal friends. At the end of our visits Ralph went home with WildCare's latest magazines and often with items from the gift shop.

Shortly after Ralph's passing, I went to WildCare alone and told the animals that their friend had physically left us, but would be with them in the spirit realm. I raised my water glass and toasted the memories.

REVEREND RALPH, MY FRIEND

When Bill, my partner since 1991, decided that 2011 would be a good time to get married, we wanted to keep it small and in our home. I asked Ralph if he would officiate our marriage. He had never done this before. His eyes lit up, and he said that he would be honored to do so. Ralph took it very seriously and researched marriage licenses, legalities, ceremonies, and asked friends and colleagues such as Sheldon Norberg for advice and suggestions. To become licensed, he became a card-carrying member of the Universal Life Church.

As many weddings are, ours was one near disaster after the other!

■ Fig. 35. Bride and groom Gail Colombo and Bill Niemeyer with Reverend Ralph Metzner, 2011 (Photo courtesy of Gail Colombo)

This included Ralph not being on time and not answering his cell phone. In a panic we pulled up the Universal Life Church website and were ready to ordain a guest if necessary! Ralph finally arrived, and the ceremony began. The wedding incorporated many aspects of the Metzner Alchemical Divination process, including calling in the four directions, the spirits of that day and place, our guides, our ancestors, and the names of our parents. Interestingly, Ralph, who for decades had effortlessly spoken in front of thousands of people, was more nervous than we were! After we recited our vows and promises to each other he pronounced us "husband and wife." He completely forgot the "Do you take this man . . . Do you take this woman . . . I do . . . I do . . ." part! We didn't have the heart to tell him! It didn't matter because he was officially ordained clergy of the Universal Life Church, and we were legally married by the Reverend Ralph Metzner.

Self-Transformation of Beautiful Warrior
Briege Farrelly

Briege Farrelly, M.A., is a dedicated yogini and yoga teacher, medicine woman, somatic counselor, and psychospiritual facilitator.

I am taking this opportunity to describe some of the healing technologies Ralph employed as an adept therapist addressing deeper issues.

I came to Ralph with a dream in my heart, but felt broken, sad, insecure, and fearful. I was carrying many burdens. Imprints of complex trauma endured as a child had branded my psyche. "Ugly" and "stupid" were projected onto me and were part of the wounding. Many decades later, I understood that I wasn't stupid after all, but suffered learning trauma from shameful and humiliating childhood experiences. Despite the early projections, "ugly" came from an unintegrated shadow. Even though I presented well to the world, internally I felt worthless, helpless, and flawed to the core. The impulse to hide and protect was strong.

Early on, Ralph recognized the changes I needed to make. Without judgment he created awareness around what I needed to let go of and enabled me to embrace what would benefit my life. Always the fair witness, he was a treasure as a mentor on my path toward healing and wholeness. He envisioned the Beautiful Warrior within and invited her out.

At thirty-nine, I had come a long way on the road of self-reclamation but still had far to go. Caught in delusion and codependent relationships fraught with pain and misery, I was still disconnected from myself. My head was going in one direction, heart in another, and body yet another. I had just left a dark night experience in Hong Kong after living there for seven years. Aware to some degree of my shadow, it was too difficult to own. I kept running. Temporary, addictive, soothing quick fixes were easier to choose. I wanted to be a good person but had developed behavior that depicted the opposite.

I first met Ralph as a student at CIIS in the East-West Psychology master's program in September 2000. My first class was the Unfolding Self. He taught us to look and see metaphorical patterns in our experiences by learning to decode them, whereupon a psychospiritual transformation would occur. We were required to write two papers for the class using the metaphors from his book *The Unfolding Self.* I chose "From Captivity to Liberation" and "Journey to the Place of Vision and Power." Healing happened through the courage to turn inward; it was there that I would find everything for which I was searching. A process of remembering and integrating those split-off parts of self-in-exile enabled me to transform trauma into understanding and wisdom. He was clear that the key to freedom was found by being accountable and responsible for my actions, past and present.

Through my therapeutic relationship with Ralph, I began to heal the karma and trauma that had been passed on through the Irish Catholic lineage into which I was born.

Ralph taught us that the physical body was a sacred vessel for the expression of a transcendental existence—a vertical life, that of the soul.

Aspiring to soul alignment was the path of the Middle Way, a process of merging my received impressions from external material existence with my increasing inner experience of soul perceptions and life force. His alchemical teachings and divinations led us toward *coniunctio*, the alchemical natural path to union of the Lower Self (personality/masculine/solar) with the Higher Self (soul/feminine/lunar). The integration of one's life as a human being essentially starts with circling back to childhood to accept, digest, and integrate traumatic experiences. Letting go of the masks of shame and guilt, and dysfunctional conditioned habit patterns, enables the soul to settle into the body.

At times I felt frustrated that healing was not a straight road and that backsliding with indulgent old behavior was part of the process. Strengthening my masculine was necessary to stop the distraction of meaningless diversions and create healthier boundaries and structures. Ralph would say, "It takes as long as it takes!" This left me feeling both deflated, that healing was an endless road, as well as gave relief that it was a lifetime process without a timeline.

Ralph also held my feet to the fire, assisting the uncomfortable process of updating my brain, nervous system, and perceptions to bring life, flow, and vitality back to frozen, terrorized parts of my being—my feminine. I was changing my past by the way I carried it—by the way I perceived it, by learning to trust the language of my beautiful body, mind, and intuition, and perceiving life as it was. I'm told that many know what their work is, although most do not do the hard work. With Ralph's guidance, I was able to do the work to create a more harmonious, balanced relationship between my Lower and Higher Selves.

The most powerful medicine Ralph offered was all the creative ways he guided us to navigate our inner worlds. Soul, residing in the Cave of the Heart, was the bridge between the material and spirit world. His alchemical teaching on navigating the six directions we travel as human beings are now a part of my subtle awareness and consciousness. Mother Earth below, father sky above, masculine/expressive/dynamic on the right, feminine/receptive/magnetic on the left, our history and the ancestors supporting us from behind and the future we are creating in front. The inner guidance of the soul is constantly realigning and restoring balance from our center.

During my daily yoga sadhana Ralph comes to mind to cultivate deeper presence. I would think of him saying, "Always pause and check in with your body for feedback. What do you feel within your body? Was it effective? Always coming back to your Heart Center, work to create balance between right and left, masculine and feminine, expressive and receptive." I applied Agni Yoga in other spiritual practices I learned from him. When my mind is wanting to rush to the next thing, Ralph is there with his magic formula, reminding me of *intention*, *attention*, and *awareness*. He adds earth to my sadhana.

As I was preparing to write this, an email called to me—the only email that I had printed and saved from the many correspondences I had with Ralph. He wrote, "Your beautiful warrior spirit is revealing herself in your beautiful body. As I was writing this, I wondered what your 'medicine name' might be; and there it was: *Beautiful Warrior*."

A big piece of my work with Ralph was healing and releasing shame. The Jaguar session focused on releasing what was in the way of feeling empowered. We looked back at two previous experiences: (1) my life as a little girl; and (2) a traumatic move as I entered puberty. Revisiting preconception first, I connected to my pure and untainted essence. I was joy, love, and beauty inside and out. There was nothing to feel ashamed about. Then he took me to the different incidents and asked me to revisit each with the enlightened awareness of the compassionate witness. He said, "Embrace everything with the Light-Fire energy of the compassionate witness—the shame, the blame, the whole lot. Let them dissolve like clumps of ice melting in the springtime flow of the clear waters of life. The power of the feminine/magnetic comes from taking off the masks of shame, revealing and expressing one's true inner nature."

■ Fig. 36. Ralph and Briege Farrelly
(Photo by Leo Figgs)

Ralph's Earth Vision Circles taught us the value and beauty of ceremony, ritual, and the incredible healing power of community.

Visiting Marin several months before Ralph's death, I saw him for one last mentoring session. Finally, after almost twenty years of study with him, my own offerings were beginning to get traction in the world. Still comparing myself to others and feeling somewhat shameful and dismayed about being a late bloomer, I mentioned this to Ralph. Without missing a beat, he kindly said, "Early bloomer, later bloomer, doesn't matter. What matters is that you are blooming." That changed me forever!

Slowly, I have been exercising the muscle of sharing Ralph's teachings and methodology with groups. Leading a women's retreat a year ago was transformative for both me and those participating. As I offer his gifts to others and in the process reclaim more of myself, I have learned to trust myself and trust life.

You'll Always Have a Place in My Heart
Jamy Faust

Jamy Faust, M.A., is an energy healer, psychotherapist, and family constellation facilitator. She has launched the Mystery and Alchemy Training (MA'AT), offering the Metzner Alchemical Divination modality and more. She cofacilitates immersion programs in their method of family constellation therapy.

Looking back, I see that 2005 was a fateful year for me as my life took on a steep trajectory. That spring, I was surprised to be invited to a small gathering here on the East Coast to ingest the sacred mushrooms known as Teonanacatl, the flesh of the Gods, Los Niños ("little saints") as they are called in the Mexican Mazatec traditions, and more.

I'd experienced sacred mushrooms many years earlier when on my twenty-first birthday friends bestowed me with a gift-wrapped honey jar of the Hawaiian strain. I spent that birthday evening in awakened divine bliss and was being shown the nature of all things, the Pure Lands beyond space and time.

A year later, due to this experience and having graduated from the University of Hawaii, I joined the Neuropsyche Analytic group whose focus was on Tibetan Buddhism meditation practices and their effect on the mind. I moved with them from Honolulu to a coffee farm we purchased on the Big Island of Hawaii, still trying to grasp my birthday experience. There I began a life-long exploration into the astonishing world of consciousness expansion. Psychedelics weren't part of these meditation practices or initiations, but part of our studies included such texts as the Tibetan Book of the Dead and *thangka*[19] interpretation. Still intrigued, it was a comfort to read *The Psychedelic Experience* by Leary, Alpert, and, of course, Ralph, to help me grapple with a small part of what I'd experienced. That tattered book is still a mainstay in my library.

---

19. Tibetan Buddhist paintings on fabric depicting a Buddhist deity, scene, or mandala.

■ Fig. 37. Jamy Faust and Ralph
(Photo courtesy of Jamy Faust)

Thirty years later I found myself in a small gathering returning to those very same visions and conversing again with those divine beings, revisiting the awakened state of being, beyond my personality. How could this possibly be, that my consciousness would open to such similar visions so many years later? I was shocked, and in awe, to say the least.

As a group member I urged our wise circle leader to share how he'd learned about working like this; that is, to lead others ceremonially after ingesting these substances in a sacramental way through prayer and respect for the plant spirit teachers, and then gently guiding us to explore the inner realms of our consciousness. He pointed me to a table outside our ceremony room displaying the brochure of Ralph Metzner and his MAD program, the Metzner Alchemical Divination training to start that summer. I felt I had to attend, I was being called or—more to the point—pushed.

BEGINNING THE METZNER
ALCHEMICAL DIVINATION TRAINING

I crossed the pool deck at Westerbeke, a retreat center in Northern California, and a small group of two women and a slender, smiling man stood beneath an awning of the clay-tiled roof of the Mission-style building. As I approached, I realized that the man was Ralph Metzner and the women were his assistants for the MAD training that I'd enrolled to attend for the week.

"It's nice to see you again," I said to Ralph, not knowing where those words came from, as I'd never met him in this lifetime prior to that moment. While smiling widely and looking at me closely, little did I realize that he was welcoming me into a world of which I'd never dreamed.

Almost three dozen folks had gathered for Ralph's MAD training. Some of these dear ones are still my friends today. I had no intention of learning more about psychedelics and their effects. Rather, what drew me to this training was to learn more about what had happened to me and my consciousness at age twenty-one, and again thirty years later, and their astonishing similarities. In turn, Ralph had no intention of teaching us about psychedelics, or their effects, though many may have expected that. Instead, he was training us to evolve, expand, and explore our consciousness through divination practices of entrainment, using the rattle and the drum, as the ancient shamanic practitioners had done. He taught us how to navigate our consciousness through states of awareness, so that when we magnify our intention, focus our attention, and amplify our awareness, we can develop expanded states without medicinal supplementation. Learning his approach was a profound asset to my work in the world.

Ralph spent individual time with each of those whom he didn't know personally; he was generous with his time with me. We had so much in common that it felt uncanny. I shared the brochure of my world work with him and Teilhard de Chardin's quote included on its first page, "For you, there is only one road that can lead to God and that is fidelity—to remain constantly true to yourself, to what you feel is highest in you. The road will open up before you as you go." Ralph exclaimed, "We are doing the same work!"

We quickly realized that we shared a wonderful connection with Bert Hellinger. My husband Peter and I had completed five years training in family constellation work with Bert. Ralph had just translated Bert's book from the German, *On Life & Other Paradoxes: Aphorisms and Little Stories*, in 2002.

I learned of Ralph's unyielding interest in alien abduction, and was well acquainted with Harvard University's Dr. John Mack, whom I knew personally based on my husband's experiences many years prior. And last but not least was our mutual interest in perceiving energy fields and the healing energy of radiant Light-Fire itself. Ralph had studied and taught the process of Actualism while I'd been offering and teaching Barbara Brennan's Hands of Light work for many years. Ralph was right—we were kindred spirits!

As the Westerbeke training ended, I was invited to join Ralph at an upcoming gathering in the Northwest. Again, with excitement and anticipation, I accepted. From that moment onward, Ralph invited me to attend his two-yearly gatherings that occurred in the United States and which I attended for the next dozen years.

During one of his Southwest gatherings, Ralph asked me to facilitate a family constellation process for him. Several of the gathering's participants stood in as representatives for an issue on which he wanted clarity. Over time, I continued to facilitate constellation sessions for him using figurines rather than "live" representatives. The figurines we used were sometimes as simple as the salt, pepper, and sugar packets on a conference dining room table! The mutual appreciation we had for the power of the family constellation methodology was a sweet blessing upon our collegial relationship.

Our rapport deepened. He invited me to assist him in a gathering not far from Lucerne, Switzerland, at the foot of Mount Pilatus where his European MAD training was meeting for their first time. I met many of his friends, colleagues, and students while continuing to expand my understanding of who Ralph was—a scholar of consciousness, master alchemist, philosopher—and of his effect on others. It was an incredible experience, being there at the foot of the Alps, that felt as though we were all being held in the palm of God's hand.

Ralph was familiar to me in ways that were unexplainable. Was it that we had maternal Scottish and paternal German heritages in common? Or that the moons in our horoscopes were both in Aries and rising signs in Sagittarius? Did we really share past lives with the twelfth-century Benedictine abbess and Christian mystic Hildegard of Bingen of Germany, as once came to me in a dream? Had we been students of the sixteenth-century Swiss-born physician, philosopher, and alchemist Paracelsus, as I'd received in a premonition while visiting the scholar's Salzburg tomb years prior? Perhaps it was just simply that Ralph reminded me my dear uncle Jimmie whom I took care of for many years. They shared the same May 18 birthday though ten years apart. Nevertheless, there was an unexplainable bond that I felt deeply. There was a deep recognition between us beyond romantic or familial; it was a soul love.

During one entire year of our work together, Ralph taught me, through phone sessions, the teachings of Actualism created by Russell Schofield. He did so with my promise that I would not in turn teach them to anyone else, but only to use them for myself. I've kept this promise. These teachings are very akin to my own study of Barbara Brennan's work mentioned earlier, and with whom I had been a student and teacher prior to meeting Ralph. The teachings of Actualism that I learned through Ralph have strengthened my connection with high-frequency, never-extinguishing, pure white Light.

My life circled around his biannual gatherings. I continued mentoring with him for many years by Skype. My world was changing enormously. I had begun offering his style of ceremonial gatherings shortly after the MAD training completed, always with his blessing.

I loved having Skype sessions with him when as the screen opened and our faces appeared he'd exclaim, "There you are!" Those words warmed my heart.

By this time, my husband Peter had joined Ralph's gatherings with me. During our time of studying with Ralph, Peter and I wrote a book bringing family constellations, energy-field work, and Ralph's teachings together. It was essentially our mutual work with Ralph that allowed the creation of the book's final section, "Agreeing to Our Soul Nature." Certainly, we had learned the art and craft of family constellations from that "wise old owl" Bert Hellinger, as Ralph liked to call him. But it was Ralph's divinatory sessions that opened us to the profound understanding and felt sense (and sight) of the Soul Council, Ancestors, and Spirit Guides. We are still honored that Ralph wrote our book's foreword.[20]

In the summer of 2018, Ralph wrote to me that he'd been diagnosed with the lung disease idiopathic pulmonary fibrosis (IPF). He liked to call it the "tattered sail syndrome." He anticipated that he'd have another two years or so to live. I made sure we had our Skype sessions scheduled through the winter as well as a flight to Sonoma to visit with him the following April. I'd really hoped to see him in person that spring, though, sadly, it never came to pass.

On the March Monday evening before he died, I had a profound dream in which I had entered the ground level of an empty parking garage with many floors. I found myself standing in front of the elevator doors with Ralph. He was wearing a regal emerald-colored velvet robe with one of his Nepalese smoking hats upon his head. We entered the elevator and pressed the top button to floor number 10. The doors opened and laid out before us appeared a rainbow-colored bridge surrounded on both sides with puffy cumulus clouds. Together, we walked across the bridge and as we reached the other side, Ralph disappeared into the clouds.

---

20. Jamy and Peter Faust, *The Constellation Approach: Finding Peace through Your Family Lineage* (Berkeley, CA: Regent Press, 2015).

Two mornings later, I learned that Ralph had transitioned in his sleep during the wee hours of the morning with Cathy sleeping by his side. My friend Michael who texted me of his passing also included with the text a photograph that Ralph had by his bedside. It was one that was taken during our last gathering together depicting me next to Ralph with our friend Diane and my husband Peter on each side. I was incredibly touched that I was "nearby" him at his last moments.

In my return text I shared with Michael that I would begin the Tibetan prayers now for the next forty-nine days so that Ralph would pass easily into the Light. Praying this way for our dearest Ralph spread throughout his community of loved ones through texts, emails, and phone calls. A website through Caring Bridge was set up. Many posted memories and photos of Ralph on the website, along with the following prayer.

Although it is a shortened version of the Heart Sutra and not the full extent of the prayers that are recited by monastic Tibetans, many of Ralph's family, friends, and colleagues did join in. It was to be chanted once, twice, twenty-seven, or 108 times daily for the full forty-nine days for his safe passage through the bardos and into the Light. We began on March 16 and ended May 1, 2019, with this Sanskrit mantra:

O Nobly Born Ralph, listen carefully to our prayers,
Om Mani Padme Hum
Gate Parasam Parasamgate Bodhi Svaha
Om Vajra Satva Hum
Om Mani Padme Hum

I continue to offer ceremonial gatherings. I've begun to pass on his Alchemical Divination teachings and see that part of our soul agreement was to do so after he left his mortal coil. It was one of the main purposes of our meeting. I devote my work to his honor with gratitude, each and every day. Ralph has a seat as a Spirit Guide at my Soul Council's table, and there he always has a place in my heart.

Green Psychology

Terrapsychology's Debt to Ralph Metzner
Craig Chalquist

Craig Chalquist, Ph.D., is core faculty in East-West Psychology at CIIS and former associate provost of Pacifica Graduate Institute. He teaches at the intersection of psyche, story, nature, re-enchantment, and imagination through courses on depth psychology, applied folklore, ecotherapy, and his own field of terrapsychology.

Ralph specialized in consciousness studies, including the use of psychedelics for personal transformation. Those who know his work would also mention his cross-cultural studies of expanded ways of knowing, including via the fabled roadway of folklore, and myth in particular. He countered mainstream psychology's materialist emphasis on what can be measured with an integral corrective approach, always insisting that our research, scientific or otherwise, take whole persons into account. He was a psychologist who wrote, practiced, and lectured on behalf of the neglected dimension of soul.

However, those of us in the field of ecopsychology also know him as a mentor who emphasized how human health and the health of ecosystems are interdependent. He was, in fact, an early ecopsychologist. Shortly after Roszak, Gomes, and Kanner edited and published the innovative volume *Ecopsychology: Restoring the Earth, Healing the Mind*, Ralph came out with *Green Psychology: Transforming Our Relationship to the Earth*,[1] a collection of writings drawn from decades of deeply honoring nature. As was usually the case with him, he reached the edge of revelation well before the rest of us.

---

1. Theodore Roszak, Mary Gomes, and Allen Kanner, eds., *Ecopsychology: Restoring the Earth, Healing the Mind* (San Francisco, CA: Sierra Club Books, 1995); Ralph Metzner, *Green Psychology: Transforming Our Relationship to the Earth* (Rochester, VT: Park Street Press, 1999).

RALPH'S WORK WITH ECOPSYCHOLOGY

An omission needs addressing in our early writings on terrapsychology, the growing field of studies, ideas, and practices for reimagining and restorying how deeply and intimately our psychological life is involved with our surroundings, whether human-built or more than human. Ralph is not mentioned or cited. I write to correct this and to gratefully, if belatedly, acknowledge our debt to his work.

Why the oversight, then? I believe it's because Ralph's work and thought so thoroughly permeated our ideas and practices right from the start that, to borrow a phrase from Gestalt psychology, they quickly became ground rather than figural. For example, in his book *Green Psychology*, he asks: "Cannot what we have learned from working with troubled individuals and families help us deal with this collective psychopathology, this profound alienation of the human psyche from Earth?" This important question is what drives so many of us with a dual background in both psychology and working in the natural world—whether that of environmental advocacy, nature-based therapy, deep ecology, permaculture, gardening, biodynamic farming, and the like. It is a question we all live, often without articulating it.

FORMING A MORE COMPLETE PSYCHOLOGY

Green Psychology and much of Ralph's later works can be thought of as a declaration of liberation for psychology, imprisoned almost since its inception by agendas of prediction, control, measurement, and power, sold to the public under the white coat of scientific objectivity. Abraham Maslow compared that kind of narrow psychology with the drunk who looked for his wallet not where he had lost it, but beneath a street lamp, because the light was better there. [2]

Ralph preferred the term *green psychology* to *ecopsychology* because he did not want the sprouting field to devolve into just another

---

2. Abraham Maslow, *Motivation and Personality* (New York: Harper & Brothers, 1954).

academic department or subdiscipline within psychology. Which is, of course, exactly what happened. By contrast, I wrote an article in the December 2020 edition of the *Journal of Ecopsychology* offering other analyses.[3]

Mainstream psychology might be defined as the objectively disguised art of collecting data to direct attention to individual pathologies. "Rather," Ralph notes, fighting this, "we are talking about a fundamental re-envisioning of what psychology is, or what it should have been in the first place—a revision that would take the ecological context of human life into account."

His type of green psychology did not stay timidly on the empirical side of the road. It journeyed deeply into Indigenous knowledge and praxis, biology, theology, mythology, philosophy, mysticism, history, systems theory, dream studies, plant medicines, and the humanities in general. Why? Because *we* show up *out there*, not just in laboratories, where only what's measurable puts in a brief appearance. We cannot understand fish by studying them in fishbowls; we cannot understand ourselves by isolating us from the world. Empirical research is only one way of knowing, and its conclusions mean little unless integrated with wider kinds of inquiry.

We should also bear in mind that by calling for a green psychology, Ralph himself did not mean a merely political push. Emphasizing politics, economics, or any other single arena of human concern merely replicates the sort of one-sidedness that cannot cope with the thickets of interrelatedness and consequence we face as monolithic single-track agendas fall apart on every side. What he offered was new visions of who we are and how to be here with each other.

---

3. Craig Chalquist, *Terrapsychological Inquiry: Restorying Our Relationship with Nature, Place, and Plant* (Abingdon, UK: Routledge, 2020).

PSYCHOCARTOGRAPHY

Places tend to gather folklore of the kind Ralph wrote so movingly about throughout his career. He was among the first to suggest that we Westerners quit pillaging the myths of lands that we find exotic and attend instead to our own lost stories.[4]

Years before my book *Ventral Depths*,[5] a terrapsychological exploration of the Great Central Valley of California, described places there in terms of alchemical operations, Ralph suggested that alchemy—not just an attempt to convert lead into gold, but a Hermetic wisdom path for millennia—brought a symbolic language for illuminating ecological and biospheric transformations on the one hand and their echoes within human interior life on the other. Alchemy had served as an imaginative practice ever since it came forth from Egypt so long ago. Ralph's book *Ecology of Consciousness* applies alchemy to "a program of radical empirical research on personal, familial, collective, and planetary transformation." He suggests "that the language of alchemy, both Eastern and Western, updated with contemporary scientific concepts, can provide the appropriate paradigm for a worldview that integrates rational science and intuitive mysticism."[6]

The program embodies story as a tool and expression of profound appreciation. The grand universe story contains nested within it innumerable other stories: the story of the galaxy, the story of the solar system, the story of planet Earth, the story of life on Earth, the story of animal and human life, and the story of human culture.

Ralph observed that just as particular places served as altars to characteristic deities, so have divisions of time: days, weeks, and longer

---

4. For example, the story "The Black Goddess, the Green God, and the Wild Human" in Ralph's book *Green Psychology* (see above) explores key pagan goddesses and gods that personify our relationship to nature, place, and Earth.

5. Craig Chalquist, *Ventral Depths: Alchemical Themes and Mythic Motifs of the Great Central Valley of California* (El Cerrito, California: World Soul Books, 2011).

6. Ralph Metzner, *Ecology of Consciousness: The Alchemy of Personal, Collective, and Planetary Transformation* (Oakland, CA: New Harbinger Publications, 2017).

cycles associated with a spirit or daimon, goddess or god, what Jung would have called an archetype.

Ralph himself reflects the archetype of the far-seeing Magus, the wizardly presence associated with figures like Thoth, Hermes Trismegistus, Merlin, and Lugh. People and the planet are better for all the magic he left us.

The Maternal Mythic Milieu of Ralph Metzner
Alastair McIntosh

Alastair McIntosh is known for modern Scottish land reform, environmental protection, and social justice. His books include *Poacher's Pilgrimage: An Island Journey*, which advances an ecology of the imagination, and most recently, *Riders on the Storm: The Climate Crisis and the Survival of Being*. He is an honorary professor at the University of Glasgow.

You know how it is these days. You go to a conference, and they give you the program and your pen and badges in a cotton bag. Everybody makes out it's saving the environment, and having just arrived, you're happy at the contribution this might make to offsetting your bad carbon karma. All is well, until back home the rueful day comes when you have to clear out a closet-full of cotton bags. And, as the bard of Scotland, Robert Burns, put it to a mouse whose nest his plow had overturned:[7]

> *The best-laid schemes o' Mice an' Men*
> *Gang aft agley,*
> *An' lea'e us nought but grief an' pain,*
> *For promis'd joy!*

---

7. "To a Mouse, On Turning Her Up in Her Nest with the Plough," November 1785, available on www.scottishpoetrylibrary.org.uk. The phrase *gang aft agley* means "go all awry."

Notice the empathy with nature in that poem. Another verse has it:

> *I'm truly sorry Man's dominion*
> *Has broken Nature's social union,*
> *An' justifies that ill opinion,*
> *Which makes thee startle,*
> *At me, thy poor, earth-born companion,*
> *An' fellow-mortal!*

Burns penned those lines in 1785 in his home county of Ayrshire, just south of Glasgow from where I'm writing this.

THE 13TH ITA CONFERENCE
IN KILLARNEY, MAY 1994

In this Gedenkschrift contribution I will pay tribute to the impact of that event and use it as a springboard to reflect on Ralph's Celtic—to use that term loosely—ancestry on his mother's side here in Scotland.

It was probably in the fall of 1993 that I'd seen a call for presentations, and submitted a proposal to speak about the bardic—one might say, *shamanic*—underpinnings of our pioneering work on land reform in Scotland. The conference was called "Toward Earth Community: Ecology, Native Wisdom and Spirituality."

■ Fig. 38. 13th ITA Conference, Killarney, Ireland, cotton cloth bag (Photo courtesy of Alastair McIntosh)

Ralph, as conference program director, accepted my proposal, which also meant that I could afford to attend the conference along with an astonishing 1,600 other delegates. As Cathy Coleman (his wife) would later tell me, "It reached maximum enrollment and was financially successful too."[8] Such was how I came by the cotton bag. Later, I enlarged it by splicing in a length of green cotton fabric from an old pair of trousers. It became the carrier for a drum I'd made with a rainbow eagle motif that I used on the campaign trail. Through the Contemporary Collecting Programme, that drum now forms part of the permanent collection of National Museums of Scotland as a "disobedient object" representing modern Scottish land reform.[9]

A lot of heady water has passed under the bridge since then. Not only did we succeed in striking the iconic spark that brought the seven thousand acre Hebridean Isle of Eigg—once "cleared" (i.e., evicted) of much of its population—back into community ownership, but we also stopped a multinational corporation from turning the majestic mountain Roineabhal on the neighboring Isle of Harris into the biggest roadstone quarry in the world.[10] Land reform legislation followed, formally abolishing feudalism and creating a community right-to-buy. Some 3 percent of Scotland is now held in five hundred community land trusts.

IMPACT ON SCOTTISH LAND CONSCIOUSNESS

My part as one of the leaders in these campaigns lay mainly in following an emergent land consciousness. In this respect the International Transpersonal Association's Irish conference came at the perfect time.

---

8. Cathy Coleman email, October 14, 2020. The 1,600 figure was what was said at the conference itself. Elsewhere, I have seen the figure stated as 1,500.

9. See the museum curator's Sarah Laurenson's video *Collecting the Present: Land Reform* available on YouTube, from about 2:50 minutes in. Also, find her on X (formerly Twitter) as @SarahALaurenson and see the May 11, 2020, thread.

10. Alastair McIntosh, *Soil and Soul: People versus Corporate Power* (London: Aurum, 2001).

Vast areas of Scottish land were—indeed, still are, for this is work-in-progress—owned by private interests who can exert considerable control over ordinary people's lives. Such is a legacy of events around the so-called Highland Clearances, the dispossession of the clansfolk from their lands mainly in the eighteenth and nineteenth centuries. This, part of the "internal colonization" of the British Isles such as in Ireland, had led to the Famine, and in England, the Enclosures.

I had a strong vantage point as a lecturer in human ecology at the University of Edinburgh. But as the work gained traction, and as newspaper headlines were made, it ruffled powerful feathers. Our teaching center was notoriously closed down in 1996. To carry on, as an unemployed writer and activist, took a particular strength. Much of it came from having had my ideas from preexisting Scottish poets and historians further refined, endorsed, and supported in friendships that came out of the ITA's conference integration of ecology, trauma psychology, activism, and consciousness. It was only a three-day event. But never underestimate the power of what a person like Ralph and his team could constellate.

Just to give a hint at other speakers by whom I was fired up, we heard:

- The poetry of David Whyte, and his powerful rendition of W. B. Yeats' shamanic "Wandering Aengus" with its line "because a fire was in my head."

- The Irish presenters, such as Sister Imelda Smith, who led the welcoming ritual. Not for the first time, I experienced in my mind what Scottish tradition calls "the carrying stream," a great river of silver fire that was the Old People of Scotland. I don't easily cry, but Imelda's ritual of calling in "the voices of the land" from all four corners of the world had tears streaming down my face as my head ignited while we sung the responses.

- The Ojibwe activist Winona LaDuke, whom I remember explaining to her six-year-old daughter Waseyabin that "there are white

Indians in places like Ireland and Scotland, but you just don't hear very much about them."

- The psychotherapist Jane Middleton-Moz, who talked about the "lateral violence" that breaks out in colonized peoples when they can't deal with "intergenerational violence." She said that "children are the canaries of the community."
- The history of consciousness evolution and planetary survival in the face of violence, presented by Stanislav Grof.
- Then there was Ralph himself, the conference coordinator. I still have the Canadian journal *Interculture* that I happened to be reading at the time. I wrote on the cover something that I heard Ralph say that resonated: "Stories tell us about our past; visions tell us about our future."[11]

DARSHAN WITH RAM DASS

There was such generosity at the conference, too. There were all those bright-spirited volunteers who sat at desks, missing most sessions. And there was the bookshop owner, who'd laid out an enormous spread, most of which sold; but rather than flying back the unsold stock, he loaded me up with all that I could manage as a gift to our Centre for Human Ecology library.

You can imagine what rocket fuel the whole jamboree was for me, a junior figure on such a distinguished stage. Indeed, a stage that profiled most of the distinguished figures who had come out of the 1960s counterculture era, and were ushering in an axial tilt into the emergent new millennium. It would be no exaggeration that the conference that Ralph coordinated was life-changing for many, and I recall some of the Irish participants even saying, "This will change Ireland."

---

11. My note dates that quotation as on May 25, 1994, the day after the conference closed. Other presenters out of the many parallel sessions that had to be chosen from include Nuala McDowell Ahern, Edward Goldsmith, Vandana Shiva, Jill Purce, Rupert Sheldrake, Darrell Posey, Matthew Fox, Delores Whelan, Erik van Lennep, Bron Taylor, David Abrams, Helena Norberg-Hodge, Satish Kumar, and Sulak Sivaraska.

A most precious memory that lingers with me was an encounter with Ram Dass, whose keynote address was "The Spirit of Service." He was present at the preconference presenters' gathering, and he was obviously tired from travel. Over most of the weekend he was nowhere to be seen. But then, I think it was the Sunday afternoon, I was walking through central corridor of the conference venue, the Great Southern Hotel, when who should approach from the opposite direction.

I felt a surge of delight. Here was my chance to Be Here Now with himself. He'd recognize me as a presenter. I had an access point. At which, suddenly I realized that the last thing the poor man probably wanted was to be buttonholed by yet another punter who could go on and say, "I've met Ram Dass." As we closed toward each other, he slightly lifting his head in recognition, a different spirit came on me. I lowered my head to a bow, averted my eyes to the ground, and walked silently on past with my palms together and raised in the *namaste* position.

No transient conversation could have added depth. Only later did I realize, this had been darshan. The sense of a blessing has never gone away.

DARSHAN WITH RALPH

On the evening that I arrived by train from Dublin, and in a less silent but also lasting darshan, I was shown into a lounge at the Great Southern to meet Ralph face-to-face. There he was with Cathy, hosting a small group of other presenters who had arrived early over refreshments. There was no mistaking which he was. The Irish press, tickled at the prospect of such a 1960s-style "happening" in Killarney, had already found its form in cracking jokes about his "greying pigtail."

Ralph brought me warmly into his circle. The in-joke of presenters from the Celtic lands was that "an international conference" meant an American one, but this was not the usual cultural tourism. As the event got underway, it was clear the guests bore gifts. Here was a wave of returning diaspora consciousness. Here was a mirror to ourselves that would advance us in the process of discovering, and recovering, our own Indigenous origins.

I wrote up the impact that the conference had on me in *The Trumpeter*—the Canadian journal of ecosophy (or ecological philosophy), in 1996.[12] So doing was hugely important. When I lost my job that year, I moved directly to write the book for which I'm best known, *Soil and Soul*, and the *Trumpeter* article provided me with a starting point and framework.

ORIGINS OF THE PSYCHEDELIC REVOLUTION

Because my developing thinking was so boosted by Ralph's conference, I sent him a copy of *Soil and Soul* when it came out. In correspondence appreciating this in 2011, he mentioned that he and his daughter had recently spent a fortnight in Scotland visiting places where he had lived as a child and adolescent, as well as where he had gone to school at Gordonstoun. As his mother was from the little farming market town of Stewarton in Ayrshire, "the focus was on my daughter seeing her ancestral places."[13]

Twelve miles north of Stewarton, on a tributary of Glasgow's River Clyde, is the mill town of Paisley, famous for its brightly colored swirling teardrop patterns known as "Paisley shawl" or "Paisley pattern." Originally brought back from Persia and India, these had found their own legs in Scotland, not the least through their metacultural resonance with the remarkably similar motifs of Celtic art.

There's an amusing passage in *Allies for Awakening* where Ralph tells how his daughter, when she was nine, "came home from school one day and delightedly referred to some paisley pattern designs she saw somewhere as 'ooh, ooh, how psychedelic.'"[14] In the email he offered to

---

12. Alastair McIntosh, "Community, Spirit, Place: A Reviving Celtic Shamanism," *Trumpeter* 13, no. 3 (Summer 1996): 111–20; available on www.alastairmcintosh.com, search under the Published Articles tab. *Trumpeter*, founded in 1983 by Alan Drengson, is still very much thriving under the auspices of the University of Athabasca.
13. On a Post-it note and in email of October 10, 2011.
14. Ralph Metzner, *Allies for Awakening* (Sonoma, CA: Four Trees Press, 2022), 6.

send my choice of one of his books, and it was natural that I chose *Birth of a Psychedelic Culture* that he and Ram Dass had authored the previous year with Gary Bravo.

On its dedication page is a photo from the 1996 Harvard Project Reunion of what I've always thought of as the original psychedelic triumvirate of the counterculture—Alpert, Metzner, and Leary—prophet, priest, and holy fool. There's Ralph in the picture, born of his Scottish mother and German father. His shoulder gives support to a very old Timothy Leary, this being just before his passing. Tim is regaled in a baseball cap that proclaims: "100% Irish." And Ram Dass (Richard Alpert), who was, of course, of Jewish provenance.

"So there you have it," I once had occasion to quip to Ralph, mindful of those fading jokes where three men walk into a bar. "That tells you everything you need to know. The psychedelic revolution was set off by a Scotsman, an Irishman, and a Jew."

A GERMAN SCOTTISH FAMILY AND TRANSPERSONAL CALLING

Ralph's father, Wolfgang, was German, and a successful Berlin publisher. He met Jessie "Jill" Laurie, his Scottish wife, in 1932 in Geneva when he was a student at the university. She worked for the League of Nations, the forerunner of the United Nations, which would suggest a competence with languages. The family, in penury, fled at the end of the war to northern Germany to escape approaching Russian armies.[15] Taking advantage of Jill Laurie's Scottish provenance, Jill and her three sons then left Germany. As his brother Robin takes up the story:[16]

---

15. This information is in his obituaries. See Neil Genzlinger, "Ralph Metzner, LSD and Consciousness Researcher, Dies at 82," *New York Times*, April 4, 2019; "Ralph Metzner 1936–2019," *Sonoma Index-Tribune*, March 29, 2019. Cathy Coleman told me it was she and Ralph's younger brother Robin who provided the childhood information here.
16. Email October 16, 2020, from Robin Metzner to Cathy Coleman, addressing some of my queries.

Ralph was 10 when we first came to the UK and I was 8. Neither of us spoke a word of English. All our childhood days were spent in Berlin where we only spoke German and read or had read to us German stories of which there are many. Jill was incredibly busy as she had to support us and my maternal relations, with whom we lodged in Stewarton in grossly overcrowded conditions . . . Apart from that we were at boarding schools in England and Edinburgh, as a result of which we were only in Stewarton together for a very short time, a few months. Ralph was there the longest and actually attended the local primary school, which was a bit of a rough house.

EDUCATION AT GORDONSTOUN

For his secondary schooling Ralph went to Gordonstoun, a top Scottish "public" school. That terminology developed at a time when "public" meant a nonchurch school. Paradoxically, today it means a private school, and with elitist overtones.

He attended Gordonstoun boarding school through an exchange his father arranged, and a Scottish boy went to a similar boarding school in Germany. Ralph had asked to go to boarding school in Scotland, rather than in Germany where his brothers went. He said that he always felt more of an affinity with the West. This would be followed by Oxford University, Harvard, and then a life in California.[17]

Gordonstoun, for all its overtones, was an avant-garde experiment in pioneering education. It was founded on the estate of a Scottish aristocrat, Sir Robert Gordon of Gordonstoun (d. 1656), and became a school in 1934 when the Berlin-born Jewish educator, Kurt Hahn, fled Germany in 1933 after being briefly imprisoned by the Nazis. He had written to the pupils at his pioneering Schule Schloss Salem School in southern Germany, telling them they had "to break with Salem or break with Hitler."

17. Email from Cathy Coleman to me, October 29, 2020.

One of the pupils had been Prince Philip of Greece and Denmark, the school being owned by his brother-in-law's family. When Hahn left for Gordonstoun, Philip followed to complete his education, and went on to meet Princess Elizabeth who later became queen. Their son, King Charles, was also sent to Gordonstoun.

In Ralph's 2011 email to me about revisiting with his daughter where he'd lived "as a child and adolescent," he said that they had gone not only to his Ayrshire mother's "ancestral places," but also to Gordonstoun, nearby Findhorn, and the Highlands. In having so done he made the observation that Ralph's period of schooling overlapped with Hahn's headmastership.[18] The Berlin educator (with his Berlin pupil) remained at his post until 1953, when he retired on health grounds and went back to Germany. He was eventually buried in Salem in 1974.

In researching this piece, I phoned up Maxwell MacLeod, the son of Scotland's most influential twentieth-century Presbyterian churchman, Lord MacLeod of Fuinary, the founder of the ecumenical Iona Community. I asked MacLeod what it would have been like at Gordonstoun in Ralph Metzner's time in 1950 when Ralph started there at age fourteen, and through 1954 when Ralph graduated and went to Oxford.

If I might meld a telephone conversation and emails, Maxwell put it to me thus: "Gordonstoun was just a big Highland estate. Kurt Hahn chose it for the climate, the east being less wet than the west. He wanted to import Teutonic principles of education to Scotland."[19]

School life was legendary for its austere regime. Maxwell continued: "Every morning you'd get up at five-past-seven and the house master stood outside the house and you ran with just your shorts on for a morning run, then your warm wash and cold shower."

Every day you had a discipline test. You were asked, Have you

---

18. Email October 10, 2011.
19. Conversation March 10, 2021, and emails March 13, 2021.

performed your training plan? Two warm washes—one in morning and one in evening; two cold showers; sixty skips with a jump rope; five press-ups; and one hour's study. And then you added your own discipline—an extra activity you'd take on. A prefect would ask each boy what discipline he'd performed.

Hahn's educational principles were rooted in Plato's *Republic*. His guiding motif was "education for democracy," with students being encouraged to participate in the school's running.[20] His educational principles, *The Seven Laws of Salem*, that he imported to Gordonstoun from his previous venture, were:

1. Give the children opportunities for self-discovery.
2. Make the children meet with triumph and defeat.
3. Give the children the opportunity of self-effacement in the common cause.
4. Provide periods of silence.
5. Train the imagination.
6. Make games important but not predominant.
7. Free the sons of the wealthy and powerful from the enervating sense of privilege. [21]

Perhaps importantly, we might note the value placed on times of silence and training the imagination. Some boys struggled with the regime at Gordonstoun. King Charles is said to have been miserable there, famously describing it as "Colditz in kilts." It seems that Ralph not only survived but thrived. At Gordonstoun he was at the top of his class, even though he was a German boy who had to learn English.

I ask you stand. And raise the traditional toast:

---

20. Michael Knoll, *Schulreform through "Experiential Therapy" Kurt Hahn—An Efficacious Educator* (Eichstaett, Germany: Catholic University, 2011).

21. Emily Hanford, "Kurt Hahn and the Roots of Expeditionary Learning," APM Reports (website), September 10, 2015.

Ralph Humphrey Guenther Metzner, son of Wolfgang
   Metzner and Jill Laurie.
A great German, a great Scotsman, and a great American.
The immortal memory.

As Above, So Below
Sam Mickey

Sam Mickey, Ph.D., earned his doctorate in philosophy and religion from CIIS. He is an adjunct professor in the Theology and Religious Studies department and the Environmental Studies program at the University of San Francisco. He is an author of several books on ecological philosophy and spirituality, including *On the Verge of a Planetary Civilization: A Philosophy of Integral Ecology* and *Whole Earth Thinking and Planetary Coexistence: Ecological Wisdom at the Intersection of Philosophy, Religion, and Ecology*.

What do you learn when you learn about yourself? In many wisdom traditions, inquiry into one's own consciousness opens out onto the whole world. Consider this saying from Dōgen Zenji, the thirteenth-century Japanese Buddhist who founded the Soto school of Zen. "To study the Buddha way is to study the self. To study the self is to forget the self. To forget the self is to be actualized by myriad things. When actualized by myriad things, your body and mind, as well as the bodies and minds of others, drop away."[22] In brief, "What Buddhists call the self is the entire universe."[23]

One can see that the many traditions, numerous rituals, symbols, scriptures, and beliefs are oriented toward connecting the self to the world, the microcosmic to the macrocosmic: when yoga practitioners align their posture with the axis of the world; when taiji practitioners

---

22. Eihei Dōgen, *Moon in a Dewdrop: Writings of Zen Master Dōgen*, ed. Kazuaki Tanahashi (New York: North Point Press, 1985), 70.
23. Eihei Dōgen, *Moon in a Dewdrop*, 164.

harmonize their flow of energy with the energy of Earth and the cosmos; when a Christian touches holy water, which corresponds with the baptismal waters of Jesus and the cosmic waters from the beginning of God's Creation; or when an alchemist sees the transformation of the self as a transformation of earth, air, fire, and water.

The principle underlying these correspondences is summarized by a refrain that appears in *The Emerald Tablet* (*Tabula Smaragdina*), a text attributed to the legendary Hermes Trismegistus. "That which is above is like that which is below, and that which is below is like that which is above."[24] As above, so below. This was an insight I wanted to explore in more depth. Where does the exploration of my own mind converge with an exploration of the elemental? In other words, I was interested in ecological psychology or an ecological worldview, which is what Ralph Metzner outlines in *Green Psychology: Transforming Our Relationship to the Earth.*[25] After reading that book and several of his other books while I was in graduate school, I knew that focusing on ecological consciousness would be central to the rest of my life.

I only applied to one school for my doctoral degree, the California Institute of Integral Studies (CIIS), a relatively small, private graduate school based in San Francisco. I did not know much about CIIS, but I knew that it was where Ralph was teaching. His teachings and practices on ecological consciousness, altered states, and alchemical divination provided the capacious and compassionate perspective that I was seeking. His mentorship, CIIS, and the culture of the San Francisco Bay Area have been an ongoing source of nourishment for my life and work.

Since completing my Ph.D., I teach courses at the University of San Francisco on ecological ethics and religion, I have written and edited

---

24. Hermes Trismegistus, "*The Emerald Tablet* (*Tabula Smaragdina*)," in *The Alchemy Reader: From Hermes Trismegistus to Isaac Newton*, ed. Stanton J. Linden (Cambridge: Cambridge University Press, 2003), 28.
25. Ralph Metzner, *Green Psychology: Transforming Our Relationship to the Earth* (Rochester, VT: Park Street Press, 1999).

several books of ecological philosophy, and I work with the Yale Forum on Religion and Ecology. I still return to Ralph's books, and *Green Psychology* stands out, playing a pivotal role in my life. It stands out because it is ahead of its time, a reminder that his contributions to consciousness and culture are still taking root.

Two decades since its initial publication in 1999, *Green Psychology*'s insights are still relatively new to many researchers and scholars in psychology and environmental studies. One thing that is not new is the critique of the technological rapacity of extractive industries and, more generally, human-centered (anthropocentric) attitudes that treat humans as separate from and inherently more valuable than the rest of the natural world. Psychological and historical analyses of the split between humans and nature have been relatively common since the 1960s. What makes Ralph's thinking different is that it does not rest with critique. It also points the way forward, imagining what a new, ecological worldview would look like.

Ralph attributed this to his conversations with the cultural historian Thomas Berry, who is one of the people to whom *Green Psychology* is dedicated. I recall Ralph saying that Thomas would tell him that there are enough people theorizing about what is wrong with our current worldview, and what is needed is for people to offer new stories for the reintegration of humans with the Earth community. We need a vision of a viable future, one in which human consciousness is aligned with its ecological context. Still today, there is an overwhelming abundance of critiques of current social systems and cultural values. Images of a transition to a peaceful, just, flourishing Earth community are comparatively rare.

With humility and simplicity, Ralph's writings and teaching lay out guidelines for transitioning to an ecological worldview, including ecological reorientations of science, philosophy, politics, economics, and religion, drawing on diverse sources of knowing, such as alchemy, yoga, mysticism, shamanism, and psychoactive plant medicines. Academic studies of religion and ecology have grown considerably since the 1990s, but even in those contexts, discussions of plant medicines and esoteric spirituality are still relatively infrequent. The taboo around studying psychoactive plants is gradually disappearing, due in part to Ralph's articulating the issues in a scholarly way.

An ecological worldview calls for humans to think, feel, and act as members of a self-organizing planetary system, a living Earth—Gaia. After the development of the Gaia hypothesis by James Lovelock and Lynn Margulis in the 1970s, the scientific community was reluctant to speak of Gaia, as it connotes something like personhood or even divinity of the planet. Still today, scientists will speak of Earth systems sciences, rather than say the name "Gaia."

People have been aware of the importance of thinking globally for many decades, as ecological crises have made it glaringly apparent that human actions ripple across the planet, refusing to stay local. However, even when people think globally and account for the complexity of Earth systems, a psychospiritual connection to Earth is often left out of the equation.

In contrast, Ralph would have us direct our attention to analogies between person and planet, seeing Earth processes as "Gaia's alchemy," and not merely as the mechanical operations of a system.[26] After all, the Hermetic axiom "as above, so below" encapsulates the ancient idea that there is an analogy, a pattern correspondence, between the planetary macrocosm and the human microcosm. This correspondence reaches across many different oppositions, "Thus we could substitute any of the following pairs for 'macrocosm' and 'microcosm': universe/human, heaven/earth, spirit/matter, divine/human, world/person, inner world/outer world."[27]

All beings participate in the physical, psychic, and spiritual powers of existence, whether human or nonhuman. Indeed, the elements that compose all things are themselves "Living, intelligent, autono-

---

26. Ralph Metzner, *Green Psychology*, 25.
27. Ralph Metzner, *Green Psychology*, 25.

mous, spiritual forces, with modes of expression on many levels."[28] The
greening of psychology is not only about recognizing the ways that the
natural world shapes human consciousness. Ralph was focused on recognizing consciousness in the natural world, attuning to the intelligent
and spiritual forces of Earth and the cosmos, finding humankind and
the universe intimately intertwined. As above, so below, indeed.

Heeding the Call of the Soul
Brian Nattrass

Brian Nattrass, J.D., Ph.D., is a managing partner of Sustainability Partners, Inc.,
and is coauthor of *The Natural Step for Business, Community Sustainability Toolkit*
and *Dancing with the Tiger: Learning Sustainability Step-by-Natural Step.* Ralph served
as his dissertation chair in the Transformative Learning Program at CIIS in 1994.

Simply stated, of all the influential men in my life over the course of its
now seventy-five years, I hold Ralph to be the most profoundly positive
of all. I am deeply grateful for the insights and guidance that I received
from Ralph. In this essay I will describe a life-changing vision quest.

Growing up in the highly constrained spiritual landscape of prairie
Alberta in the 1940s and 1950s, I felt a profound yearning for which
I had no name, experiencing aching pangs for that which I could not
identify. Finally, in 1965, at the close of my first year at the University
of Alberta, and under the intense pressure of final exams for which I
was woefully unprepared, I felt myself inexplicably drawn for the first
time to the religion section of the main university library. There I
stumbled upon—or was guided to—the 1927 Evans-Wentz translation
of *The Tibetan Book of the Dead*, or, *The After-Death Experiences on
the Bardo Plane*. It changed my life forever. I knew then that I needed
to find a teacher who could guide me in the inner realms described in

---

28. Ralph Metzner, *Green Psychology*, 32.

these ancient teachings. But in Edmonton, Alberta, in 1965, at nineteen years of age, I had no idea how to find that person.

Then in 1971, after my second year of law school at the University of British Columbia in Vancouver, I came across a book entitled *Maps of Consciousness*, written by Ralph Metzner. Like *The Tibetan Book of the Dead* six years before, it opened a window to a new and revolutionary way of thinking for me, one that I readily gravitated toward. And with one very obvious advantage—Ralph Metzner was alive and on the path, not a historical figure in a dusty tome.

Inspired by these writings of pathways to inner worlds, in 1971 I undertook my first intentional deep inner journey with LSD. I conscientiously prepared set and setting as counseled by Ralph, waited until evening, lit a single candle in a dark room, and then waited with excited anticipation for something to happen. I was not disappointed. It was classic: leaving my body, soaring into the heart of the universe, meeting a friendly and welcoming God, being given life lessons—which like a diligent law student I blindly scribbled down in the darkness on forty pages of legal-size note paper. I eventually returned to everyday conscious, but with my mind irreversibly opened.

Over the next nineteen years I lived a full and active life, practicing mainly corporate law, writing Canada's first book on corporate finance for entrepreneurs, and getting married. We were blessed with our daughter Sarah, and at the same time I actively continued the inner search. It was like trying to ride two horses at the same time whose gaits are not aligned: switching back and forth from the outer world to the inner world, but not quite connecting the two and feeling that I was not fully succeeding at either. I read more of Ralph's work, including *Opening to Inner Light: The Transformation of Human Nature and Consciousness* (1986),[29] and the more that I read, the more intrigued I became and the stronger I felt the inner pull, and the more restless and dissatisfied I became with the conventional life that I was leading.

---

29. Reprinted under the title *The Unfolding Self* (2022).

Finally, I couldn't stand the inner conflict any longer. So in 1990, at the age of forty-four, I chose to wholeheartedly undertake an authentic, nondrug vision quest. Connections led me to a Canadian shaman living in the interior wilderness of the Selkirk Mountains of British Columbia, who was known to lead people on vision quests.

The price of admission was to go on a water-only fast for twenty-one days. This was to both raise the level of my energy field and to prove and strengthen my resolve and openness to receiving an inner vision. Three weeks without any food of any kind culminated in twenty-four hours of building a sweat lodge, chanting, building an enormous fire to heat the rocks for the sweat ceremony, followed by an extremely intense four rounds of blistering heat of almost suffocating intensity. It was after midnight, and after each round of searing heat, I did not have the breakthrough insight for which I was longing.

The shaman stated that most people experience their vision after one intense round of near-burning heat and rhythmic chanting in the sweat lodge. Failing that, almost everyone receives it by the end of the second round. Absolutely everyone receives it by the end of the third round. Everyone except me. I had nothing after four excruciating rounds in the totally dark and sweltering confines of the wilderness sweat lodge.

Dejected, and filled with negative self-talk, I hauled myself naked on hands and knees in the pitch blackness, weak and superheated, into a freezing cold mountain stream flowing directly from a nearby glacier. As soon as I collapsed into the frigid water, having given up my quest and let it go, large red letters appeared and flowed across my eyeballs in the utter blackness of the mountain night like words on the tape of a stock ticker: "BUSINESS FOR A BETTER PLANET." *Business for a Better Planet.* I had absolutely no idea what this meant! It was 1990, well before the corporate environmental movement had been born or I had even heard the word "sustainability."

Totally inspired by Ralph's writings on alchemical divination, and my psychedelic experiences of twenty years prior, I made the major life decision to take the words of my vision completely seriously and pursue it fully. Over the next four years, that decision was supported and confirmed by many highly synchronistic and fortuitous events as I left the practice of law, determined to discover what Business for a Better Planet actually meant. It was during this life-disruptive yet richly creative period that I experienced the reality of the famous words on the power of commitment that are often, but mistakenly, ascribed to Goethe.

> Until one is committed, there is hesitancy, the chance to draw back, always ineffectiveness. Concerning all acts of initiative (and creation) there is one elementary truth, the ignorance of which kills countless ideas and splendid plans: that the moment one definitely commits oneself, then Providence moves too. All sorts of things occur to help one that would never otherwise have occurred. A whole stream of events issues from the decision, raising in one's favor all manner of unforeseen incidents and meetings and material assistance, which no man could have dreamed would have come his way. Whatever you can do or dream you can, begin it. Boldness has genius, power and magic in it. Begin it now. (William Hutchinson Murray)

After I left the practice of corporate law, I made the further decision that I needed to educate myself in ecology as well as in the nature and processes of personal and organizational transformation if I wanted to understand what the words of my vision quest, Business for a Better Planet, actually meant.

So in relentless pursuit of that understanding, in the summer of 1994, I enrolled in a three-week immersion course in Deep Ecology led by Buddhist scholar and environmental activist Joanna Macy, which took place in the redwood country of Northern California. Joanna casually mentioned something that forever altered the course of my life.

She told me Ralph Metzner, whom I only knew and admired through his writings, was leading an experimental, online doctoral program in transformative learning at the California Institute of Integral

Studies—a school that as a Canadian lawyer I had never heard of. At the exact time that I was looking for an appropriate doctoral program to pursue my understanding and interpretation of the words of my vision quest—and which had to be nonresidential so that I could remain in Canada close to my daughter Sarah who was only five years old in 1994—I discovered this pioneering program on transformational learning that sounded perfect! It was incredible to me.

As soon as the Deep Ecology course was over, I drove straight to San Francisco to meet with Ralph for the first time to discuss enrolling in his doctoral program on transformative learning. As the quotation above states, "a whole stream of events issues from the decision, raising in one's favor all manner of unforeseen incidents and meetings and material assistance, which no man could have dreamed would have come his way."

For the next five years, from 1994 to 1999, Ralph was my dissertation supervisor at CIIS. Of his many essential contributions to my life during this period, the most important was how to integrate inner guidance with outer life. What I learned from my time with Ralph in particular, and my studies at CIIS in general, is that seers, sages, shamans, and scientists—inquiring minds of every age and every culture—all grappled with the nature of reality with the tools available to them. What was really critical for me was that Ralph had the personal credibility and stature in my eyes such that he was able to validate my own direct apprehending of the nature of reality. He inspired in me confidence in that "knowing"—such as the life-changing guidance received in my vision quest—my own *alchemical divination*, to use Ralph's words.

Based on my doctoral studies at CIIS and research on organizational learning and corporate environmental sustainability for my dissertation, entitled "The Natural Step: Corporate Learning and Innovation for Sustainability," my wife Mary and I came at last to grasp the meaning of my vision of Business for a Better Planet that I had received almost a decade earlier.

In 1999 Mary and I coauthored our first book, *The Natural Step for Business: Wealth, Ecology and the Evolutionary Corporation*.[30] This was the right book at the right time and became a best seller in the world of corporate sustainability books. It launched our careers as management consultants in the domain of environmental, social, and governance (ESG) matters with some of the world's most well-known brands.

Thanks to Ralph's inspiration and influence, we have been actively engaged in the work of sustainability strategy development, and world-view and behavioral transformation, in many major corporations and government agencies for almost twenty-five years, helping them to understand and mitigate their impacts on both the natural world and the human communities where they do business. Today, we continue to evolve in our understanding and implementation of Business for a Better Planet to help further the positive environmental, social, and governance transformation of organizations around the world—particularly with respect to the burgeoning climate crisis, which the corporate world is finally beginning to take seriously, spreading beyond early adopters.

As a fitting close to these words of appreciation, love, and respect for Ralph that I am writing near Vancouver today, a $312 million Veterans Village was announced for British Columbia, which will be home to Canada's first Centre for Clinical Excellence for veterans and first responders with PTSD. The new village will include government-sanctioned clinical trials into plant-based therapeutics and psychedelics such as cannabis, psilocybin, and MDMA, as well as ketamine. The announcement ended with the statement, "Eventually the centre will open for treatment to the public once clinical trials meet with regulatory approval."

I know Ralph is smiling.

---

30. Brian Nattrass and Mary Altomare, *The Natural Step for Business: Wealth, Ecology and the Evolutionary Corporation* (Gabriola Island, Canada: New Society Publishers, 1999).

Ecological Interconnectedness
Jan Edl Stein

Jan Edl Stein, M.F.T., is a licensed psychotherapist and director of Holos Institute where she provides clinical supervision and directs a certificate program in ecopsychology.

This tribute was spoken at Ralph Metzner's memorial on May 24, 2019, at the Unitarian Universalist Church in San Francisco.

I stepped into the shoes of Alan Levin to take over the helm of Holos Institute—a nonprofit counseling and educational center based upon principles of ecopsychology. Ralph was a close friend of Alan's and supporter of Holos and ecopsychology. Ralph's circle was wide.

While Ralph's fame is based on his studies of psychedelics and explorations of consciousness . . . he was first and foremost a clinical psychologist and his orientation was fundamentally ecological. Let's not forget that his website and associated nonprofit is named Green Earth Foundation. In 1999 he published a book called *Green Psychology: Transforming Our Relationship to the Earth*. Ralph was one of the pioneers who understood the radical shift in consciousness that is needed to turn around the human relationship to the environment. He was also one of the early proponents of expanded states of consciousness—what Joanna Macy has coined "the ecological self."

I invite you to imagine Ralph standing here quite dapper in his iconic cap and colorful vest, and speaking in his soft, lyrical voice: "*Green Psychology: Transforming Our Relationship to the Earth*! . . . we are talking about a fundamental re-envisioning of what psychology is, or what it should have been in the first place—a revision that would take the ecological context of human life into account."

Ralph came to speak at the very first Holos fundraiser. He was energetic, enthusiastic, and full of good vibes! Underneath everything was his comprehension of an ecological consciousness and what was happening to our planet. At his core was a being of pure love for this Earth.

Ralph had the extraordinary capacity to see this interconnected dimension and apply it to all levels of human awareness. He held a profound awareness of our ecological crisis. Ralph's legacy calls forth a deep ecology that I sincerely hope will come to permeate our lives. I am deeply honored to have known him.

Artistic Expression

Geomancy and Goddess Imagery
Christopher Castle

Christopher Castle is a British-born painter and printmaker. He exhibits his work widely in the United States and Europe. The theme of his work is ancient consciousness and art, focused on ancient cosmologies and the traditions of sacred place. He regularly sojourns to Romania and Kathmandu, Nepal.

When I think of Ralph I see his gentle humanity and a slightly wry smile layered with a wisdom of ages. For years I knew Ralph only as the coauthor of *The Psychedelic Experience*. In 1965 in Paris I had my first LSD trip. My young eyes were stripped bare, leaving me wondering how to integrate such extreme vision into daily life. A door was flung open and no one seemed to know how to approach the vista beyond. Where were the maps? Not easily identifiable in any Western tradition that I'd ever heard about. In a few days I was to embark on my first days at art school, and suddenly I had been introduced to the timely gift of a completely unique visual experience.

Back in London, even in my first few days at college, I could recognize the few other "experienced" students. Soon I was pointed toward *The Psychedelic Experience* by a friend and immediately rushed to Watkins bookstore, that wondrous cave of esoteric riches, where I bought my copy.

At the earliest opportunity my friends and I took our next journey with LSD, accompanied by the guidance spelled out in this unique guidebook. Based on careful reading we were curious, excited, and filled with anticipation. Already familiar with the Evans-Wentz translation of the *Tibetan Book of the Dead*, the adaptation to psychedelic language was fascinating to me. The trip was utterly transformed by the powerful and precise Tibetan structure of bardo worlds. Instead of being blown around by the cosmic winds, we had a guide who would take us in and out of the energetic fields, returning us with a new understanding. The triumvirate of Leary, Alpert, and Metzner became heroes with the key to these realms of mind and spirit.

My work in painting and printmaking developed over the next few years as I explored the ancient landscape of Britain, and then Europe. I had begun to realize that the prehistoric megalithic sites that pervaded the historically layered landscape invoked a kind of consciousness that paralleled the knowledge of the East.

Some years later after moving to California I heard that Ralph Metzner was academic dean at the California Institute of Integral Studies. Through other contacts there I had arranged to show my paintings and prints in the hallways of the Institute. By then I had opened a small gallery in Point Reyes Station in West Marin County called Spotted Fawn, after the Hopi name for the Earth and its sacred places.

At Spotted Fawn Geomantic Arts we held events and exhibits based on the subject, bringing numerous specialized speakers and artists from around the United States and from Europe. I wanted to meet Ralph and at last I was brought into his office at CIIS. I have to admit to being in awe, but I was soon put at ease by Ralph's personable nature and openness. We had a brief conversation and he encouraged me to put on a show for my etchings based on the prehistoric Goddess figurines of Europe along with landscape paintings of ancient stone circle sites.

Soon after, Ralph's book *The Well of Remembrance* was published, demonstrating his broad knowledge and understanding of mythology in Northern Europe. The mythic layer of history is a major key to the full story that geomancy suggests. The important figure of an Earth Goddess is often referred to directly or obliquely in ancient myths while folk art and folktales with their place-specific roots manifest aspects of the meaning of the Goddess. At this time, I was fortunate to meet archaeologist Marija Gimbutas whom Ralph hailed as substantiating his work in this area.

■ Fig. 39. Marija Gimbutas
(From the collection of
Ralph Metzner)

Humanity's loss of the sense of the feminine and the subsequent imbalance of male and female is seen for example in the relentless exploitation of the natural world. The long history of male dominance is in sharp contrast to that revealed by the archaeology of prehistoric feminism that the pervasive female deities indicate.

I often felt that this connection with Ralph was somehow preordained. We had several encounters over the years, and I was always thrilled that he would bring his insights to the various projects I worked on. My

■ Fig. 40. Christopher Castle and his wife, Yana Womack, with Ralph and Cathy, 2013 (Photo from the collection of Ralph Metzner)

own work with Goddess imagery has been an exploration of another layer of consciousness, comparable to that which Ralph showed through his work. This Goddess imagery work has vital importance today in restoring and redefining broader cultural depth and balance.

Cosmic Manners: A Song for Ralph Metzner
Leigh Marz

Leigh Marz advises cross-sector collaborations and is coauthor of Golden: The Power of Silence in a World of Noise.

Ralph was my mentor and friend, and—for a decade—I served as a board member for the Green Earth Foundation, which he cofounded with his wife, Cathy.

A few months after Ralph's passing, I attended a medicine circle—it was my first since his death. I'd hoped Ralph might pay me a visit me. He did—by way of song.

In this particular circle, we closed the evening with each member offering a spontaneous and original song to consecrate aspects of our journey. We were reminded that this was not a performance; it could include words or be sung as a wordless melody. We did four rounds of singing, passing a rattle and a talking stick—or in this case a *singing* stick—around the circle. This song, "Cosmic Manners," came to me in one of those rounds.

For those of us who are *mortified* by the idea of singing publicly—much less composing a song on the spot—it is an extraordinary exercise in humility and trust. It's also a potent way to begin the integration process without reengaging our habitual forms of narration. I recall Ralph using this method at times, I believe, for these very reasons.

The term "cosmic manners" describes the guidance and, occasionally, the etiquette that Ralph offered for when we're in a nonordinary state of consciousness. In this simple song, I'm speaking to three lessons

I learned from Ralph. I invite you to add your own lessons, or verses, to this melody.

Cosmic Manners

Chorus
I learned my cosmic manners from
Ralph Metzner, I call him friend though
Some knew him better.
I do, however, have the
Great pleasure
Of tending to the things that
He loved most. (2x)

Verse one
His beloved wife, Cathy,
His daughter, Sophia,
His stepson, Eli, and his
Twenty-something books! (2x)

Lesson one: We honor the memory of our teachers and friends by tending to the people and things they loved most. In doing so, we build a bridge between the worlds.

Repeat Chorus

Verse two
If you come across a guide, be sure to be polite,
And ask them to join you by your side. (2x)

Lesson two: When we meet an entity—an animal spirit, an ancestor, or an energy form—don't forget to *ask permission* if we'd like them to become our guide. Don't assume that just because they've shown themselves that they are ours for the taking—*ask*. It's just good manners!

Repeat Chorus

Verse three
Intention, Attention, Awareness. (4x)

Lesson three: The words Intention, Attention,
   Awareness are instructions for nonordinary states of
   consciousness.

First, we set our Intentions—What is our question? What do we want to better understand or remember? If we're in circle, our Intention will be spoken aloud. If it is wandering or untethered—he'll ask you to refine it. We hold our Intention throughout the journey.

Next, we become receptive and attentive. If we have guides—which Ralph certainly encouraged—he'd often say we "pay" our guides by paying attention to what they show us. Ralph emphasized the importance of reciprocity in this relationship.

And finally—with a clear Intention and receptive Attention— we've met the conditions for Awareness. Typically, we are shown many things—our Awareness is what we are able to absorb and, potentially, integrate into our lives.

Ralph frequently emphasized these words—Intention, Attention, Awareness—by enunciating each (since they sound a bit similar in English) and distinguishing them from one another.

These three words were important enough to Ralph that he posted them in his office, on his mirror where he got ready in the morning and at night, and—at the end of his life—at his bedside.

The musical score for "Cosmic Manners" is available on the Green Earth Foundation website, www.greenearthfound.org.

The Bardo Blues
Phil Wolfson

Phil Wolfson, M.D., is the president and CEO of the nonprofit Ketamine Research Foundation and directs the training of KAP practitioners through the Ketamine Training Center. He is the co-creator of a new psychotherapy modality based on use of the legal psychedelic medicine ketamine—Ketamine Assisted Psychotherapy (KAP). Phil is author of *Noe: A Father-Son Song of Love, Life, Illness, and Death*. He and Ralph shared a psychotherapy office for several years.

I knew Ralph for many years. He helped me in some difficult times. He was a deep and marvelous therapist and took me through a depression with unforgettable kindness and several skillfully applied medicine sessions that I can still recall decades later. And, in turn, I helped him as he aged. There was an abiding friendship and mutual respect for our different styles.

■ Fig. 41. Phil Wolfson and Ralph (Photo by Cathy Coleman)

Let me tell of the passions, creativity, and confidence that would erupt from the man. In an ayahuasca group he led, a notable woman of the tantric sexual persuasion was disruptive, taking up the space, and blocking Ralph's leadership. He tolerated it for a while, attempting to keep her in, but her intrusions and fuss were too much for the group to meld and continue. He did not mince words, drew himself up, and escorted her out of the hall and out of the building. On return he settled the group down for the ecstatic and profound experiences and integration that moved us into an impeccable flow and unity. I learned from that to have the courage to set boundaries no matter the "who."

At Albert Hofmann's one hundredth birthday party in Basel in 2006 Ralph took to the stage in a most unforgettable moment of the celebration. The stage was full of our psychedelic brethren, the diminutive birthday boy to Ralph's right, the audience full of the all of us. One hundred years of life with vitality, proof that psychedelic medicines did not limit longevity, spirit, or the fun of being alive with all its ups and downs. *Au contraire.* It was our celebration, an embrace of the fecundity and richness of this persistence to expand our beings, no matter the penalties or judgments. After all, history is ultimately about who it is who tells the story.

So, to get on with it, Ralph is center stage and begins to dance and sing, leading a Sufi-like move that he teaches all of us and he sings and we dance and trance. He is beaming. It is for Albert and all of us facing our own fate at some unknown moment. Albert is moving, the stage is full of dance and chorus, a thousand people moving in unison in the auditorium and Ralph is teaching, leading ecstatic dance, celebrating Albert and life and impermanence, inspiration and daring. And the entrancement of being an adept who knew he had much to offer and did not hesitate to do so.

All Hail Ralph Metzner! For all he became and the grand offering of his life, wisdom, creativity, courage, and uniqueness.

The Chorus of the Bardo Blues
I'm comin' through the Bardo
I'm comin' through the Bardo
I don't know if I'll make it
I don't know if I'll make it
Or make it through alive
Or make it through alive
I've got the Bardo Blues
I've got the Bardo Blues

RALPH METZNER

The Winged Heart Rises
Jais Booth

Jais Booth, M.A., is a lifelong artist whose art is linked with four decades of discipline and study in Eastern and Western forms of alchemy. She started the Red Door Gallery and Collective in Oakland, which showcased art that transforms individuals. After the Red Door closed, she cofounded the Liminal Art Salon as part of Star Mountain School of Liminal Art.

After the heyday of the late '60s in San Francisco, in 1972, at the age of twenty-four, I was given a copy of Ralph Metzner's new book, *Maps of Consciousness*. I read it from beginning to end, riveting through the chapters on the I Ching, tarot, tantra, alchemy, astrology, and Actualism. I had been on a journey to find a spiritual teacher, and by reading this book I learned about the School of Actualism in Valley Center, California. At that time Ralph was the supervising teacher at the Center where lightwork energy classes were taught.

After a trip to Northern California to pick up my belongings so that I could move to Southern California, I returned to the school—and I entered upon the most amazing, in-depth teaching of the actual design of human consciousness I have ever encountered. I have trea-

■ Fig. 42. *The Winged Heart Rises* © Jais Booth 2019

sured memories of the many sessions Ralph led, both in small group classes and at the retreat center, Star Mountain, in Idyllwild.

The story of our connection would have ended there but for Fate. After years of putting aside my lifelong love of art for spiritual learning and teaching, a hunger to fulfill that part of me arose and could no longer be denied. I sold my condo in Costa Mesa, California, and moved back to the Bay Area to study for my master's degree in the Arts and Consciousness program at John F. Kennedy University in Berkeley, California (JFKU). The reconnection occurred through our mutual friend, Alan Levin, who had recommended JFKU.

I was on my way to a discovery of art as influenced by deep spiritual work that profoundly affected my life. All the exhibitions and creative work I did after JFKU were influenced by Actualism Lightwork and the sessions I had with Ralph. I was also grateful to experience Ralph's work as a psychotherapist, and well as the guided subsequent explorations with lightwork on the creative process. After graduating, I spent a couple of years exhibiting at the Red Door Gallery and Collective in downtown Oakland that I had founded with another JFKU graduate. After the gallery closed, I formed the Liminal Art Salon® with a poet friend, Cheja, and we continued exhibiting with two significant shows: *Oracle: Visionary Art Expressing the Prophetic Voice* (2011) and *The Poet and the Artist in Aphrodite's Garden* (2014).

This last show was a very important part of my reconnection with Ralph. In June 2014 Ralph participated in a panel discussion of his book *The Six Pathways of Destiny*.

I am very grateful that my life and my destiny have come under the wing of a teacher and mystic such as Ralph Metzner. My painting *The Winged Heart Rises* (2019) was influenced by Ralph leaving us on this physical plane for another journey.

Invocation to the Web of Ralph's Life
Silvia Nakkach

Silvia Nakkach, M.A., M.M.T, is a Grammy-nominated musician and a pioneer in the field of sound and consciousness transformation. An interdisciplinary educator, vocal artist, author, and a former music psychotherapist, Silvia serves on the faculty of CIIS. For many years, she has collaborated with Claudio Naranjo's SAT Institute, and she has devoted more than forty-two years to the study of Classical Indian Music under the direction of the late Maestro Ali Akbar Khan and other living masters of the Dhrupad Chant. Silvia is the founder and artistic director of the International Vox Mundi School of Sound and the Voice. She has released many CD albums, and her latest book is *Free Your Voice*. Visit www.voxmundiproject.com.

■ Fig. 43. Silvia Nakkach and Ralph (Photo by Cathy Coleman)

I met Ralph in March 1982 at the Slide Ranch Paul Winter Music Improvisation workshop, where a combination of my broken English and open voice drew Ralph's attention. We played music in a small group, laughed, and then he drove me home. At the time I was living in Claudio Naranjo's house in Berkeley, helping Claudio with his books.

Ralph and I had a lot to talk about. He was interested in Afro-Brazilian Yoruba magic and trance that was part of my upbringing and musical life. Ralph became my musical friend. We collaborated on workshops, CDs, and magical journeys to the depths of Amazon mysteries.

Ralph always answered the phone when I called late at night, and he was a master of quantum listening—"listening to more than one reality simultaneously"—as defined by Pauline Oliveros. Quantum listening is a continuum field of listening at the edge of local and nonlocal realms, far beyond hearing. *Diving for Treasures*, his poetry book, is an apt description of how Ralph listened to the interdependence of self and many worlds and ways of spiritual longing.

In the spirit of what Ralph called *re-membering*, I wrote a sound poem titled "Invocation to the Web of Ralph's Life" as an invocation inspired by words and sacred presences of Ralph's books and poems. The complete invocation can be accompanied by the music titled "Raga Orb," by Matt Levine, available on YouTube (www.youtube.com/watch?v=MUib4GAOKaA).

You Are Here!

because...

...the sea is blue
and in love
with the sky

...Mother Earth is still
GREEN
thriving
for more time
without end

...your trees sing in harmony with
the seasons of
the Great Forest

...your enlightened
nature has arrived to **the EDGE of Everywhere**

...your visions of the
beyond-ness
will continue
unfolding EVERYWHERE

...your innocence
is playing the
infinite music
of the
spiritual
overtones

...your CURIOSITY
for the
deep mystery
will never end

because...

...your heart has
opened to the **DEEP**
LONGING of
the Enchanters —
the ones who
journey through
the power
of sound
to **attract**
the spirit world

...WE have been
charmed by the **melodiousness**
of your teachings...
and the **COLORS**
of your mind

because...

You are here because
I am with you
and the words
written in this song
are the same that are
written in my heart

You are here because
    you can't
        stop
listening
    to the
        BREATH
of God

because... # You Are Here!

You are here because
        you have indulged
        the boundless imagination
        of the poet and
                the seer

You are here because
    your poems became
        chants
and chants have made
your voice *timeless*

You are here because
your Prayer for
        the *Web of Life*
        has elicited the
tasteful groove
of *amrita* - the ageless
nectar of *deathlessness*

because...

You are here
because
    your search for
harmonizing humanity
with EARTH and SPIRIT
    is vital

You are here because
        the door to the
back of your heart
        was left OPEN,
and WE are inside and
        don't want to leave

You are here because
    the Goddess has
fallen in love with your
    transcendent wisdom
and your **SILENCE**

You are here because
you have conquered
the *Great Hall of Peace*
that comes after
        all is fulfilled

You are here because
    you are the *Great Father*
        of all-embracing Light
The light that knows
        no more struggle

because...

You are here because
    your net of treasures
    is interconnected
to the INFINITE —
    like the dreams
    of the *Awakened One*

You are here because
I am with you
and the words
written in this song
are the same that are
written in my heart

You Are Here!

because...

...**you are** guarded by
the Jaguar, the Dragon,
and the
Wolf of the North

...**your body** has merged,
turning, and
spinning with the
Great Serpent Mother

...**your** music is forever
pulsing with the streams
of *the River of Time*

...**your** laughter delights
the heart of the **dakini clouds.**
They are dancing
with you freely.
Now there is no trace of pain

...**you are** the master of
remembering how to re-member.
Now there is hope of **Wholeness**

because...

...**your** compassionate
wisdom found
the **PEARL**
and the way
back to the Kingdom

...**you** have
heard the
voice of divination
and made the
UNSEEN realms your
home. Now there is the
sound of OM

...**you are** welcomed
and adored
by the majesty
of the Mother-Father

...**your** ancient voice
lures our
protective allies,
and **WE thank you!**

...**you** have become
one with the spirit medicine
that is here to stay,
and WE thank you!

because...

You are here because
I am with you
and the words
written in this song
are the same that are
written in my heart

You Are Here!

because...

...because you are the **Great Mother**
who compassionately manifests
in whatever form is necessary to heal
the neglected CORNERS **of the human psyche**

because...your generous awareness
is like the love of the father
watching over his
children playing at life

because...you are
SET FREE
having drunk from
the **Well of Remembrance**

because...your
unobstructed confidence
in healing the
human is like the human
ESSENCE of the sky,
unborn and naturally
abiding as the same

because...you have discovered
a way to bless us from the
quietest place

because...

because...
the Mother of Time
has granted
you the
unconditional
treasure of
pure samhadi

because...you
are the STORYTELLER
who left
us millions of words
filled with mysteries
still to be revealed
by our
worldly sleepiness

because...we will be
forever flowing together
INTERCONNECTED
in the Wheel of Samsara

because...

You are here because
I am with you
and the words
written in this song
are the same that are
written in my heart

You Are Here!

because...you are
resting now in the
twilight throne of
the **Victorious One!**

because...

because...you are the
Grateful One! Who tenderly
shared
DIVINE gratitude
even during the
time of the *Last Breath*

because...we need to tune INWARD
and listen to the
spiritual overtones of our beings

because...you have
passed through the
GATELESS GATE
and now walk freely
between *Heaven and Earth*

because...

because...as you said:
"When I die, I'm only dead! I'm not gone.
Now rebirth is coming... Looking at the Wheel
As the Worlds are turning
I am coming...
I am coming through the Bardo!"

because...

You are here because
I am with you
and the words
written in this song
are the same that are written
in my heart and today sings your
Bardo Blues!

Mystical Living: Classical and Improv
Maria Mangini

Mariavittoria Mangini, Ph.D., FNP, is Professor Emerita of Nursing at Holy Names University in Oakland, where she was the director of the Family Nurse Practitioner program for twenty years. She cofounded the Women's Visionary Council, a nonprofit organization that supports investigations into nonordinary forms of consciousness and organizes gatherings of researchers, healers, artists, and activists whose work explores these states. She has written extensively on the impact of psychedelic experiences.

Until recently, I didn't know that Ralph trained as a classical pianist as a child. In his sixties he took up jazz improvisation, and by the first time I heard him play, he had been studying jazz weekly for years, playing, singing, composing, and even producing two CDs.

I first heard Ralph's music at a Holiday Inn in San Jose, California. We were at the first "official" Psychedelic Science Conference, and Ralph's post-conference seminar was assigned to the room next to where the Women's Visionary Council was also presenting an event. He was playing an upright piano, and his enthusiasm for the tune had recruited all of the participants in his workshop to a loud sing-along about humanity's metaphysical predicament.

Next door, the WVC members were more quietly comparing notes on what we had seen and experienced at the conference, strategizing about how to correct the continuing absence of women from most of the conference platforms, and how to align our desire to be seen and heard with our ideas about privacy and security. Coming through the wall, Ralph's group's unabashed rendition of "The Bardo Blues" was energetically very different from our workshop, where we weren't really in a jolly mood, and I went over to see him about the clamor.

Although Ralph graciously reduced the volume, he also laughingly encouraged us to celebrate the occasion: practices and people, mostly women, who had been deeply under cover were beginning to bring their wisdom and experience into the light. He memorably suggested that it was time to give up some of our habits of secrecy and concealment, to sing out, and to have more fun! He invited us to join the merriment, as he had often invited interested spectators and inquirers to join in the various iterations of cosmic theater that he had been producing since the heyday of the psychedelic pageant[1] at the Hitchcock estate in Millbrook.

I didn't really get to know Ralph until this century, but when we met I recognized his ability to engage with the inexplicable, the mysterious, and the peculiar as something characteristic of the goings-on at Millbrook, even though, by the time I arrived there, the scene had devolved, literally and figuratively, into a goat rodeo—"an operation or undertaking involving an unnecessarily large number of people, most of them contributing nothing or who would actually impede progress." The police were hovering, eviction was threatened, and, yes, there was a temperamental mother goat in the yard. The inhabitants were still expecting the improbable and were alert for the miraculous.

More than a year before, I had accidentally stumbled onto an experience of LSD-inspired insight, but I had no idea how to reach that place again. "Experienced" people were not numerous then, and Millbrook seemed like a magical paradise populated by people who were adept at navigating various states of consciousness. I was fascinated, but the experiment in mystical living was breaking down under the unending stream of visitors. In order not to be sent home, I learned to blend into the background so as not to bring displeasure on whoever let me in, or cause trouble for their accommodating minors. This turned out to be a useful habit during the decades when the use of substances to alter consciousness was held to be a thoroughly criminal act. Even after my abiding appreciation for psychedelics brought me to undertake the formal study of their possibilities in a doctoral program, I suffered from a

---

1. In the mid-1960s the Castalia Foundation produced psychedelic theatrical events.

habit of backward-glancing, worried that there would be consequences for my unorthodox interests.

I was fortunate that nursing, a spacious profession, was ready to allow me to study any subject that interested me, as long as I would consider it rigorously. Still, when, early in my doctoral career, a senior researcher wrote to me dismissing my plan to interview people about the long-range impact of their historic psychedelic experiences as unscientific, I wondered whether I was completely out of line.

In his view, neither using my membership in the research population to gain access to a study sample nor my interest in investigating lived experience fit established scientific standards that demanded detached statistical measurement and the exclusion of null hypotheses.

I was aware that his objections were the result of his unfamiliarity with the process of qualitative inquiry, but he was entrenched in a position of power, and I was a beginning researcher. I had just published a 40,000-word article on LSD as a possible treatment for alcoholism, and I was still trying on my new identity as a scholar. It seemed to me the study of psychedelics was uniquely suited to qualitative investigation rather than empirical reductionism.

To use a musical analogy, my ideas about how to orchestrate a composition on the transformative potential of psychedelics did not seem to harmonize well with his. I wasn't ready for a solo, but I was hoping to improvise with an ensemble, rather than to have each note directed by a conductor. Apparently, I did not know the score, and I was not being invited to play along.

The habit of trying to remain invisible might have settled into a permanent occupational deformity, but I got some timely help from Ralph in the first summer after I completed my doctorate. I was attending one of many events at which Ralph was a featured and honored speaker. During a question-and-answer period, someone asked him about the potential of psychedelics to be used to treat the abuse of other substances, specifically alcohol. To my everlasting surprise, Ralph turned to answer the questioner by saying, "You should ask Dr. Mangini here about that. She is an expert in that area." This was the first time that anyone had used my new title, and the first occasion on which I was acknowledged as having expert knowledge of specific scientific content. This recognition, by an eminent person whose work I knew and whose friendship and regard I valued, was an important turning point for me. Ralph made me welcome in the world of scholarship.

That was twenty years ago. I no longer need to conceal my interests, and I have begun to teach some of the history of both psychedelic enthusiasm and suppression. I'm grateful for the opportunities I've had to share a forum, an audience, or another chance to express an opinion with Ralph. We didn't always agree, but we always had a spirited discussion. Ralph will, of course, be remembered as a psychedelic pioneer. His intellectual curiosity, his capacity to move among diverse realms of consciousness, his reasoned exposition of patterns that connect, and his fearless willingness to confront complex issues, all made him a formidable figure, and one who was unafraid to express some decided opinions and some radical ideas. He also is remembered as a gracious and generous teacher and colleague who used his distinguished status and his acknowledged authority to blaze trails for new players. He invited those who worked and played with him to extemporize on the spot, to work out riffs and variations, and occasionally to take a solo.

Ralph embodied an attitude, an approach, and a way of thinking that was remarkable in its spaciousness and grace. He was like a friendly neighborhood idea-musician with whom one could get together for a relaxed and improvisational thought-jam session. This contrasted with my earlier experience with the more inflexible version of psychedelic science, like the difference between classical music and jazz.[2]

With classical music there is a composer and a conductor who controls each musician's input to create a harmonious but hierarchical and

---

2. I am indebted to Eugene Holland for the jazz classical analogy. Eugene W. Holland, "Studies in Applied Nomadology: Jazz Improvisation and Post-Capitalist Markets," in *Deleuze and Music*, eds. Ian Buchanan and Marcel Swiboda (Edinburgh: Edinburgh University Press, 2004), 20–35.

static composition, in conformity with a code established in advance. In jazz improvisation there is no need for a consistent leader and the music is a process of continual creation, new every time it is played. The players' parts intersect and blend as a democratically developed vision in which the process is more important than any finished product. It's really good for one's musicianship to jam with someone who has a lot more chops than you do, and I am so grateful that I sometimes got to play with Ralph.

Conversations with Ralph
Susan Wright

Susan Wright, Ed.D., is a semiretired Canadian living in Vancouver, British Columbia. She is a teacher, writer, scholar practitioner, artist, and world traveler, and specializes in the development of consciousness through coaching and workshop facilitation.

I began this writing by reflecting on my experience of being at annual retreats with Ralph in the high desert, and the way he ingeniously designed and facilitated the space for my explorations, the revelations I

■ Fig. 44. Portrait of Ralph Metzner by Susan Wright

experienced, and the resulting slow climb out of a deep dark night[3] that had overtaken my life for several years. I wanted to use this opportunity to express my gratitude for the gift of these inner world journeys.

I intended to tell the story of how at one retreat Ralph had helped me with the idea that I could combine art in some way with an exploration of dying. I had recently lost a half-dozen loved ones and was reeling from the weight of so many deaths. Through our divinations, I was able not only to mourn them but to confront my own death as well, emerging with a sense of peace and gratitude that transformed my sense of self. I have since created and facilitated over twenty workshops called "The Art of Dying" to normalize the discussion of death and the preparation for it. Each of the six sessions in the process includes an art form. Because Ralph always wanted to know, "What are you going to do about it?"

Ralph was also the inspiration for me returning to painting. He encouraged me to integrate my experiences through simple art processes, like intersecting mandalas on large sheets of newsprint. I found these exercises on the mornings after our journeys especially helpful. They allowed me to reconnect with my creative self through colorfully expressing my insights in drawings. I had painted as a young person, following in my artist mother's footsteps. But when she died I discarded it and turned my attention to achieving material success in the outside world. Now, in my sixties with more time, I had been stirred to paint again.

That was the idea for my contribution. Something different happened. I struggled to describe the impact Ralph had on a very difficult few years in my life, how with his guidance I had reclaimed the lost relationships with my mother, my wild feminine, and Mother Earth, integrating the masculine/feminine poles of my psyche into a mystical

---

3. I tell the full story of my journey with Ralph over these years and his pivotal effect on my life in my book, *Dark Night: Reclaiming the Discarded Other on the Journey to Wholeness* (Vancouver, Canada: TPC Publications, 2020).

Oneness. As a distraction, because the writing seemed far too esoteric, I began searching for a photograph I could include with this submission. Unexpectedly, I found a picture of Ralph that called out to me, seeming to exude the qualities I had been trying and failing to describe in words—his intelligence, compassion, intense interest, wisdom, and caring. I decided to paint his portrait.

At first, I was uncertain about how it would unfold. I have been doing portraits of family members lately but I didn't know Ralph well outside his role as a guru, sage, teacher, shaman, and wise elder. I wasn't sure I could capture his essence in acrylics. Little by little, though, he began to speak to me as I added the paint. We communicated in an unspoken correspondence between his emerging image and my layering of color on the canvas, slowly intuiting through our inner dialogue where to apply the paint, a line here, a highlight there, then standing back to see what it had to say. We continued this dance over the course of a week. I would paint for a couple of hours, then sit in my chair across the room and engage with him, seeing and sensing him, until I could discern where I needed to go next. Back and forth we went as he slowly emerged from the canvas, his gentle eyes and boyish grin guiding me toward a resolution, just as he had done many times before.

As I was painting, I was also reliving all the hours I spent with Ralph on retreats, recalling the huge impact he had on my life, all the ways in which I have been made whole, re-membered. In a way, portrait painting is remembering too, beginning with a bounded openness, an intention, and allowing the lights and shadows to emerge, the face to take shape as it materializes out of the canvas.

I thought the process might be seen as one of Ralph's divinations, an exploration of our depths to unveil inner truths, to connect with our Divine being, and guide us toward our futures. Only this time I was the diviner, allowing the inner nature of who he was to come into view in a correspondence between my hand and his spirit.

But that is only one side of the conversation. The other is the continuing impact Ralph has had on me as the painter. What further hidden knowledge might he share with me? How might this bond between artist and subject offer me a further insight or integration? As I have thought about it, I am left with the feeling that this has been a continuation of my grieving process, revisiting a phase of my life that changed me significantly and the person who catalyzed it. A ritual expression in this portrait and these words—Ralph was a man of ritual—mourning his loss and all the others that drew me to him in the first place. Only now I am able to face into these necessary losses, including my own mortality, with the spiritual mystery of death a comforting companion.

The portrait is now finished. Well, a portrait is not really ever finished, maybe complete for the moment, and I am almost ready to let him go. It has been lovely to have him around. I hope I have captured my affection and respect for Ralph, and my immense gratitude. I remember one evening as our group scattered for the night, calling out to him, "Vous êtes un genie, Ralph!" He simply smiled, then turned toward his cabin. I was in awe of his grace and wisdom. I am still.

Death, Conscious Dying, and the Afterlife

Ralph Metzner: Bodhisattva
Chellis Glendinning

Chellis Glendinning, Ph.D., is a retired psychologist whose specialty has been recovery from traumatic experience. She is also the author of seven nonfiction books, two novels, a poetry chapbook, a bilingual opera, and hundreds of essays in newspapers and journals. Her latest books are *In the Company of Rebels* and *Objetos*. She lives in Chuquisaca, Bolivia.

◆ ◆ ◆

In Buddhism, a bodhisattva is a person who is able to reach nirvana but delays doing so out of compassion so as to save suffering beings.

Ralph Metzner was a bodhisattva.

He was ever dedicated to his life's mission—up to his last days— learning, teaching, and writing for the good of all sentient beings. He was sharp of mind, as humble as a pebble, and a master of living in wide-eyed wonder. But most relevant to the one quality I wish to high-light: he was generous beyond bounds.

Of course, I had heard of Ralph long before I met him. He was a card-carrying member of the Harvard trio of consciousness travelers that in 1963 found its ground for exploration in a farmhouse in Millbrook, New York. All three were clinical psychologists and naturally shared a passion for discovering the nature of reality as well as the possibilities offered by LSD for exploring it.

I saw that white clapboard dwelling on a motor trip with W. H. "Ping" Ferry some thirty-five years later. It was far grander than it appeared from the road. It had fifty-five bedrooms and during its three-year High Holy Days was visited by such luminaries-of-the-times as Allen Ginsberg, Charlie Mingus, Rosemary Woodruff, Alan Watts, Humphrey Osmond, and R. D. Laing.

Meanwhile, I was a University of California/Berkeley radical stu-dent of social sciences, both via books and via the streets. When the 1969 issue of the *Whole Earth Catalog* came out, we all rushed to thumb through its diverse submissions and ponder living in a handcrafted log cabin lit by a kerosene lamp. That year the catalog presented a review of Charles Tart's *Altered States of Consciousness*. Except for marijuana smoking, one acid trip, multiple hits of mescaline, and my naturally itinerant consciousness, I knew little on the subject. Tart's book looked enticing. Ergo, when Ralph began to share his insight into, and experiences of, altered states through books and classes, I took note.

We finally did meet at a 1994 gathering at England's Dartington Hall of our mass-technology-critiquing Jacques Ellul Society. There big-system conceptualizations using sociopolitical language dominated the analysis, yet Ralph's choice of words presented a softer, often humorous, yet adamantly resolute take on the topic. After seeing him in action, I ordered his books and tapes that had diamond-like facets of mind-travel, shamanism, and alchemical transformation.

Of particular interest to me was *The Well of Remembrance: Rediscovering the Earth Wisdom Myths of Northern Europe*. In these ancestral legends, with their separation of spirit and nature, lay the foundation of European expansionism, just as they revealed the visionary possibilities of ceremonial plants contained in their practices.

But I didn't really know Ralph, so how rare it was that we launched our friendship via letters, emails, and packages after I moved from my land-of-birth to the *altiplano* of Bolivia. I was sending out my Bolivia Letter to an ever-morphing group of friends and colleagues. The Letter is an entirely irregular endeavor that to this day goes out maybe three times a year, maybe once a year, or not at all. As if by a tap on the shoulder from the spirits, I had included Ralph as a recipient and—lo and behold!—he mindfully wrote me back *immediately* after reading each one. I mean, within a half hour. Often he praised me for the compassion he saw in me, always encouraged me to continue documenting the cultural differences I was encountering. I was astonished . . . first that he perceived such qualities through mere words—and then that he cared enough to cheer me on in my explorations.

One day I sent out a note asking if anyone would like to participate in a tea exchange. You see, when I arrived in Bolivia, the country had not yet jumped headlong into the corporate global economy. I think we could all agree that such is a political/ecological quality worthy of admiration; the food in the market—sold by the grower/collector and purchased from a blanket on the ground—was local, probably organic, and available only in season. So there were few packaged natural-food products and certainly no tea from England! But after a few years the lack of choice began to wear on me. The entire stock of available black tea consisted of *té clásico* and *té clásico con canela*, in the case of the latter mixed with cinnamon, all bundled and boxed by the Bolivian tea company Windsor.

But let's face the cold facts: if you're a fanatic of internationally-grown-and-marketed tea to the point of even devouring books on the history of the tea trade, after a spell you can get a longing for an old favorite—which in my case was Lapsang souchon. I sent out a proposal to my friends: I offered to send quantities of what Bolivia Letter recipients in the United States, Canada, and Europe did not have— lozenges made of the infamous mind-bending Bolivian *coca* leaf[1]—and in exchange they would send me packets of, you guessed it, Lapsang souchon. The outpouring of desire for the sacred leaf exploded like a cascade of mountain water on the rocks below.

Needless to say, Ralph was the first to sign up. And so began the Great Tea for Coca/Coca for Tea Exchange that came to define our friendship. It went on and on and on—for years in fact—whereas for the other participants the trade occurred just once. There were deviations. Knowing I had collected enough Lapsang to last three lifetimes, he sent me a surprise: the most divine tin of organic sencha, and in exchange I would dutifully pack off coca lozenges, coca candies, *mate*

---

1. The coca products I mailed to friends are more than legal in Bolivia; they are de rigueur. They are made of the coca leaf pure and simple. Cocaine—NOT! Through cocaine's chemical-drenched process of manufacture the leaf gains its "illegal" status because it is mixed with other substances to produce the extremely dangerous extremely addictive—and extremely profitable—drug that is rightfully feared.

de coca, sometimes in a handwoven bag for carrying, always placed in a snap-shut tin to stave off the growls of U.S. customs' German shepherds.

The bamboo tea strainer he mailed was a telling gift. Knowing Ralph, if I hadn't pried he would *never* have mentioned the trouble he endured to get it. I learned that a virtual labyrinth of failed attempts had sent him to multiple health food stores and, having had zero success at finding such the sought-after artifact, instead of admitting defeat, Ralph actually ordered one online specifically for me.

Through this ongoing exchange I enjoyed myself immensely, and I was well aware that he would go out of his way to find items I requested. He also enjoyed sharing his delight in the articles I had sent: he relished chewing a coca pastille when he was stressed because it invariably set him at ease. He also used it for travel to his various lectures and investigative journeys to meet academics, shamans, and peers in the field of consciousness.

Then, as my seventy-third birthday approached, I wrote in the Bolivia Letter that some twenty-five years earlier I had received startling information in a dream: I would die at age seventy-three. Ralph responded immediately! His tone in this correspondence was a break from his usual gentle placidness; a demand of urgency had suddenly arisen. He started out with "Dear good friend Chellis" so I sensed that some tough-love wisdom was to follow. He went on:

As for the guessing game of what age will it be that the grim reaper comes knocking at your door, we only know that indeed he will come (how do we know it's a he, anyway?), but not when or what our exit ticket will be. For myself, I've put in a request that my train leave for the other side when I'm sleeping.

But as for coinciding with what you call "Collective Demise," you're all set, and so am I, and so are we all. The collective demise of human civilization on this planet is happening now and will continue. Of course, there´ll be some humans left, scattered here and there around the planet, as it sheds half or more of the livable environments and 50% or more of its human populations.

> And meanwhile, yes, indeed, "it's a flaming royal gift to be alive." So drink wine and snuff *coca* with friends and dance to the music.

He signed the note "Your pen pal Ralph."

Ah, the disappearance of a friend we have woven into our lives with loving threads! Each time it slaps us in the face, we are confronted with the startling realization that, even without afternoons of sipping tea together, we have depended on that person's very existence to grow the roots of our own.

This world without Ralph's presence is essentially and forever unthinkable . . . yet what a gift was his last letter. What a bodhisattva he was in every moment! In his straightforward, caring way, Ralph managed to soften the terror of turning the age I had long held as my exit ticket—and put a frame around our beautiful tapestry by preparing me for navigating the bewilderment and sorrow of his departure.

How to Channel: The Gift Ralph Gave
Matthew McKay

Matthew McKay, Ph.D., is a psychologist, author, and publisher/founder of New Harbinger Press. He is a professor of psychology at the Wright Institute in Berkeley, California.

In June 2009, Ralph Metzner gave me something of immeasurable value, something that would change my life. He showed me how to initiate channeled communication with my murdered son despite having no psychic or clairaudience abilities whatsoever. Ralph told me that Jordan was just a "thought away," and that a simple divination could open the door. I followed his instructions.

In the intervening years, Jordan and I have had hundreds of conversations. At first I was primarily concerned with getting reassurance that his soul survived death, and that he fared well in the afterlife. But soon enough I began asking larger questions about the nature of the spirit world and why souls incarnate to such a difficult planet. The answers filled me with love—for Jordan and all the souls separated from me on the other side; for Ralph, who showed me the path; and for All, the way we join all of consciousness in our quest to learn and evolve.

What became apparent to me, in the months following the revelation I experienced, was that all souls—living and dead—are inseparably joined. We are held together by a common purpose to learn how to love more deeply. We do not incarnate to be judged or found worthy. We are here to encounter every barrier to love that the physical world can offer, and yet embrace and care for each other. I could not have known this without channeling.

Since Ralph taught me the channeling protocol, Jordan has revealed our history as souls (*Seeking Jordan*, 2016, New World Library), a spiritual process for recovering from trauma (*The New Happiness*, 2019, New Harbinger Publications, and *The Luminous Landscape of the Afterlife: Jordan's Message to the Living on What to Expect After Death*, 2021, Inner Traditions); and a treatise on the nature of love (*Love in the Time of Impermanence*, 2022, Inner Traditions).

These communications from Jordan's soul, and the wisdom they convey, have reduced the fear of death and uncertainty for thousands of people. And they have offered a spiritual path for those who face the traumatic effects of life on this planet.

None of this would have been possible without Ralph Metzner's lifetime study of the curtain between life and death—and the means by which it can be parted. The process he taught me, which I follow to this day, is as follows.

How to Channel

- Channeling is enhanced with ritual. Identify a comfortable, safe environment where you will reach out to the other side.

- Select an object that connects you to the soul you wish to contact on the other side. This could be something they once possessed or gave to you. If you wish to contact guides, souls with whom you have no personal relationship, or the All (collective consciousness), use a talisman such as a mandala, Celtic knots, or even photographs of sky, sea, sunset, and so on, to symbolize the connection to Spirit.

- Select something for eye fixation—a candle is ideal, but you could use anything with a bright, shiny surface. Hold in one hand the object that connects you to the other side, or place it below the candle.

- Have a notebook at hand in which you'll record your conversations with the other side. It's helpful to use the same notebook for multiple channeling sessions so you'll have an ongoing record for these important communications.

- At the onset of channeling, establish the intended spiritual address. Set an intention that you are connecting to a particular entity.

- Fix your attention on a candle or other object of focus, and begin a brief meditation. Allow awareness to settle on your diaphragm, the center of breath and life. As you observe your breath, count each outbreath (one . . . two . . . three . . . and so on till you reach ten). When thoughts arise, return your attention—as soon as you notice them—to your breath. Continue meditation through two or three rounds of ten outbreaths, letting your mind slow and settle, and slipping into a receptive altered state. There is nothing hard or esoteric about this—just wait until your thoughts are coming with less frequency and urgency, and there's a beginning sense of calm.

- As your meditation closes, visualize an orb of light, the color of the sun, about six inches above your head. See the light elongate upward, stretching infinitely from the top of your head into the world of spirit. This is the channel, opening by your mere intention to do so. Departed souls, and the entire community in spirit, are waiting and willing to communicate. They want to talk to us for many reasons, including (1) showing what awaits us on the other side and helping with the fear of death; (2) reassurance from our loved ones that they continue in a life after death; (3) giving advice and guidance for the challenges of incarnate life; (4) offering deep knowledge about the purpose of life, plus the evolution of our individual souls and all of consciousness; and (5) induction into a felt sense of love as the connective tissue holding everything.

- When you are ready, write your first question in your journal. This is a conversation, and conversations usually begin with questions.

- Now wait. Listen for the first words to form inside your mind. Write whatever comes—even if the first words make no immediate sense. Write without judgment. Write with the full anticipation that the soul on the other side has something to say. And with patient listening you'll learn what it is. After writing down the first few words, listen again. In time more words will come to finish the sentence or start a new one. Keep listening. The answer to your question will slowly take form.

- When the channel goes quiet, write a new question and repeat the above process. Answers at first may seem hesitant—arriving in brief phrases. Over time, the channel gets stronger and communications more fluent. Practice will improve your skills. What were one-word or brief messages grow into more complex and rewarding conversations. You may experience downloads of ideas that you later must find words for. Or the messages may come at a speed that your pen can't match. This is not a problem. Keep asking clarifying questions and listening at the channel door for answers.

- Keep writing questions and answers until you experience an internal quiet, and you feel ready to close the channel.

- Thank the soul or entity on the other side for their love and knowledge.
- Between sessions think about the things you'd like to know, or wish help with. Consult your channeling notebook to review what you've learned so far.

Channeling requires no special powers and works for most who try it. In truth, it is nothing more than realizing the awareness that we are all connected, living and dead, holding each other in a web of eternal love. That's what channeling is, and that's what Ralph gave me.

Afterlife Journey of the Soul in Jewish Mysticism and Tradition
Simcha Paull Raphael

Reb Simcha Paull Raphael, Ph.D., is founding director of the DA'AT Institute for Death Awareness, Advocacy and Training. He received his ordination as a rabbinic pastor from Reb Zalman Schachter-Shalomi (1990). He works as a psychotherapist and spiritual director in Philadelphia. He is author of numerous publications including the groundbreaking *Jewish Views of the Afterlife*.

DOCTORAL DISSERTATION

From 1979–1988 Ralph Metzner served as academic dean of the California Institute of Integral Studies, where I was a doctoral student in Integral Counseling Psychology. After completing my coursework, in the summer of 1980, I reached that juncture when I had to select a dissertation topic and committee. Ralph Metzner, Ph.D., was a natural choice as head of my doctoral dissertation committee. He brought to this work more than simply the administrative portfolio of academic dean of CIIS.

First of all, my dissertation topic, "Judaism's Contribution to the Psychology of Death and Dying," was an exploration of life after death in Judaism with applications for working with the dying and bereaved. Only in the avant-garde transpersonally oriented program of the CIIS, which Ralph helped to envision and shape, could one write a psychology dissertation on survival of consciousness after death.

Ralph brought the synthesis of his Harvard University psychological training and his creative explorations of visionary states of consciousness to his work at CIIS to help spawn an environment for in-depth study of the human psyche. Being a student at CIIS in the late 1970s felt to me similar to what it might have been like in ancient Greece at the time of the philosophers, with new winds of thought permeating every corner of our intellectual and spiritual *weltenschaung* (worldview). And without any doubt, Ralph was one of the midwives of that environment.

Secondly, my other doctoral dissertation advisor, Reb Zalman Schachter-Shalomi, founder of the Jewish Renewal movement and widely known teacher of contemporary Kabbalah, was a long-time colleague of Ralph's. They had met in the 1960s at the home of Timothy Leary in Millbrook, New York. And (as I recently discovered) Reb Zalman had published an article on his own psychedelic journey in Ralph's anthology *The Ecstatic Adventure*.

TRANSPERSONAL PRINCIPLES
UNDERLYING THIS PROJECT

In retrospect, I can see that specific principles that guided my work, influenced by the emerging psychology of consciousness of CIIS, were ideas that had appeared in Ralph's writings.

First of all, in his 1964 book *The Psychedelic Experience* (co-authored with Timothy Leary and Richard Alpert), Ralph and his colleagues endeavored to present a *phenomenological depiction of states of consciousness*. Without judgment, evaluation, or reductionist interpretation, this directly describes nonordinary, suprarational states of mind and being. *The Psychedelic Experience* drew on the Tibetan Book of the Dead as a model to describe what happens to the human mind as consciousness separates from the body and to compare these states of being with the psychedelic experience.

In my research and writing, I likewise used a phenomenological approach to look at little-known afterlife teachings in Jewish mysticism and tradition. My research explored a wide swath of historical ideas on life after death in three millennia of Jewish sacred texts. I got to wade through obscure—but fascinating—texts on life after death in Judaism. I never had to validate the use of a phenomenological approach because Ralph already supported it, and, even more, phenomenology had become a standard academic approach at CIIS in the 1980s.

Secondly, another operating objective guiding my work was similar to that which Ralph had written about in the mid-1970s in his book *Maps of Consciousness*—where he described the journey of consciousness in multiple spiritual paradigms of world religions. My research focused on the afterlife journey of the soul and correlated states of mind in Jewish mystical texts; but given the world religions/interfaith orientation of CIIS, also on Theosophy, Tibetan Buddhism, and contemporary near-death experience literature.

I worked to create a cartography of the afterlife journey. That question of what a cartography of the postmortem journey would look like became the guiding focus in my exploration of biblical, apocryphal, rabbinic, medieval, kabbalistic, and Chasidic texts on the afterlife.

I was not only interested in the "what?"—what does Judaism have to say about life after death?—but also the "so what?"—if consciousness survives bodily death, so what do we do about that? How does an assumption of postmortem survival of the consciousness affect ways we companion the dying and comfort the bereaved?

Ralph grounded his own research in visionary states of consciousness in psychological healing work with clients. He developed a unique way of combining the spiritual and the psychological, the cosmic and the practical. In the spirit of my CIIS training, the ultimate applied goal of my research was to be of service to others in the healing of both psyche and spirit, particularly with regard to the human encounter with dying and death.

THE FOURFOLD MODEL OF THE AFTERLIFE JOURNEY IN JEWISH MYSTICISM AND TRADITION

What follows is a brief summary of what my research revealed. Essentially, I found within the Jewish sources a fourfold model of the afterlife journey that has parallels in religious traditions around the world.[2]

Readers may be interested in the following summary of current and historical Jewish literature as a context for comparison of both after-death and psychedelic-induced states of consciousness.

1. Separation of Consciousness

The first stage of the postmortem journey in both traditional and mystical Jewish sources is called Hibbut Ha-Kever, "the pangs of the grave." It is a relatively brief process of the separation of consciousness from the body.

In this earliest stage, as consciousness leaves the body, Jewish sources describe a series of visionary phenomena experienced by the disembodied consciousness. For example, we find the following in the medieval mystical text, the Zohar.

On seeing deceased ancestors:

Rabbi Shimon said: Have you seen today the image of your father? For so we have learnt, that at the hour of a man's departure from the world, his father and his relatives gather round him, and he sees them and recognizes them, and likewise all with whom he

---

2. The Tibetan Book of the Dead presents three stages, or *bardos* (transit stages), of the afterlife journey. I maintain that the second stage, Peaceful and Wrathful Deities, is in some sense parallel to the heaven and hell depiction in other traditions.

associated in this world, and they *accompany his soul to where it is to abide*. (Zohar I, Ron a)

On seeing mythic or archetypal guides:

When one departs this world . . . they see many strange things on their way and *meet Adam, the first person, sitting at the gates Gan Eden*, ready to welcome all who have observed the commands of their Master. (Zohar, I 65b)

On the postmortem life review:

When God desires to take back a person's spirit, *all the days that they have lived passed before God in review*. (Zohar I, 221b)

Always fascinating to me was that the twelfth-century Kabbalists were reporting the exact same kinds of dying and after-death visions as chronicled in NDE reports and being seen in hospital rooms and intensive care units today. This affirmed for me the universality of the inner dimension of dying; it is clear that our medical establishment still has a long way to go to understand the inner intricacies of the transpersonal and transcendent experiences people have as they are dying.

Another noteworthy observation from my research, specifically with regard to practical application of afterlife teachings, was discovering a connection between contemporary Jewish ritual practices and ancient afterlife teachings. For example, a traditional Jewish mourning practice is the observance of *shiva*, a seven-day ritual of communal mourning immediately following a burial (the word *shiva* means "seven"). One is said to "sit shiva," literally sitting on low stools and being surrounded by family and friends who gather to comfort the mourners and remember the bereaved. If done with intentionality and communal support, observance of shiva tends to be an efficacious grief ritual, helping mourners deal with grief and loss.

At the conclusion of seven days of shiva, a traditional practice is for mourners to walk around the block. Psychologically this act is seen as a reentry into the world; having taken time out of ordinary life to mourn a loved one, the bereaved begin to slowly reenter life. On a spiritual level, walking around the block is a symbolic act in which the mourner accompanies the spirit of the deceased on its journey. It is as if the mourner says, "We can walk you only this far . . . now you have to go the rest of the way on your own to be 'gathered to the ancestors,'" as it says in the Hebrew Bible (Gen. 25:8, Abraham; Gen. 35:29, Isaac; Gen. 49:29, Jacob).

2. Purification

Subsequently, the second stage of the postmortem journey in rabbinic and kabbalistic sources is called Gehenna. This is a state of the purgation and purification of the soul. Essentially what this means is that after death there is a psychic, emotional residue one individual has to process—a working through of the incomplete layers of guilt, shame, regret, failed expectations, of lived life.

Unlike in Christianity, the leaders of rabbinic Judaism—many of whom were contemporaneous with St. Augustine, the author of *City of God*[3]—did not espouse a belief in eternal damnation. In Jewish sources, Gehenna is a maximum twelve-month process of purgation. Texts such as the following replicate images of a medieval penal colony, portraying Gehenna in a Dantesque fashion:

[These are the] punishments in Gehenna, and Isaiah saw them all . . . He saw two men hanging by their tongues; and he said, "O You who unveils the hidden, reveal to me the secret of this." He answered, "These are the men who slandered, therefore they are thus punished." (*Keitzad Din Ha-Kever*, 1–3)

---

3. Gerald Walsh, et al., trans., *St. Augustine—The City of God* (Garden City, NY: Image Books, 1958).

I came to understand a very important point that has been foundational in my study of afterlife teachings in general: *depictions of heaven
and hell in religious literature are not literal but are symbolic of states of
mind.* This is something Ralph Metzner recognized in his own work,
and he supported me as I worked to understand these kinds of traditional heaven-hell images through the lens of transpersonal psychology.

3. Arriving at Levels of Being and Knowing
The third stage of the afterlife journey is called Gan Eden, the heavenly
Garden of Eden. As to be expected, this realm of postmortem experience is
depicted in "heavenly" terms. One text describes Gan Eden as having "two
gates of carbuncle, and sixty myriads of ministering angels." In terms of
the journey of consciousness this text speaks of how "angels remove from
one the clothes in which they had been buried, and clothe them with eight
robes of the clouds of glory" (*Masekhet Gan Eden*, 1–2). In other words, at
a certain point in the postmortem process, we leave behind our terrestrial
identity—"the clothes in which they had been buried"—and awaken to
the higher realms of knowing and being. In the heavenly Garden of Eden,
we harvest the fruits of our lifetime of accrued spiritual experience, and we
continue evolving to higher levels of being and knowing.

4. An Experience of God
In some mystical texts (though not all) we find a fourth dimension of
the afterlife journey of consciousness referred to as Tzror Ha-Hayyim,
"the source of life." Yes, Judaism does include reincarnation.

In one of his later books, *The Cycle of Life of the Human Soul,*[4]
Ralph tracks a similar and more expanded journey of the soul, as the
subtitle of the book indicates: *Incarnation–Conception–Birth–Death–
Hereafter–Reincarnation.* Clearly, these ideas are replicated cross-
culturally, and they also occur in plant medicine experiences that Ralph
explored and described in his writing.

---

4. Ralph Metzner, *The Life Cycle of the Human Soul* (Berkeley, CA: Regent Press, 2011).

FROM GRADUATE STUDENT TO AFTERLIFE SCHOLAR AND TRANSPERSONAL GRIEF COUNSELOR

Little did I know it at the time, but the work I did on my doctoral dissertation not only established the direction of my life's work for the next four decades (and counting), but also provided me with opportunity to stay in touch with Ralph until the very last days of his life.

Over the years I have also continued research and writings as a scholar of afterlife teachings. I expanded the work of my dissertation into a book, *Jewish Views of the Afterlife*, which was published in 1994. In delineating little-known teachings on postmortem survival over the course of three millennia of Jewish thought, this book has been groundbreaking in the Jewish community and beyond. I have also had the chance to teach this material widely, in university psychology and religion departments, Jewish congregations, churches, senior centers, youth groups, and community centers across the United States and Canada, as well as in England and Israel.

The book has become a classic resource for study of life after death in Jewish mysticism and tradition. I have always been grateful to Ralph and CIIS for opening the way for me to do this kind of innovative study, especially given that life after death was not a topic of respectable inquiry in most academic settings (and still is not to this day).

RECONNECTING WITH RALPH

In 2009 a second expanded edition of the book was published; and a third, twenty-fifth anniversary edition of *Jewish Views of the Afterlife* was published in 2019. As the new book was being prepared for publication, I asked Ralph if he would write an endorsement for the back of the book. At that time, late 2018, Ralph's health had been deteriorating but he graciously offered to write the endorsement. It certainly meant a lot to me that he agreed to do so; and I believe that for Ralph, having one of the graduate dissertations he had supervised four decades earlier be published as a twenty-fifth anniversary edition book meant a lot to him as well.

Once the book was released in early spring 2019, Ralph was sent a copy. His endorsement on the back cover was actually the last contribution to a publication he saw in his lifetime. Two days before Ralph died, his wife, Cathy Coleman, relayed to me that his copy of *Jewish Views of the Afterlife* arrived, and Cathy made sure that he saw it. Cathy saw it as a sign that his time to enter the afterlife was near. Ralph Metzner died on March 14, 2019.

After a lifelong journey exploring the depths and heights of human consciousness, it was as if the universe was saying, "Ralph Metzner, you've done your job, and you've done it well." May Ralph's indefatigable spirit of creativity continue to shine. I am ever-grateful that Ralph was a mentor, guide, and teacher in my life. His legacy lives on.

AFTERWORD BY CATHY COLEMAN

Regarding the Hibbut Ha-Kever, the first stage of the postmortem journey described above as consciousness leaves the body, when one sees deceased ancestors, I want to relate that about thirty hours before Ralph died, as he was falling asleep and in a liminal state, he said, "I am going home to my father . . . I am going home to see my mother . . . I am going home to see my son Ari . . . I am going home to see my good friend Angie . . . I am going home to see my good friend Tim Leary."

It was these five that he named . . . and the next night, about four-to-six hours before he died, he repeated the words about his mother and father. Tim Leary being among this group of five affirmed his close connection with Tim. I suppose they were all there to greet him at the gate.

I repeat from Simcha's text:

Rabbi Shimon said: Have you seen today the image of your father? For so we have learnt, that at the hour of a man's departure from the world, his father and his *relatives gather round* him, and he sees them and recognizes them, and likewise all with whom he associated in this world, and they *accompany his soul to where it is to abide.* (Zohar I, 218a)

Friend, Inspirer, and Companion
Roger Liggenstorfer, Christine Heidrich, and Markus Berger

Markus Berger is an ethnobotanist, drug researcher, author, and lecturer. He has written numerous books and articles on drug research and ethnobotany and is editor-in-chief of the magazine for psychoactive culture *Lucys Rausch*, copublished by Nachtschatten Verlag. He is also an organizer of congresses and events on psychoactive culture.

Christine Heidrich grew up in Hanover, Germany, and studied architecture at the University of Hanover and history and theory of architecture at ETH Zurich. She lives in Switzerland, where she works as an architect and as a cultural mediator for museum exhibitions and writes books and texts on recent architecture. As a part-time translator for Nachtschatten Verlag she has translated numerous works, including those by Ralph Metzner and Stanislav Grof, into German. She is co-owner and designer of Switzerland's first absinthe bar.

Roger Liggenstorfer is a Swiss author and publisher of various books focused on psychedelics and drug policy. He is the founder and managing director of the publishing house Nachtschatten Verlag in Solothurn and the initiator of several events on psychonautics and drug policy. He is the founder and president of Eve & Rave Switzerland and the manager and co-owner of Switzerland's first absinthe bar.

On March 14, 2019, at 4:20 hours, Ralph Metzner embarked on his last journey. He passed over at his home in California at the age of eighty-two years.

Ralph Metzner leaves behind a rich inheritance. He authored more than one hundred scientific contributions, around twenty books, and held countless lectures and workshops, including about the Alchemical Divination method he established. In collaboration with his wife Cathy, he set up the Green Earth Foundation. He served as professor at the California Institute for Integral Studies and maintained his own psychotherapy practice.

Ralph perfectly prepared the conclusion of his life: He donated his private library to Purdue University in Indiana, wrote three more books, and ordered his affairs. He left this earthly existence as he had imagined: Peaceful and in his sleep.

Ralph counts among the most important trailblazers who enabled us to reclaim the spirit and the worldview of Indigenous shamanism for our modern civilization—without blindly copying the rites of other ethnicities. Influenced by the Tibetan Book of the Dead, he explained to us like few others that, based on insights from psychedelic experiences, death is not to be understood as the final point of existence. He drew on examples from spiritual traditions for explanation:

> According to Buddhism and other philosophies in the traditions of East and West, we enter other dimensional worlds when leaving this one in order to grow and to learn—and finally reincarnate into another round of living on Earth. Each Dying is followed, after a while, by another birth. After each birth and rebirth there will be, after a while, another death. When thinking about birth and death in this way, one will notice a subtle yet profound shift in attitude— we can reach a point from where we can accept our numerous births and deaths with inner serenity"[5]

We mourn our friend, author, inspirer, pioneer, and companion Ralph Metzner, in the knowledge that his influence, his inspiration, and his spirit will move on and live on.

---

5. Ralph Metzner, *Welten des Bewusstseins: Welten der Wirklichkeit* (Solothurn, Switzerland: Nachtschatten Verlag, 2015), 17 (translated from German).

Ralph's Report on the "Here Now" in the "Here After"
Michael Ziegler

Michael Ziegler was ordained in the Jewish Chasidic lineage by Rabbi Zalman Schachter-Shalomi. He has been a pioneer in the development of spiritual and somatic programs. He worked with the Green Earth Foundation in support of Ralph Metzner's legacy.

Michael presided over Ralph's memorial celebration on May 24, 2019, at which he spoke this "report."

> I am here with my father, Wolfgang,
> my mother, Jill,
> my son, Ari,
> and my great-niece, Susie.
> I send my blessings to my new grandson,
> Gracian Cole Jacobson.
> I am sitting
> In the shade of the World Tree
> This part of the garden is next to Mimir's Well.
> It is filled with San Pedro Cactus and has a
>   comfortable hot tub.
> My pendulum doesn't work here—
> So I am busy exploring new kinds of awareness
>   practices.
> Perpetual Love-Bliss-Indivisible is available—
> But there are so many things I have yet to discover.
> Nearby, I hear Rumi and Blake exchanging poems
>   under the garden wisteria.
> George Gurdjieff is dancing the enneagram on the
>   lawn.

Socrates has gone to the house for wine,
Leaving Leo Zeff, Carl Jung, and Angie Arrien to
    discuss the Culture section of the Multi-Verse
    Tribune.
Odin, Jehovah, Milarepa, Oshun, and Krishna are
    tag-team wrestling on the lawn.
Mozart will be collaborating with George Harrison and
    John Lennon for a noon concert in the Zocalo.
At the gate to the Temple,
Timothy Leary and Terence McKenna are telling
    stories
and have drawn a crowd.
Inside the sanctuary,
Russell Schofield is doing Agni Yoga while
Maria Sabina chants and Michael Harner drums.
In the Laboratory up the hill,
Sasha Shulgin and Albert Hofmann are inventing clever
    palindromes while crafting novel tryptamines.
Enkidu is explaining the politics of gender in Gilgamesh
    to Marija Gimbutas, while Zecharia Sitchin listens in.
This afternoon, Richard Wagner will premiere a new
    opera: Isis, Osiris, Anubis, and Sekhmet are playing
    themselves.
In the evenings,
I am making new alien friends from other galaxies.
They bring to our conversations exciting new
    perspectives on art, science, and the numinous.
Later, emerging from the deep Silence,
a Goddess brings out a delicious tureen of my favorite
    tomato soup to share.
She is helping me understand the implications that this
    present
Eternity is an infinite amount of time.

Family

Extraordinary Dad
Sophia Metzner

Sophia Metzner, M.S.W., is the daughter of Ralph Metzner and Cathy Coleman. She is a child and family social worker in the area of foster care and adoption.

It is with profound honor that I write about my father and reflect on our time together in the physical world. I am grateful to have shared such a deep connection with him in this life. I want to portray his life as a father, a role he played with love and gratitude. His loving smile, gentle laugh, and infinite wisdom are forever imprinted on my heart.

As a child, I knew my dad was unusual, different from other dads. He was not your usual soccer dad. I cannot remember him ever attending a game, although he would always ask me about it so sincerely with his undivided attention that I felt supported. My mom attended every game and told me that she made sure that my dad was there for at least one game each season. He was not the dad who donned an apron and grilled food for gatherings, or spent weekend afternoons watching sporting events with friends. However, he did attend all of my school events, music recitals, singing performances, and theater

■ Fig. 45. Sophia Metzner
and her dad, 1990
(Photo courtesy of
Sophia Metzner)

productions when he was not traveling, and he was especially proud of my performance as Edward in Shakespeare's *King Lear* in my senior year of high school.

I knew that he was supportive of all of my interests and proud of my accomplishments, even those at which he was not present to witness. My deep connection to him made me feel he was always cheering me on. I grew to know that he was held in high honor and regard in the world, and over the years I began to appreciate the special dad that he was. To me, he was simply my dear dad, who incorporated his deep work, his understanding of the world and of people, and his ability to help people heal, into his role as my father. Our relationship was deeply cherished by both of us.

Throughout my childhood he would talk to me about the power of healing energy, using colors, hues, and lights to envelop the body and the mind as a tool for deep relaxation and envisioning wellness, as well as for manifesting new ideas and thought patterns. My dad began leading me in guided light meditations from around age five. As a young girl, the invitation to pick a beautiful color to wear as a "cloak" and imagine it as a light streaming through my body was a joyful experience.

The meditations helped me overcome debilitating anxiety attacks, insomnia, and nervousness. When I was an adolescent I began to understand how deeply meaningful the knowledge and practice had become. Having developed this helpful practice from a young age, I continue to use it in my daily life. This experience with my father gave me my own glimpse into some of the deep work that he did with many people who knew him as their teacher, healer, and guide.

I have saved all of the cards, notes, and letters from both of my parents over the years. It is a treasured gift to be able to read through the notes and letters my dad wrote to me. In re-reading some of the notes since he died, I am struck by how deeply touched he was by the work I do with children. He acknowledged my passion and love for the work and was proud that I had found a well-suited career path working with different aspects of child and family services.

On the days leading up to my father's death, I had many sweet moments with him sitting by his side, holding his hand, and being present. It was heart-wrenching, sad, and overwhelming to watch his rapid decline, and yet my love poured forth. I was grateful for every single look into his eyes, every kiss and hug, and every time we greeted and said goodbye. He would say, "Here she is, my beloved daughter." And as I departed, "I love you, Sophia. I always have and I always will. I will always be your dad."

What follows is a letter I wrote to my dad about four months before he died, which my mother suggested that I do to prepare myself for his death, and to communicate my thoughts. I read this letter to him in a moment of solitude as he sat quietly on his bed shortly before he died. He had lost nearly all of his energy at this point, and could not respond with the words I know he was thinking in his mind. He looked at me with a twinkle in his eye and said, "Thank you, Sophia. I love you."

Dear Dad,

You are my beloved father. You have given me an incredible life, a life of learning, laughter, love, and letting be.[1] You have taught me to love unconditionally, to accept what is, to be present in the moment, and to always be the best that I can be. You have taught me to be honest, humble, and responsible.

You have guided me through the most challenging times of my life. You have always been my teacher, my guiding light. You have taught me to connect with the deepest parts of myself, to get in touch with my own inner wisdom and strength, and you have taught me how to connect with others in deep and sacred ways.

I know how deeply cherished you are by your friends, colleagues, and students for your incredible wisdom. It is an honor and privilege that you have been my father.

---

1. These words are mostly from a mantra/toast Ralph came to be known for: life, love, laughter, and letting be.

My memories of our times spent together in my childhood are forever imprinted on my heart. I cherished our walks in the neighborhood. I remember you reading to me every night, especially the Berenstein Bear books. We wrote a children's story together called *Kyler the Alien Boy*. I cherish the memory of playing board games together and with my brother Eli.

I appreciated the patience and dedication you had for helping me with difficult homework, and for facilitating my academic success. I particularly remember you helping me understand *The Odyssey* and *Siddhartha*. You supported and encouraged me to learn, grow, and achieve.

When I went through periods of extreme anxiety in high school, you guided me through the challenges and reminded me that I was loved. You spoke to me with kindness, heart, and understanding. I appreciated your unconditional love even through disagreements, arguments, or misunderstandings.

We took special trips together. I cherish the experience of family trips, among them Mexico, Costa Rica, and Hawaii. My most treasured memory is our trip together to Scotland, Germany, and Italy to visit the places where you spent your childhood and young adulthood, and when we visited Damanhur in Italy, one of the most wondrous places in the world.

You have been blessed in your lifetime with many wonderful friends, and I felt grateful to have met some of them. You touched the lives of countless people: acquaintances, admirers, close friends, students, colleagues, family members, and most profoundly, Eli, Mom, and myself.

You are a most remarkable man, and I feel blessed to have known you as my father. Thank you from the bottom of my heart for giving me this special life, for supporting me, loving me, and teaching me. I love you, and hold you in my heart as I go forward in my life, making you proud.

With love always,
Sophia

My dad always said to me, "We can meet in our dreams." Whenever I went away on a trip or was away for a period of time, he would remind me that he would always be there for me in the dream world. Since his death I have had several remarkable meetings with him in my dreams. I cherish them, and have recorded the details. This was something I learned from him. He always kept a notepad, pencil, and flashlight by his bed so that he could record his dreams as he had them. He then later in the day wrote them out and worked with them as he saw fit. Through the teachings that he passed on to me, I am able to continue to connect with him, and for this I am grateful.

■ Fig. 46. Ralph and Sophia in Scotland, 2015
(Photo courtesy of Sophia Metzner)

Adventures Growing Up with Ralph
Elias Coleman Jacobson

Elias (Eli) Jacobson, M.S., is associate director of digital media and conferencing services at Brandeis University. He is the stepson of Ralph Metzner.

When I was eleven, my mom and Ralph took me to Manaus, Brazil, to the International Transpersonal Association Conference. Ralph was a lecturer and my mom directed a youth conference in which I partici-pated. One evening Ralph took me to a Santo Daime temple deep in the Brazilian Amazon rainforest to do ayahuasca. While it was my first time doing anything like that, it did not seem all that strange to me at the time.

Ralph was my stepfather and has been in my life since before I can remember. I had three parents: my mother, my father, and my stepfather. They all knew each other through an intertwined web of academic and social circles. Their eccentricities and adventurous spirits led to some of the retrospectively wild and interesting experiences I had growing up.

Though most people who knew Ralph are much more versed in his teachings, I can provide a little insight into what it was like growing up in a home with him. Ralph was an incredibly important person in my life. While he was one of my three parents, we maintained a dynamic that included both boundaries and opportunities that made our relationship different from that of a typical parent/child. I am lucky to have had Ralph parent me and to have had him influence and inspire me.

Ralph was a writer and a teacher, though I had no idea what it was he wrote about or taught for the majority of the time I was living with him. He also traveled a lot, and although I knew where he would go, I had no idea what he was *actually* doing on those trips. All I knew was that he was usually going to "lead a workshop" . . . whatever that meant. As a kid, you don't think to ask, "What kind of workshop?" He might have told me, but I never did pry for much information, and eventually I figured it out.

I thank Ralph for my connection to and appreciation for nature and the planet. We often walked together, which is where we would do most of our talking. He spent so much time sitting at a desk writing, but moving his body and being out in nature remained incredibly important to him. Walking and talking with Ralph gave me some of my best memories whether it was exploring a jungle in Costa Rica, traipsing through gardens in Hawaii, or just walking the dogs around the neighborhood. He taught me to love being in nature and to appreciate the natural world.

Every night at the dinner table, Ralph reminded us of our connection to the "Great Goddess Earth" as he said grace, thanking her for "the nourishment of our bodies and the healing of our lives." At every dinner with friends he would toast to the four Ls, "life, love, laughter, and letting be." Writing about this now makes me realize how much of an impact these key phrases had on me.

Though Ralph was deeply connected to nature, Mother Earth, deities, and the revelations of consciousness and alchemy, he could also disconnect from it all and be a normal dad. I looked forward to Friday nights in the mid-1990s when my mom had some other commitment and Ralph would order a vegetarian pizza from Dominos and he, my sister, and I would watch *The X-Files*. You probably wouldn't expect it, but when I would commute with Ralph from San Francisco and Sonoma, we'd often stop halfway at Burger King for a fish sandwich and fries. It was a sharp contrast to some of the other experiences he shared with me.

Ralph taught me to drive. We were in San Francisco and I had just gotten my permit. Ralph turned to me and said, "Eli, do you want to drive home?" I remember being both terrified and excited at the opportunity, thinking, "Is he out of his mind?" San Francisco to Sonoma was at least a full hour away and involved driving across the Golden Gate Bridge and starting and stopping on many steep hills. I kept cool and said "sure" and we both lived to tell the story. That experience has stayed with me because it demonstrated his faith and trust in me.

Ralph provided many eye-opening opportunities for me, including travel to foreign countries and experiencing other cultures, supporting me to go on a vision quest when I was sixteen, taking me to a Native American sweat lodge, and participating in a handful of ayahuasca ceremonies. As an adolescent, I would have been less willing to partake in some of these activities if they had been suggested by my mother or father, but my unique relationship with Ralph made me more receptive to these experiences.

■ Fig. 47. Ralph and Eli at Eli's Evergreen College graduation, 2007
(Photo courtesy of Cathy Coleman)

Ralph had a great sense of humor and he was an engaging story-teller. He had an uncanny ability to listen deeply—and an innate desire to help heal. He was the healer in our family and provided homeopathic remedies, bandages, or perhaps a magic healing crystal. He loved "life, love, laughter, and letting be." He had a great zest for life and was loving and kind.

Ralph's life on Earth came to an end just three weeks after our son Gracian was born. Ralph was incredibly excited about the arrival of his grandson, and I don't think I've ever seen him so elated as when he met Gracian via video call those few times during those weeks that their lives overlapped. It seemed there was an important connection between the two of them, as Gracian had just arrived and Ralph was preparing to depart.

I miss Ralph dearly and was lucky to have him as a parent, friend, and teacher.

The Sacred Hoop of Partnership
Cathy Coleman

The Sacred Hoop, more commonly known as the Medicine Wheel, is a symbolic concept used by generations of various Native American tribes that can refer to stages of life, aspects of life (spiritual, emotional, intellectual, physical), the four seasons, directions, and other meanings. The Medicine Wheel consists of the Four Directions, as well as Mother Earth, Father Sky, and Spirit Tree.

I had the honor, privilege, and joy to walk with Ralph on numerous paths . . . as his student, as administrative colleagues at CIIS where he served as academic dean, as cofounders of the Green Earth Foundation, as fellow journeyers and experimenters, as parents, as his spouse—and now working to further his legacy.

RALPH AS MY PROFESSOR

I arrived in San Francisco in early July 1981 to begin a doctoral program in counseling psychology at CIIS. Ralph Metzner was the first name I heard when I arrived in San Francisco, as my housemate with whom I had prearranged to live had just finished taking a class from Ralph.

I took seven courses with Ralph over the duration of my studies at CIIS. The Altered States class I took with Ralph was considered a "must take" class at CIIS for most students, and it was always full. The seven classes I took from him in Eastern and Western psychology were the subjects that I loved most. Engaging in these academic explorations with Ralph was my first union with him.

In addition to the fact that Ralph could lecture prolifically on numerous subjects and weave them together, he also graded papers promptly and commented thoroughly. He gave each paper a careful read, raising questions and offering encouragements and ideas for future exploration. Both his efficacy and thoroughness of grading students' papers were standouts of Ralph's professorship.

Ralph and I strongly connected in an astrology class he taught at CIIS the summer of 1983. Astrology was a subject of deep interest to both of us that we shared over our years together. Both of us were practicing astrologers, though after we came together in partnership, he focused on his psychotherapy practice and left the astrology practice to me.

Ralph served as guide/mentor to East-West students in their final terms when we were writing integrative papers and drawing on our cumulative studies. My integrative paper was on the Demeter-Persephone mythology, a theme that would play out in our unfolding lives together as I would become the mother of our daughter, Sophia.

As a professor, Ralph offered to CIIS not only his knowledge but also his willingness to explore and experiment with ideas, topics, courses, and curricula. While Ralph demanded rigorous scholarship, no topic was too strange for him.

RALPH AS COLLEAGUE

Ralph was the academic dean at CIIS when I arrived as a student. Less than a year later, I became a part of the staff. He was the supervisor of my supervisor, Harrison Voigt, and they hired me in April 1982 as director of admissions and financial aid.

Ralph was a good administrator in many ways, including managing a well-balanced budget in the face of limited funding. However, he preferred teaching, writing, and psychotherapy over administration. Ralph was quick, decisive, innovative, and productive. I came to CIIS just after the school received its accreditation in late 1980, which Ralph was instrumental in helping to attain. Also that year the school changed its name from the California Institute of Asian Studies to the California Institute of Integral Studies, which was his suggestion to the board of trustees when they had trouble agreeing on a new name.

As academic dean he added a degree in Social and Cultural Anthropology and was instrumental in incorporating the programs of Somatic Psychology, Drama Therapy, and Expressive Arts Therapy from the defunct Antioch College. Former CIIS President John Broomfield, who served 1983–1990, noted in the acknowledgments to his book *Other Ways of Knowing* (1993): "For seeing ideas and encouraging me in new directions . . . particularly Ralph Metzner, whose avid search for new understandings surrounded us with innovative thinkers."

I was promoted to director of student services (admissions, financial aid, international student affairs, registration, graduation, etc.) at CIIS and reported to the president. For nearly a decade Ralph led the academic side, and I directed the administrative/student services side of the school. This work relationship was our second union.

Ralph had an appetite for generating profound new academic courses and programs. His pioneering spirit, intelligence, and knowledge about Western and Eastern systems of thought, and an astonishing range of other subjects contributed to the flourishing of the uniqueness of CIIS. In addition, Ralph embraced and practiced CIIS's spiritual values.

Putting Ralph's contributions in context, after he died I received numerous messages from people reflecting on what Ralph gave them, taught them, or meant to them. For example, Fariba Bogzaran, a dream researcher, author, artist, and one of his students at CIIS, wrote:

> Ralph was a very important mentor to me. When I started at CIIS in 1986, he was the academic dean and he was the only person at school with whom I could share my ideas about lucid dreaming and transpersonal experiences. He was wholeheartedly supportive of me doing my thesis on this topic when it was at the time a cutting edge research. I wanted to do qualitative research for my subject, but he was strongly against it. He said, "The topic is obscure and if you do a method that is not fully accepted, no one would take you seriously." He encouraged me to use hard science for my research and he was absolutely right. As soon as I finished my study, it was recognized immediately. As a visionary, it was a lonely path to pick a topic less understood by many, but Ralph was always there to discuss the most unusual subjects. I feel grateful to have had him as my mentor.

Fariba's message illustrates that one could discuss any far-out topic with Ralph; he would ponder and encourage students to do the best research that would have the most far-reaching, effective results; and he would continue to be your loyal colleague, collaborator, and friend.

RALPH AS HUSBAND

In late April 1986, a few weeks before he would turn fifty, Ralph invited me to lunch. This was unusual for Ralph, as he rarely broke from work for socializing. The lunch date was set for May 6. Between his invitation and May 6, I attended the National Council on Geocosmic Research (NCGR) Astrology Conference in Washington, D.C.

I was browsing in the Yes Bookstore after the conference and Richard Nolle's book *Chiron: The New Planet in Your Horoscope, The Key to Your Quest* practically jumped off the shelf. I purchased it, and I devoured it on my plane trip back to California. I was excited to tell Ralph about this new planetary discovery. Chiron symbolizes the maverick, the mentor, and the holistic healer. Transiting Chiron was at 11 degrees of Gemini, exactly conjunct the Descendant in Ralph's horoscope that day of our first (lunch) date, and nearly conjunct his natal Chiron.

The Descendant in the horoscope is the place indicating mate/marriage. The Descendant also symbolizes close one-to-one relationships such as mentor-student. Transiting Chiron was close to his natal Mercury-Chiron conjunction at 14 and 15 degrees of Gemini, respectively. This configuration symbolizes his maverick mind and his mentorship of many students and others. Doors to new worlds of understanding had been opened for me with the reading of this book on Chiron, and I consequently opened new worlds of understanding for Ralph. My sharing of the discovery of Chiron for us "coincided" with the door opening to our long love relationship.

On our walk back to CIIS in the Haight-Ashbury neighborhood of San Francisco, Ralph poured out his desire for us to be in a relationship together. He said that his intention was to obtain my agreement before his fiftieth birthday that was a few weeks later, and before his upcoming vision quest to mark the occasion.

I was in shock. I had an immediate vision of a flashing yellow light and told him that's what I saw. He said, "That means proceed with caution." Of course it did. Ralph had been active in my dreams the previous year; I had been courted in the dream world. He had an intention for our relationship which matched the visions and dreams that had informed me.

The next day I walked into his office and said "Yes!" However, it was complicated, as I was married and he was in another relationship. We ventured forth honestly and courageously with our partners and each other and eventually worked things out. There was an undeniable synchronicity between the Yes Bookstore, where I purchased the book on Chiron, and my response to his surprising, awe-inspiring invitation, "*Yes.*"

Two years later we would marry on July 16, 1988, on Mount Tamalpais by Native American Elder Richard Deertrack of the Taos Pueblo. Our wedding vows included prayers each of us gave for the Four Directions, Mother Earth, and Father Sky.

Ralph undertook another vision quest before our wedding and sought to obtain a vision for our life together. He wrote about this inspiration:

While in the mountains, I'm asked to go on two symbolic walks, to obtain a vision for my upcoming marriage to Cathy. In the first, I am to test my commitment to her by climbing down a steep and rocky canyon and find her spirit. Finding her and the commitment was easy. The second was a repeated walk (in the day, and at night) along a high ridge, to find my vision for our relationship. The path wound through cool, shade-giving clumps of trees and across sunny, open meadows, covered with wild-flowers. I talked with her in my mind—her soul is as a field of wild-flowers. I saw us walk-

■ Fig. 48. Our wedding; from left: Cathy, Ralph, and Richard Deertrack,
Taos Pueblo officiant, July 16, 1988
(Photo courtesy of Cathy Coleman)

ing together, meeting and interacting with many other individuals
and groups, working in creative collaboration, dancing in ritual play.
"Togetherness in open space" was the mantric marriage formula I
was given. I danced for my love. Cathy liked the marriage walk
vision.

Indeed, we traveled together, in open spaces. This vision describes
our third union, that of our thirty-year marriage. How amazing that
Ralph would intentionally seek a vision for our marriage by doing a
vision quest!

From my prior marriage I had a son, Elias, who was three when
Ralph and I married. Then in 1989 Ralph and I had a daughter,
Sophia Marija, named after Marija Gimbutas, one of his teachers and
mentors. Ralph was a loving, encouraging parent to both children.

■ Fig. 49. Ralph and Cathy, 1988 (Photo courtesy of Cathy Coleman)

Ralph had a son, Ari Krishna Metzner, who was born May 6, 1966, and died in 1974 at age eight from a bicycle accident. Of course, this was the greatest tragedy of Ralph's life. Our lunch date that initiated our marriage was on the twentieth anniversary of Ari's birth, although Ralph did not realize this synchronicity at the time. We held Ari as part of our family circle.

In 1990, when Sophia was one and Eli was five, we moved to Sonoma, Northern California, creating a home where Ralph would live for the rest of his life, and where I still live. Our home and family life served us both as an anchor for work and travels.

As I have related, we shared an astrological worldview. Before we were in relationship, Ralph wrote about astrology in his book *Maps of Consciousness*, did astrological consultations, and wrote articles on astrology. He had a strong knowledge of astrology, but over the years increasingly deferred to me, asking me to help him understand his clients through this cosmic lens. He often referred his clients to me for readings. We shared this framework of meaning through the unfolding of our lives.

We did some maiden voyages with psychedelic medicines to test them, and these journeys were not always smooth. A memorable night was our first ibogaine experience with Terence McKenna in the living room of our Fairfax, California, home. I received a powerful image that night of an upside-down black goddess with a full head of wild black hair. Ibogaine is known to foster strong connections with ancestors, and I have felt a strong past life connection with black African forebears. A few days later, Ralph declared that the vision must have been the Goddess Oya, the black Yoruba goddess of wind and tornadoes, cemeteries, and the border between life and death. He then often referred to me as the Tornado Goddess(!).

Ralph and I had uncommon common interests, and there was no topic, esoteric, alien, or otherworldly that was too mysterious for us. However, learning to collaborate on ordinary, mundane affairs could be challenging. One of our memorable arguments was over my purchase of a lawn mower. Ralph insisted that we have a gardener take care of the yard, and so the lawn mower was returned to the store. Another argument was over my purchase of a used piano for my son Eli to learn to play. Ralph insisted that we get rid of it, whereupon he purchased a new piano and started taking piano lessons himself. We had to learn how to negotiate household purchases and decisions in a way that honored both of our needs, and we got better at doing this over time.

EXPLORING PAST LIVES

In addition to experiments with psychedelic medicines, we had other unusual experiences together. At the invitation of Ralph's friend Uwe Doerken (also a contributor to this Gedenkschrift), Ralph participated in a past life weekend experience offered by the Damanhur community of northern Italy. One of a person's past lives is channeled in the underground temples of Damanhur by a group of several people, based on the birth date and a photo given by the inquirer. Then one goes through a process over a weekend of unfolding and engaging with that life, led by a Damanhur-trained facilitator. Ralph invited me to attend the second one that he attended here in Northern California. One could do this process five times: four at any place where the workshops were held, and the fifth in the cave temples of Damanhur.

I participated in three more processes over that next year and then joined Ralph in Italy at the end of his European trip in 2013 at Damanhur to do the fifth and final one. These explorations were not lives we necessarily had together; that was not a part of the past life exploration process. The final exploration at Damanhur included a synthesis of the threads of the five lives explored.

The five past lives that were channeled by a Damanhur committee for Ralph to explore, in order of exploration, were (1) an eighteenth-century Welsh nobleman; (2) a nineteenth-century Austrian aristocratic diplomat; (3) a twelfth-century American Indian male shaman; (4) a thirteenth-century Polynesian girl who was a deep diver and died young while diving; and (5) a sacred female dancer from ancient Mesopotamia.

This past life exploration via Damanhur's process was one of the most precious experiences that I had during my life with Ralph. Of my five lives explored, the first four were channeled by the Damanhur Committee. The fifth and last was suggested by me as a possible past life and confirmed by the committee.

In order of exploration, they were (1) a seventeenth-century American male pioneer; (2) a nineteenth-century Chinese businesswoman (who ran a laundry), scholar, wife, and mother; (3) an eighteenth-century German male, sensitive, introverted, independent, unusual creative genius inventor; (4) a seventh-century Native American shaman, with strong personal energy; and (5) a seventh-century Moroccan trader. The third life seemed similar to Ralph in this life; perhaps it helped me to understand him.

Friendships and fellowship played an important role in our lives. Ralph already had many friends who were also professional colleagues when I came into the relationship. Among the many were Angeles Arrien, Stan and Christina Grof, Michael and Sandra Harner, Seymour and Sylvia Boorstein, Rupert Sheldrake and Jill Purce, and Terence McKenna. As a result of our long associations with CIIS, our network and friendship circle grew with students, faculty, and staff from the school.

A group of psychiatrists who had been students of Roger Walsh at the University of California at Irvine arranged a group medicine circle for themselves with Ralph as facilitator in the late '80s. More subcircles in Southern California followed, and later many of the group moved to the Bay Area. They and their spouses and children became one of our strong familial tribes. We hosted Christmas Day dinners with this tribe for about twenty-five years. After dinner we always had a ritual talking circle. Ralph's toast to the four Ls and eight Ls became standard part of our gatherings: "life, love, laughter, and letting be." Later in the evening Ralph would toast to the eight Ls: "long life, light of love, lusty laughter, and lightly letting be."

I initiated a wider neighborhood babysitting cooperative when our children were small, and this offered date nights to us on the nights when one of the other six sets of parents were hosting all the children. This group was another tribe. One Christmas season Ralph gathered the fifteen co-op children together to practice and present the story of the birth of Christ to the astonishment of all of us. The babysitting co-op enabled precious date nights and they continued throughout our life together. An added bonus was that the children bonded as extended family.

Ralph was ever the experimenter, sometimes resulting in some far-out domestic expressions, such as:

- Bufo the Hallucinogenic Toad who lived in a large structure in our bedroom for a number of years. Ralph tried milking the hallucinogenic secretion but was not very successful, and at some point he decided Bufo deserved to live in the wild. Bufo was released in a wetlands area.
- One day a man named Harry arrived to install a wood and metal pyramid structure suspended from our bedroom ceiling over our bed. This was supposed to enhance dreams and sleep. It remained until Ralph hit his head on it one too many times.
- Ralph purchased a quarter of a large San Pedro cactus garden and had it delivered in a small U-Haul truck. Several months later

over dinner our neighbors asked what the large delivery of cacti was for. I let Ralph answer the question. The cacti were transplanted into a large garden and then a roof was erected over the garden to keep them from being soaked with rain. The cactus farm was a prominent feature of our backyard for many years.

We participated in numerous ITA (International Transpersonal Association) Conferences together: Prague, Czechoslovakia; Killarney, Ireland; Santa Clara and Palm Springs, California; and Manaus, Brazil. Ralph was the program director for the Killarney Conference in 1994; at all he was a lecturer. I produced youth conferences alongside the main conferences. I also helped Ralph with his production of a CIIS-sponsored Ayahuasca Conference in 2000 and a Gaia Conference focused on ecopsychology in 2002.

When friends, clients, and associates came to town, we often invited them for dinner, expanding our ongoing circle of fellowship. Social gatherings and dinner conversations were a hallmark of our life together. Ralph enjoyed bringing various people together who he knew would engage in fascinating conversations, notwithstanding that Ralph generally was an introvert.

He could spend endless hours at his desk writing. Yet I knew how important relationships were to him, and to us as a couple, so I fostered these social gatherings, and liked hosting them. Some had a larger, practical purpose, such as Sunday afternoon harvestings of our substantial San Pedro cactus garden. Various people joined us in cutting, slicing, and preparation for drying and later processing into hallucinogenic capsules, not to mention the product sharing.

Special mention must be made of Ralph's renowned wise Basque friend Angeles Arrien. Ralph and Angie had been engaged, but the marriage was called off. Still, they remained friends, as they shared a soulmate-like quality in their relationship. Ralph felt that they had known each other in many lifetimes. I encouraged him to spend time with Angie, sometimes reminding him to make a lunch date with her.

■ Fig. 50. Angeles Arrien
(Photo courtesy of
Cathy Coleman)

Angie was a loyal, inspiring friend, and Ralph's life was enriched by their relationship.

As my husband, Ralph was committed, kind, and always interesting. We both led strong, independent, creative lives while we walked together solidly in partnership. I was a devoted wife, and I tended to the practical matters of managing a household and raising children in addition to my career as an administrator and astrologer, especially while he traveled the world teaching and guiding groups. When Ralph was home he did his part to contribute to a well-managed household.

Ralph traveled twice annually to Europe for many years and to numerous places in the United States. When I read the tributes in this collection from the many people who worked with him while I tended the home space and some of his responsibilities, I feel honored that I was able to support the fulfillment of his mission in the world.

In addition to the wisdom and knowledge Ralph left the through his teaching and publications, and his intrepid exploration, I want to name some specific gifts he leaves as his legacy. First, he always taught that one must honor any vision, dream, or special message from the

■ Fig. 51. Family: Cathy, Eli, Sophia, Ralph at Sophia's graduation from University of San Francisco, 2012 (Photo courtesy of Cathy Coleman)

Divine and act upon it. By honoring the messages, he pointed out, one would continue to receive visions.

Second was to forgive and ask for forgiveness. He practiced the Hawaiian forgiveness ritual of Ho'oponopono. During the two weeks before he died he read the little Ho'oponopono book over and over and pondered its messages. We actively practiced apologizing and forgiving in our family, and we cleaned up the rough patches as we went along.

A third is that Ralph took the high road—interpersonally, morally, and spiritually, and I appreciated being married to a person who lived in this manner. He had an uncanny ability to forget or put aside most of his negative experiences. He could not be bothered with pettiness. He was ethical, and he honored his commitments and agreements.

Finally, the expansion of consciousness was a daily practice. His mantra was *intention plus attention equals awareness*. He had this posted in several places in the house.

He had a refined appreciation of music, and he took improv piano lessons during his sixties and most of his seventies and composed several songs, including words and music. I loved witnessing him building this new creative expression. He had a vast collection of music that he cultivated and employed in his journey work.

Lest you have the impression that Ralph was a saint, he was not easy. He was famously stubborn, obstinate, and opinionated, characteristics that were sometimes a stretch for me and others. Confidant, demanding, intensely independent, and extremely competent are other aspects of his personality that could be a challenge. They demanded equal strength from me, as well as bending and working things out over time.

Ralph was intent about settling his library before he died. With the help of Betsy Gordon and her foundation, and the fact that Purdue University houses the Betsy Gordon Psychoactive Substances Archives, Purdue agreed to take his books on numerous topics, including psychedelics, as the Ralph Metzner Collection. Our daughter Sophia and I worked on packing and shipping his books to Purdue. The night before he died, I said to him, "The shelves are clear, and the last ten of forty-four boxes are ready to ship tomorrow." He put his hands together and said, "Thank you. I am so grateful." Ensuring that his library was settled was the last act that he wanted to complete before he died. This was one of many examples that seemed to indicate that his death seemed well-timed with the completion of his life and work.

RALPH AS BELOVED IN THE AFTERLIFE

Our bond extends now to me connecting with him in the afterlife. He has visited me a number of times in my dreams in deep, loving connections, and I have met him for satisfying interactions through mediums. Through working on this tribute book, I continue to be deeply connected to him. This is our fourth union, that between his world in the afterlife and mine still here furthering his publications, influences, and our ongoing family life. This fourth union completes the Sacred Hoop of Partnership with him as my professor, colleague, husband, and beloved in the afterlife.

I want to close with this excerpt from John O'Donohue's blessing, "On the Death of the Beloved,"[2] which I shared at his memorial. I think it is a verse for all of us.

> Let us not look for you in memory,
> Where we would grow lonely without you.
> You would want us to find you in presence,
> Beside us when beauty brightens,
> When kindness glows
> And music echoes eternal tones.
>
> When orchids brighten the earth,
> Darkest winter has turned to spring;
> May this dark grief flower with hope
> In every heart that loves you.
>
> May you continue to inspire us . . .

2. John O'Donohue, *To Bless the Space Between Us* (New York: Doubleday, 2008), 170.

Acknowledgments

This endeavor has been a heart-warming collaboration to honor the life and legacy of Ralph Metzner, who continues to inspire us. For the greater community of fellow explorers, I am grateful.

Thanks to David Presti for writing the foreword. Special thanks to Monika Wikman, Vicki Darrow, and to David with whom I conferred on this project. I am grateful for my brother-in-law Robin Metzner's contribution and consultation on Ralph's early history. Thanks to Uwe Doerken for help with translations and coordinating some of the European contributions. Thanks also to Markus Berger for the gift of his meticulous final proofreading, with subject matter expertise on psychoactive substances.

I give profound thanks to my editor/agent Simon Warwick-Smith for his invaluable professional editing and for helping shape the book.

Thanks to Jack and Kathleen Silver, Michael Ziegler, Leigh Marz, Joseph Friedman, Phil Wolfson, Sophia Bowart, and Uwe Doerken for their service on the Green Earth Foundation Board and for supporting Ralph's numerous projects.

Acknowledgments of Financial Support
Sincerest thanks go to all of the financial supporters who funded the professional consulting and editing on this book, without whose generosity this book would not have come to fruition.

To Leigh Marz for spearheading the fundraising effort.

To major donors Betsy Gordon, and George Goldsmith and Katya Malievskaia.

To John Buchanan, Uwe Doerken, and Dawn McGee for large gifts. To all other donors, many of whom are contributors to this book: Ralph Abraham, Gary Bravo, Christopher Cassidy, Sally Clark, Kim Clay, Gail Colombo and Bill Niemeyer, Leslie Conton, Amy Cortese, Jean Eisenhower, Peter and Jamy Faust, Leo Figgs and Jennifer Cunningham, Carla Detchon and Tim Salz, Briege Farrelly, Lora and Frank Ferguson, Martin Fiebert, George Gilsanan, Chellis Glendinning, Malcolm Groome, Dan Gross and Ajna Pisanai, Pat Harden, Diane Haug and Robert Weisz, Lynette Herring, Scott Hill, Margaret Mellon Hitchcock Foundation, Shep Jenks, Theresa Jump, Alan Levin, Mark Kasprow, DeLee Lantz, David Lukoff, Roger Marsden and Susan Weiss, Alastair McIntosh, Astrid Matathias, Dennis McKenna, Friederike Meckel, Robin Metzner, Paul Müller, Brian Otter, Simcha Paull, Marc Perez, Janis Phelps, Tom Pinkson, David Presti and Kristi Panik, Laura Pustarfi, Valerie Rosenfeld, Alex Shester, Ilene Serlin, Jack and Kathleen Silver, Vernice Solimar, Dave Steel, Rebecca Stults, Jan Taal, Joachim Thiele, and Susan Wright.

For their support and contributions, I am so grateful, and I know Ralph is smiling in the realms of the afterlife.

Tributes on the Green Earth Foundation Website

There were numerous essays that could not be included in this printed volume due to space limitations. I am grateful for these contributions, and so that you may read their words and see their images, I have posted their essays on the Green Earth Foundation website at

www.greenearthfound.org

I want to thank the following authors of these writings: Thomas Armstrong, Allan Badiner, Andrew Beath, John Broomfield, Ronald L. Boyer, Bronton Cheja, Sally Clark, Laura Clein, Jean Eisenhower, Martin Fiebert, Gray Henry, Raymond Hillis, Mark Kasprow, Michael Limnios, Valeria McCarroll, Robert McDermott, Friederike Meckel, Antonio Nunez, Marc Perez, Tom Pinkson, Justin Samuels, Ilene Serlin, Alex Shester, Vernice Solimar, Jan Taal, Rolf Verres, Raymond Bart Vespe, and Robert Weisz.

Glossary of
Psychoactive Medicines

There are many resources for information about these important and useful psychoactive medicines. We have cited those we used for these brief definitions. For those drawn from the website Erowid.org, see the Plants and Drugs tab, then choose the "Chemicals Vault" or "Plants Vault" for a list of individual medicines.

2C-B (4-bromo-2,5-dimethoxyphenethylamine) is a psychedelic phenethylamine that first gained popularity as a legal replacement for MDMA in the mid-1980s. 2C-B was first synthesized by Alexander Shulgin in 1974 and saw its early use among the psychiatric community as an aid during therapy. Before it was scheduled, 2C-B was sold in small doses as an aphrodisiac. Common names are nexus, bees, and Venus. (Erowid, "2C-B Vault")

Ayahuasca is a powerful psychedelic South American brew, traditionally made from the *Banisteriopsis caapi* vine and admixtures such as *Psychotria viridis* (and/or other DMT-containing plants). One of its primary effects is considered to be the vomiting (the purge) that accompanies the experience. The term *ayahuasca* is sometimes loosely used to mean any combination of an MAOI (monoamine oxidase inhibitor, which function as highly efficacious antidepressants as well as effective therapeutic agents for panic disorder and social phobia) with DMT. Other common names for ayahuasca are husca, yagé, Daime, La Purga, and the Tea. (Erowid, "Ayahuasca Vault")

Cannabis is a fast-growing, bushy annual with dense, sticky flowers that produces, among others, the psychoactive cannabinoid chemicals THC and CBD. It has a long history of medicinal, recreational, and industrial use. The fibrous stalks of the plant are used to produce clothing and rope. Its legal status is rapidly changing in the United States and around the world from contraband to tolerated mind-alterant. (Erowid, "Cannabis Vault")

5-MeO-DMT—"short for 5-methoxy-N,N-dimethyltryptamine—looks just like DMT on both a macro and micro level, with a few extra atoms attached . . . That slight change makes all the difference, though. Like DMT, 5-MeO-DMT also appears in many plants and animals—including the dried powdered venom of the desert toad. While the DMT experience tends to be highly visual, 5-MeO-DMT is more like a perspective shift. Some have said it is something like a near-death experience.

"5-MeO-DMT has a traditional shamanic use as well in the form of a powerful . . . powder blown forcefully into the nose . . . Some progressive treatment centers have found it extremely useful. One such is Crossroads Treatment Center in northern Mexico, which specializes in combination ibogaine and 5-MeO-DMT therapy. 5-MeO-DMT seems to work synergistically with the ibogaine, enabling a transcendental or mystical experience. The combination helps patients recontextualize their experience and ultimately can give them inspiration and motivation.

"Each of these substances holds tremendous untapped healing power, and treatment experts and patients alike are helping to determine their unique potential. DMT, when in the form of a long-lasting ayahuasca experience, may help those attempting to open themselves up to bring back insights. 5-MeO-DMT, on the other hand, has its place as a very brief but effective supplement to an ibogaine experience as a way to experience becoming one with the universe." (Roger R., "What Is the Difference between 5-MeO-DMT and DMT?" Psychedelic Times website, February 26, 2016)

DMT (N,N-dimethyltryptamine) is a powerful, visual psychedelic tryptamine that produces short-acting effects when smoked. It is used orally in combination with an MAOI (monoamine oxidase inhibitor, which function as highly efficacious antidepressants as well as effective therapeutic agents for panic disorder and social phobia) in ayahuasca brews. The MAOI activates the orally ineffective DMT for use as a drink by inhibiting the body's own enzyme system mono-amine oxidase (MAO). It is naturally produced in the human and animal body and by many plants. (Erowid, "DMT Vault")

As far as the psychoactive effects of DMT, people have described feeling like they are traveling at warp speed through a tunnel of bright lights and shapes. Others describe an out-of-body experience and feeling like they have changed into "something else." (Healthline website)

Jaguar Medicine is a code name Ralph gave to 5-MeO-DMT, in part because of its rapid onset. **Jaguar Twins** and the **Mayan Twins** are interchangeable names for a specific method of using both 5-MeO-DMT and DMT that was developed by Ralph Metzner in the 1980s. However, Ralph wrote in his book *The Toad and the Jaguar* that although initially he experimented with using both substances, he gradually moved to using only 5-MeO-DMT, as he did not find it any more effective to use both. (*The Toad and the Jaguar*, 43)

Ketamine, 2-(2-chlorophenyl)-2-(methylamino)-cyclohexanone, is a psychedelic, dissociative anesthetic psychedelic used medically as a human and veterinary anesthetic. It is one the few addictive psychedelics and is associated with researcher John Lilly. (Erowid, "Ketamine Vault")

LSD, d-lysergic acid diethylamide (or lysergic acid diethylamide), is the best known and most researched psychedelic. It is the standard against which all other psychedelics are compared. It is active at extremely low doses and is most commonly available on blotter or in liquid form. Common names for LSD are acid, L, tabs, blotter, doses, and trips. (Erowid, "LSD Vault")

MDMA (3,4-methylenedioxy-N-methylamphetamine) is a phenethyl-amine, entactogen, and one of the most popular recreational psycho-actives. It is commonly sold as "ecstasy" (usually tablets) or "molly" (usually crystals). It is known for its empathogenic, euphoric, and stimulant effects, and it has been used in psychotherapy. As MDMA belongs to the amphetamine family, there is a "speed" component to the experience. A caution is that ecstasy tablets are notoriously impure, often containing chemicals other than MDMA. Common names are ecstasy, E, X, XTC, rolls, beans, ADAM, and molly. (Erowid, "MDMA Vault")

Methylone (3,4-methylenedioxy-N-methylcathinone; MDMC) is an empathogen and stimulant psychoactive medicine. It is a synthetic cathinone with substantial chemical, structural, and pharmacologi-cal similarities to MDMA. Methylone produces a sense of well-being and increased empathy; its effects are shorter-lasting and can be milder than MDMA. (Wikipedia, "Methylone")

Mescaline (3,4,5-trimethoxy-β-phenethylamine) is a naturally occur-ring psychedelic with a long history of human use. It is best known as the primary active chemical in the peyote cactus. A common name is mescalito. (Erowid, "Mescaline Vault")

Psilocybin mushrooms are more than 180 species of mushrooms that contain the psychedelic chemicals psilocybin and/or psilocin. They have a long history of use in Mexico and are currently one of the most popular and commonly available natural psychedelics. Common names are shrooms, magic mushrooms, sacred mushrooms, and Teonanacatl. (Erowid, "Mushrooms Vault")

Peyote, *Lophophora williamsii* and *Lophophora diffusa*, is a small, spine-less cactus that contains mescaline as its primary active chemical. It has a long history of use among the Indigenous in northern Mexico and the Southwest United States. Common names are peyote, but-tons, and mescalito. (Erowid, "Peyote Vault")

Salvia divinorum is Latin for "sage of the diviners." Salvia is a sprawl-ing perennial herb found in the Sierra Mazatec region of Mexico. Its leaves contain the extremely potent Salvinorin A, a potent K-opioid agonist, and some other compounds. It has a history of buccal use as a divinatory psychedelic, and it has been widely available since the mid-1990s primarily as a smoked herb. Its effects are considered unpleasant by many people. (Erowid, "Salvia D. Vault")

San Pedro cactus (*Echinopsis pachanoi* Syn. *Trichocereus pachanoi*, and several other *Echinopsis* species) are some of the most psychoactive species of cactus, containing phenethylamine alkaloids such as mescaline. (Wikipedia, "Trichocereus macrogonus var. pachanoi")

Syrian rue (*Peganum harmala*) is a plant that grows in parts of the United States, Asia, Africa, and Europe. When taken orally, the seeds of the plant have psychoactive, stimulating, but not psychedelic effects. The seeds of Syrian rue contain chemicals (tryptamines) called beta-carbolines, which primarily act as inhibitors of the body's own enzyme system monoamine oxidase (MAO) and are therefore called MAO inhibitors.

In ayahuasca-like preparations, the MAO inhibitors enable the oral effectiveness of DMT, which could not work without inhibiting this enzyme system (Webmed website).

Toad foam is the dried, powdered venom of the desert toad *Incilius alvarius* (Syn. *Bufo alvarius*), a source of 5-MeO-DMT. (See 5-MeO-DMT)

Books and Music by Ralph Metzner

BOOKS

Alchemical Divination: Accessing Your Spiritual Intelligence for Healing and Guidance. Berkeley, CA: Regent Press, 2009; Sonoma, CA: Four Trees Press, 2022.

Alchemical Musings. Berkeley: Regent Press, 2020; Sonoma, CA: Four Trees Press, 2022.

Allies for Awakening: Guidelines for Productive and Safe Experiences with Entheogens. Berkeley: Regent Press, 2015; Sonoma, CA: Four Trees Press, 2022.

Ayahuasca: Sacred Vine of Spirits, editor. New York: Thunder's Mouth Press, 1999 (under its original title *Ayahuasca—Hallucinogens, Consciousness and the Spirit of Nature*); 3rd edition published Rochester, VT: Park Street Press, 2014.

Birth of a Psychedelic Culture: Conversations about Leary, the Harvard Experiments, Millbrook and the Sixties. With coauthors Ram Dass and Gary Bravo. Santa Fe, NM: Synergetic Press, 2010.

Diving for Treasures. Berkeley, CA: Regent Press, 2015; Sonoma, CA: Four Trees Press, 2022.

Ecology of Consciousness: The Alchemy of Personal, Collective, and Planetary Transformation. Oakland, CA: New Harbinger Press, 2017.

The Ecstatic Adventure, editor. New York: Macmillan, 1968. Out of print.

The Expansion of Consciousness. Berkeley, CA: Regent Press, 2008; Sonoma, CA: Four Trees Press, 2022.

Eye of the Seeress: Voice of the Poet / Auge der Scherin—Stimme des Dichters. Berkeley, CA: Regent Press, 2011; Sonoma, CA: Four Trees Press, 2022.

Green Psychology: Transforming Our Relationship to the Earth. Rochester, VT: Park Street Press, 1999.

Know Your Type: Maps of Identity. Garden City, NY: Doubleday Anchor, 1979.

The Life Cycle of the Human Soul Incarnation-Conception-Birth-Death-Hereafter-Reincarnation. Berkeley, CA: Regent Press, 2011; Sonoma, CA: Four Trees Press, 2022.

Maps of Consciousness. New York: Collier-Macmillan, 1971; Rochester, VT: Inner Traditions, 2023.

MindSpace and TimeStream: Understanding and Navigating Your States of Conscious-ness. Berkeley, CA: Regent Press, 2010; Sonoma, CA: Four Trees Press, 2022.

Overtones and Undercurrents: Spirituality, Reincarnation, and Ancestor Influence in Entheogenic Psychotherapy. Rochester, VT: Park Street Press, 2017.

The Psychedelic Experience: A Manual Based on the Tibetan Book of the Dead. With coauthors Timothy Leary and Richard Alpert. New Hyde Park, NY: University Books, 1964.

The Psychedelic Reader. With coeditors Gunther Weil and Timothy Leary. New Hyde Park, NY: University Books, 1965.

The Roots of War and Domination. Berkeley, CA: Regent Press, 2008; Sonoma, CA: Four Trees Press, 2022.

Searching for the Philosophers' Stone: Encounters with Mystics, Scientists, and Healers. Rochester, VT: Park Street Press, 2018.

The Six Pathways of Destiny. Berkeley, CA: Regent Press, 2012; Sonoma, CA: Four Trees Press, 2022.

Teonanacatl: Sacred Mushroom of Visions, editor. Rochester, VT: Park Street Press, 2003.

Through the Gateway of the Heart. With coauthor Padma Catell under the joint pseudonym Sophia Adamson. Petaluma CA: Solarium Press, 1985, 2013.

The Toad and the Jaguar: A Field Report of Underground Research on a Visionary Medicine. Forewords by Stanislav Grof and Charles Grob. Berkeley, CA: Regent Press, 2013; Sonoma, CA: Four Trees Press, 2022.

The Unfolding Self: Varieties of Transformative Experience. Novato, CA: Origin Press, 1998 (under its original title *Opening to Inner Light*); Santa Fe, NM: Synergetic Press, 2022.

The Well of Remembrance: Rediscovering the Earth Wisdom Myths of Northern Europe. Boston: Shambhala Publications, 1994.

Why? What Your Life Is Telling You about Who You Are and Why You're Here. With coauthors Matthew McKay and Sean Ólaoire. Oakland, CA: New Harbinger Publications, 2013.

Worlds Within and Worlds Beyond. Berkeley, CA: Regent Press, 2013; Sonoma, CA: Four Trees Press, 2022.

RECORDINGS

Völuspa with Byron Metcalf, Hemi-Sync, 2020.

Spirit Soundings with Kit Walker, Green Earth Foundation, 2012.

Bardo Blues and Other Songs of Liberation, Green Earth Foundation, 2005.

About the Editor

Cathy Coleman, Ph.D., was Ralph Metzner's wife for thirty-one years (1988–2019). She worked at the California Institute of Integral Studies (CIIS) as director of student services and later as dean of students when Ralph was academic dean and professor. Cathy later worked as executive director of EarthRise Retreat Center at the Institute of Noetic Sciences, as president of Kepler College (of Astrological Arts and Sciences), and with CIIS's Center for Psychedelic-Assisted Therapies and Research. She was cofounder, with Ralph Metzner, and is a current board member of the Green Earth Foundation (www.greenearthfound.org). She is also a professional consulting astrologer.